Puritans, Lawyers, and Politics

Puritans, Lawyers, and Politics in Early Seventeenth-Century England

BY JOHN DYKSTRA EUSDEN

ARCHON BOOKS 1968

© *1958 by Yale University Press*
[Yale Studies in Religious Education. Vol. 23]

Reprinted 1968 with permission

Library of Congress Catalog Card Number: 68-12524
Printed in the United States of America

To my parents,

THE REVEREND RAY ANDERSON EUSDEN, D.D.,
and

MARIE DYKSTRA EUSDEN,
*who, in things material and of the spirit,
helped to make this possible*

ERRATA

p. 17, l. 20:   *for* unequivocably *read* unequivocally

p. 17, l. 23:   *for* exposed *read* espoused

p. 17, l. 25:   *for* one-and-for-all *read* once-and-for-all

p. 21, footnote 18, l. 2:   *for* Launcelot *read* Lancelot

p. 43, l. 23:   *for* Hakewell *read* Hakewill

p. 86, l. 20:   *for* treasures *read* treasurers

p. 185, l. 1:   *for* parliament *read* Parliament

p. 189, l. 18:   *for* 4th ed. *read* 5th ed.

p. 203, l. 17:   *for* Structure *read* Culture

p. 216, l. 35:   *for* National *read* Natural

PREFACE

A READER sometimes has the desire and always the right to know why a book is written. Both desire and right may be expressed about a work which deals with such diverse subjects as law courts, the church, universities, inns of court, the crown, Parliament, Puritan theology, and common law.

This book grew out of the author's interest in the relationship of religion and law. It was undertaken originally to discover what influence, if any, Puritanism and common law had upon each other in early seventeenth-century England. I planned to follow the lead of others who had investigated the role of Puritanism, or Calvinism, in its surrounding culture. The Calvinist economic ethic has been elaborately considered with special reference to the rise of capitalism, producing a theory that has yielded fruitful debate among specialists in religion and social history. The bearing of Calvinism and Puritanism upon democracy and society at large has long been subjected to provocative inquiries. Perhaps, within a modest scope, it would be helpful to examine the relation between Calvinist ideas and law using early seventeenth-century England as a testing ground.

At the outset I assumed that influence and counterinfluence between Puritanism and common law could be readily established. The divines and barristers of the early 1600's had a great deal in common. They shared a similar economic and social status, for the majority of each group belonged to the rising middle class of England. Politically, both Puritans and lawyers were minority factions struggling against the absolutism of the Stuart kings, and contact between them was extensive in the early part of the century. The divines preached and ministered in the inns of court, those legal societies where instruction was given in the law of the land. Barristers assisted in a large-scale attempt to establish a foundation that would provide financial support for Puritan preaching throughout England. Both groups joined in the attack on the ex officio oath and the ecclesiastical Court of High Commission. Puritans and lawyers were together in the House of Commons where they were close and forceful parliamentary allies against the crown.

Frequently the Puritan and common law strains were fused in the same person. Simonds D'Ewes, Nicholas Fuller, and William Prynne were hybrids of this kind. Even when a member of one group did not share the religious or legal interest of the other, there was often a personal attraction as in the case of Edward Coke, who helped finance the education of Roger Williams.

In view of this similarity and association, would there not be some instances of the influence of Puritanism on common law, and vice versa? Might it not be discovered, for example, that the early seventeenth-century restatement or refinement of the law of contract had something to do with the theory of church covenant, or that Puritan moralism had a part in the development of family law? These and other possibilities of mutual influence loomed as I began to read sermons, tracts, yearbooks, and legal reports.

Although fascinating as a conjecture, the evidence of Puritan influence on common law and vice versa did not materialize. The Puritan sermons in the inns of court never dealt, so far as I could ascertain, with the problems of the common law in the early 1600's. The divines used the same theological and devotional themes in the chapels of the inns as they did in their home parishes. The Independents who urged a compact theory of church organization gave no visible sign that they had been influenced by the common law notion of contract. No definite relationship could be established between Puritan morality and family law. The divines brought little to bear on the technical matters of the practice of law and the passing of judgment in the king's courts. Likewise, the barristers were generally mute about the preaching and teaching of the word of God and about the organization of the church.

But my research had not arrived at a dead end. Along with a negative conclusion in regard to mutual influence, it became clear that the relationship of Puritanism and common law was one of ideological parallelism. The divines and the barristers were joined to each other by more than personal association and a tactical alliance against the Stuart crown. Both were legalists; the one group spoke of divine sovereignty and the other of fundamental law; each advocated a special kind of reason as requisite for an understanding of theology or law; both groups insisted on institutional independence; and neither tolerated speculative systems of religious or legal thought. The Puritans and the lawyers even had common failings. They were narrow constructionists, prone to exaggeration, and generally un-willing to tolerate their religious, legal, and political opponents.

What is offered herein is primarily a book of interpretation. Using the abundant sources and detailed studies with which a student of the seventeenth century is blessed, answers to broad questions have been sought. What were the specific components of the parallelism? What was its meaning? Of what significance was this phenomenon in the English nation of the early 1600's and later? And beyond that, what contribution have the Puritans and the lawyers made to the life of the body politic in Western society?

The present book had its beginning in a dissertation presented to the faculty of the Graduate School of Yale University in candidacy for the degree of doctor of philosophy in 1953. The dissertation bore the title "English Puritan and Common Law Concepts of Political Authority, 1603–30." The gathering of materials for both disserta-tion and book was done in this country, save for two brief visits to England. The libraries of Yale and Harvard Universities, the Folger Shakespeare Library of Washington, and the Huntington Library of San Marino, California, have furnished the author much needed aid and innumerable courtesies.

During all the stages of research and writing, I have passed through doors opened by wise, competent scholars of the seventeenth century. I would single out William Haller, Margaret A. Judson, and Marshall M. Knappen, who, in addition to their writings, have been helpful in conference or correspondence. Chief guidance has come from those close by in my own academic household: Sydney E. Ahl-strom, Roland H. Bainton, Charles Blitzer, William A. Christian, Archibald S. Foord, H. Richard Niebuhr, Wallace Notestein, and Samuel E. Thorne (now defected to Harvard Law School). Without the counsel and critique of Richard Niebuhr and Samuel Thorne, this project would not likely have been completed. My wife read the en-tire manuscript, as did most of the above, and I found that her sense of expression and insistence on clarity were to the point. Her criti-cism, offered in love and with encouragement to proceed, is a special part of my indebtedness to others. But in the end an author leaves those with whom he has common interests and those upon whom he depends to stand alone. I take that stand in gratitude for what I have received and in awe of the responsibility that is mine.

J. D. E.

Calhoun College
Yale University
October 1957

CONTENTS

INTRODUCTION

THE STORY of the English revolt against the crown in the seventeenth century has been told many times. Once in the middle of the century and again near the end, the English people rose to assert principles of government which were to become the foundations of Western political life. The period between 1640 and 1660 has received probably more attention than any other part of the century. Concentration upon the first major climax of the 1600's, frequently known as the Puritan Revolution, is as it should be. This was the glorious age of John Pym, John Lilburne, Henry Ireton, Oliver Cromwell, and John Milton. During this period in England, particularly in the 1640's, modern democracy received form and substance. Indeed, continued research is needed before the significance of the Long Parliament, the Great Rebellion, the Commonwealth, and the Protectorate is fully revealed.

The author leaves this tumultuous age to those who have already demonstrated their competence to deal with it and to those who are yet to come. He would call attention to a less familiar part of the century, to the time just before new powers arose overnight as giants in the land to wage war, behead the king, and govern the country. The pre-1640 period lacks, perhaps, the color and the sense of direction of the later years dominated by parliamentarian, Leveller, regicide, and lord protector. But the early seventeenth century made no less of a contribution to political history than the period succeeding. That contribution is the story of this book.

In the early 1600's James I and Charles I faced a double-pronged opposition represented by the forces of religion and law. The leaders of this opposition were Puritans and common lawyers.[1] A concern

1. The term "common lawyer" is used to denote those of the legal profession who were trained in and practiced or adjudged the common law of England. By far the greatest number of English lawyers and judges were—and still are—common lawyers. Others of the legal profession practicing in the early 17th

with the church placed the Puritans in the fore of the struggle, although there was seldom an issue of any kind on which they did not raise their voices. John N. Figgis writes that in the late medieval period "it is right to treat the growth of political ideas as a branch of ecclesiastical history." [2] The dictum is still applicable to the early seventeenth century in England when the Puritans steadily contended with the Stuart Kings over the powers of the crown in the life of the church. The Puritan opposition to the throne is also marked by a challenge of the king's interference in the life of the universities. A true measure of the Puritans' animosity to the crown is found in James' characterization of these religious folk as "verie pestes in the Church and Common-weale." [3]

The common lawyers rank as leading antagonists of the throne because of their defense of the law of the land in the face of Stuart absolutism. Attorney General Francis Bacon, that staunch and wily friend of the king, recorded the observation of James that "ever since his coming to the crown, the popular sort of lawyers have been the men, that most affrontedly . . . have trodden upon his prerogative . . ." [4] The lawyers concentrated on the common law courts, upholding their independence much as the Puritans did in regard to the church. Similarly, as the Puritans fought the crown over interference in the universities, so the lawyers opposed James and Charles for royal tampering with the inns of court. Early in his reign James came to know the common lawyers for what they were—legal thorns in the royal flesh. In a speech in the Star Chamber, he referred to the "sharpe edge and vaine popular humour of some Lawyers at the Barre, that thinke they are not eloquent and bold spirited enough, except they meddle with the Kings Prerogatiue." [5]

The Puritans and lawyers were more than just institutional con-

century were the "civilians," those skilled in the civil law, and the "canonists," primarily clerics knowledgeable in both Roman Catholic and Anglican canon law. Whenever the word "lawyer" or "barrister" is used henceforth, it means common lawyer.

2. *Studies of Political Thought from Gerson to Grotius, 1414–1625* (Cambridge, The University Press, 1907), p. 31. See Charles H. McIlwain, ed., *The Political Works of James I Reprinted from the Edition of 1616* (Cambridge, Harvard University Press, 1918), intro. pp. xv ff., for the application of Figgis' generalization to early 17th-century England.

3. "Basilikon Doron," in McIlwain, *James' Works*, p. 24.

4. *The Works of Francis Bacon, Lord Chancellor of England*, ed. Basil Montagu (New York, Worthington, 1884), *2*, 494.

5. "A Speach in the Starre-Chamber . . . Anno 1616," in McIlwain, *James' Works*, p. 333.

tenders with James and Charles, quarreling with the crown over church and courts, universities and inns of court. They went to the heart of the matter. Out of the Puritan insistence on divine sovereignty and the common law insistence on fundamental law came an explicit challenge to the whole idea of Stuart kingship. Throughout the pre-Civil War years, James and Charles were harried by these formidable, contentious men of God and men of law.

Many others, joined the Puritans and lawyers against the crown in the early part of the century. Together they lamented the end of happy Tudor days and looked forlornly at the Stuart age. There were the summer patriots who spoke fondly of good old Elizabethan times and now bemoaned the decline of the nation's power on the Continent and overseas. The blame for the decay was placed squarely on the stumbling foreign policy of James and Charles. Certain university figures with pronounced democratic leanings were unalterably opposed to Stuart absolutism at home. And finally, there were the leaders of the rising middle class who sought to wrest financial independence from the crown. These were the folk who chafed under the restrictions created by the king's royal monopolies, patents, and impositions. All of these joined in the attack on the crown and made the early seventeenth century a time of vigorous opposition to the powers that be. We would explore two of the major strands in the opposition, the one religious and the other legal.

Our story begins with the accession of James I in the year 1603.[6] The Puritan and common law opposition to the crown had its roots in the 1500's, of course, and we shall refer at times to the pre-Jacobean period. As an approximate stopping place, the year 1630 commends itself for several reasons. First, the great Puritan exodus to America began in the late 1620's when Archbishop Laud and others of the hierarchy in the established church inaugurated a systematic perse-

6. Chronology is confusing in a study of early 17th-century England. Most of the documents used in this book follow the Old Style, or Julian, calendar, in which the year begins on March 25. The New Style, or Gregorian, calendar starts the year on Jan. 1. The o.s. prevailed in England until the mid-18th century, whereas the n.s. was in vogue on most of the Continent soon after its promulgation in 1582 by Gregory XIII. The chief problem arises when later writers do not specify whether they follow the o.s. or the n.s. in dealing with 17th-century England. The matter is further complicated by the fact that in the 1600's the Julian was ten days behind the Gregorian. We have adopted the procedure of rendering *months and days* as they are found, without correction. Months and days in this book are usually o.s., but should they in fact be n.s. the ten-day differential is thought to be minimal and insignificant. As for the *year,* we always follow the n.s. and consider Jan. 1, not March 25, to mark a new year.

cution of the Puritans. Laud became bishop of London in 1628 and
archbishop of Canterbury in 1633. By no means all Puritans left
their native land, but those with whom we are concerned were no
longer prevalent in England after 1630. When Puritanism rose vindictively in the 1640's, sending Laud to the scaffold in 1645, it was
not the same religious movement it had been earlier in the century.
Secondly, the Stuart crown greatly increased its control of the courts
and the judiciary so that between 1630 and the Civil War the lawyers, partners of the Puritans, were largely ineffective against the
king. The only major exception was the common law opposition in
the famous ship money case of 1637. Thirdly and most important, Parliament,[7] which had been the major assault weapon for both Puritans
and lawyers, did not meet after 1629 until the Short and Long Parliaments of 1640. In 1628–29 there was a struggle in the lower house
centering around the government of the church and the authority of
the law of the land. In this crisis, similar to that which lay ahead
in the early 1640's,[8] the Puritans and lawyers momentarily vented
their wrath against the crown. Charles' brash dissolution of Parliament in 1629 brings the seventeenth-century struggle in the House
of Commons to its first climax.

These reasons comprise the logic of stopping an intensive survey
at 1630. Reference will be made to the post-1630 period, however,
as events occurring earlier have their culmination in the decade before the Civil War, the war itself, and later. Our primary concern,
then, is with slightly more than a quarter of the seventeenth century,
but the years of 1603 and 1630 indicate a period of emphasis rather
than prescribe strict limitations.

The French historian Paul Hazard has written about the years
that lie just on either side of 1700 in *The European Mind: The Critical Years (1680–1715)*. With Gallic *ravissement* the author says,
"Never was there a greater contrast, never a more sudden transition
than this! An hierarchical system ensured by authority; life firmly
based on dogmatic principle—such were the things held dear by the
people of the seventeenth century; but these . . . were the very

7. Unless otherwise specified, the word "Parliament" refers throughout to the
House of Commons. The House of Lords played an occasional role in the limitation
of the crown, but the upper house was more inclined to side with the king than
against him. As an influential organ of government on either side, Lords was on
the wane in the early 17th century.

8. See J. W. Allen, *English Political Thought, 1603–1660* (London, Methuen,
1938), *1*, 309. Mr. Allen considers the crisis of the late 1620's to be like that of the
early 1640's in content, though not in intensity.

things that their immediate successors of the eighteenth held in cordial detestation. . . . One day, the French people, almost to a man, were thinking like Bossuet. The day after, they were thinking like Voltaire." [9] British restraint is more in order when dealing with the early Stuart period, but there is no doubt that in England from 1603 to 1630, as in France from 1680 to 1715, matters of utmost significance for modern history were taking place. We Americans should take special notice, for we cannot understand ourselves or our country apart from our beginning in the England of the early 1600's. The words of Louis B. Wright, Director of the Folger Shakespeare Library, show perspicacity: "All the fundamental concepts which make us the kind of people we are today had their modern conception in the Tudor and Stuart periods. For us, that's the milk in the coconut." [10]

The early seventeenth-century connection between England and America is particularly evident in regard to the subjects of this book. English Puritans contributed the ethos of American culture in the period of our country's settlement, a fact often recounted but never too often emphasized. Less well known is the American indebtedness to English common law. With few exceptions, the law of the land for England became the law of the land for the colonies and later the states and the nation. The fathers of the American republic read Edward Coke and other English lawyers of the seventeenth century. They recrossed the Atlantic to study the common law at the inns of court and sent their sons to do the same. The Middle Temple became in a certain sense an American inn during the colonial period. The early English seventeenth century left an enduring imprint on much of American life.[11]

We are concerned chiefly with the political importance of the early 1600's as manifested in the struggle of the Puritans and common lawyers with James I and Charles I. The two groups roundly opposed the Stuart conception of the divine right of kings with theories that God and law ruled the world. Instead of a hierarchical arrangement of institutions with the king at the apex, the Puritans and law-

9. Trans. J. Lewis May (New Haven, Yale University Press, 1953), p. xv. Originally *La Crise de la conscience européenne*, Paris, Boivin, 1935.

10. Commemorating the 391st anniversary of Shakespeare's birth, as reported in *Time*, May 9, 1955, p. 86. The Folger Library is not limited to Shakespearean material; it houses the world's second largest collection of early English (1475–1640) books. Only the British Museum in London surpasses it for this period.

11. In this paragraph, the author has depended on many insights of Wallace Notestein, *The English People on the Eve of Colonization, 1603–1630*, New York, Harper, 1954.

yers saw all institutions, including the crown, standing independent
of one another and responsible only to God and law. Authority had
been "distributed" among the institutions of society according to
specific laws, which were the marks of God's sovereignty and law's
supremacy. There was interdependence among institutions, but no
subordination of one to another. The Puritans and lawyers worked
with the old idea of the limitation of power and applied it in a new
political setting. In so doing, they fashioned one of the indispensable
elements of contemporary democracy. Their concept of limited power
takes a place alongside other contributions to modern political life.
It ranks with the "rights of Englishmen" and the attendant conception of liberty which came out of the Puritan Revolution, and with
the idea of equality found across the Channel in France at the end
of the next century.

The Puritan–common law adaptation of a medieval understanding
of political power and authority was uniquely applied to Parliament,
the new political force of the age. Puritans and lawyers brought to
the House of Commons not only their grievances for redress but also
their conception of authority. In later times, Parliament's exercise
of the full powers of rule, once possessed by the crown, was tempered
by the early seventeenth-century idea of authority. The influence of
the Puritan–common law opposition was felt subsequently in the development of political sovereignty and the concept of the state. The
Puritans and lawyers contributed a climate of opinion in which modern pluralism could flourish. Indeed, Anglo-American society has
developed in its characteristically pluralist way because of theological
and legal roots which reach down to the early 1600's in England.

Despite the importance of the Puritans and the lawyers, their
political thought is elusive. It does not unfold as political *Weltan-
schauung*, but rather emerges in the course of a jumbled history. The
stages of the history frequently do not even accord with each other.
Puritan divines uphold a church established by the crown and yet
attack James' exercise of ecclesiastical power. Sir Edward Coke
seems to maintain now the supremacy of the judiciary in Dr. Bonham's Case, now the sovereignty of the king in the case of the *post-
nati*, and later the plenitude of Parliament's powers. One follows the
course of Puritan and common law political thought much as one
drives through a large city on a cross-country trip. The route signs
are confusing or nonexistent in the urban maze, red lights impede
progress, and streets entered prove to be one way in the wrong direction. The traveler need not, however, be confounded by the jour-

ney if he will always bear in mind the nature of the two groups. To treat the Puritans and lawyers as political theorists would be to view them as they refused to view themselves.

The subjects of our study were ministers of the gospel and judges or practitioners of the common law. Politics was not their major concern; the church and the law sufficed for the employment of their terrifying energy. Questions of political authority became important for them only when particular germane concerns were challenged by James and Charles. What resulted from the conflict was not a neat political theory but a loose-jointed conception of the meaning and application of political power. Despite their imprecision, the Puritans and the lawyers fashioned major determinants for Western political history.

I THE PURITANS: PESTS IN CHURCH AND COMMONWEALTH

IT IS DIFFICUCT to single out the leaders of the Puritan opposition to the crown. No such thing as a "Puritan party" existed in the political life of the time. No pronouncements on the state of nation and church were delivered regularly by certain divines. Would that the Puritans had been consistent politico-ecclesiastical tractarians, as the divines of the Oxford Movement were in the nineteenth century. However, it is possible to identify the recognized leaders of Puritanism as a *religious* movement in early seventeenth-century England. Help is given by the testimony of certain church historians who lived close to the time, such as Baxter, Clarke, and Fuller. Further aid is rendered by Messrs. Davies, Haller, Knappen, Mosse, Miller, Woodhouse, and other modern authorities. But finally one depends on the literature of the age to find the answers to such questions as Who were the authoritative preachers of the time? Who were the persuasive teachers? Who molded religious thought in pamphlets and books? Who built the "Puritan ethos"? The answers do not come easily.

It gradually became clear as research progressed that certain divines, writers, and educators held earned positions of leadership in early seventeenth-century English Puritanism. Painfully aware of the sin of omission, the author finally selected for close study ten Puritans who appeared to be formulators of the movement. Although the ten were an amorphous political group, there is no doubt that they were politically important in Stuart England. The gospel which came forth from their sermons, tracts, and lectures had a relevance for the times. For them there was no withdrawal from public affairs. The positions held by these Puritans gave them every opportunity to express the "connectionalism" which they believed to exist between Christian faith and the world. They were the spokesmen at important church councils and assemblies, such as Lambeth, Hampton Court, Dort, and Westminster. With few exceptions they were popular, convincing preachers. All left behind manuscripts, books, commentaries, pamphlets, or sermon collections. Each held at least one influential ecclesiastical position in early seventeenth-century England. Their appointments included London pastorates, preaching assignments in the House of Commons, major teaching or administrative posts in Cambridge or Oxford University, masterships and lectureships at the inns of court, and chaplaincies to the royal family. In their manifold activities our clerical subjects bore witness to the generalization that "Puritanism is incurably political."

No ranking of the leaders is possible, but some classification based on the character of their lifework is feasible.[1] Certainly *John Preston* (1587–1628), *Richard Sibbes*, or Sibs (1577–1635), *William Gouge* (1578–1653), and *Thomas Gataker*, or Gatacre (1574–1654), were among the most forceful preachers of Jacobean England. Preston, "Dr. in Divinity, Chaplaine in Ordinary to His Majesty, Master of Emmanuell Colledge in Cambridge, and Sometimes Preacher of Lincolnes-Inne,"[2] thundered out his Calvinist message to king, common lawyer, student, parliamentarian, and whoever would harken. He was one of the moving spirits of the time. William Prynne, speaking of his days as a legal apprentice, acknowledged the influence Preston had exerted on him as he listened to the great divine preach in Lincoln's Inn. Sibbes likewise had an enthusiastic following because of his ability to speak the word. He, too, was a preacher to lawyers, serving as lecturer at Gray's Inn, and also a university administrator, acting as master of St. Catherine's Hall in Cambridge. His pulpit style was more personal than Preston's; he was known as the foremost devotional preacher of the age. Sibbes along with William Perkins helped to lead John Cotton into the ministry, a happening of considerable importance for the intellectual history of colonial America. Gouge and Gataker were persuasive London divines with large hearings. The former was rector of St. Anne's in Blackfriars, where his congregation included many lawyers and officials of state. Gataker, like Preston and Sibbes, preached to the lawyers in their

1. For a listing of biographical sources, consult the bibliography. In general the articles in the *Dictionary of National Biography* are reliable, particularly those by C. H. Firth and J. Bass Mullinger.

2. As he or his editors listed his titles on the frontispiece of nearly every one of his publications.

inner circle while serving as lecturer at Lincoln's Inn. Both Gouge and Gataker were chosen as delegates to the Westminster Assembly and were members of the special committee appointed by Parliament to prepare the document later known as the Westminster Confession.

Two of the ten belong together as fiery, pamphleteering apologists for early seventeenth-century Puritanism: *Thomas Scott*, or Scot (1580?–1626), and *William Prynne* (1600–69).[3] Both wielded a vitriolic pen; both were violently anti-Catholic. Writing polemics was their life. Carlyle called Prynne "my unreadable friend," and he could have said the same about Scott. The latter was, for a while, chaplain to James I, then rector successively in Norwich and Ipswich, and finally preacher to the English garrison at Utrecht in Holland. Prynne, who combined the roles of common lawyer and Puritan (though never ordained), was probably the most prolific pamphleteer of the age.

The remaining four were either leaders of Puritanism in the universities or writers a cut or two in quality above the pamphleteers. No academic retreat marked these four, simply a different expression of the Puritan calling. *Paul Baynes*, or Bayne (d. 1617), *William Bradshaw* (1571–1618), *Samuel Ward* (1572–1643), and *Richard Holdsworth* (1590–1649) belong in this group. Baynes was at once an accomplished commentator on Ephesians and Colossians and a preacher of repute. Bradshaw and Holdsworth were likewise known for their preaching. Baynes succeeded the famed William Perkins (1558–1602), the principal architect of Elizabethan Puritanism, as lecturer at Great St. Andrews in Cambridge. While ministering in that post, Baynes is said by Sibbes to have accounted for the latter's conversion. Bradshaw, one of the first fellows of the Puritan-dominated Sidney Sussex College in Cambridge, was the author of the definitive *English Puritanisme* and *A Protestation of the King's Supremacie*. Ward was appointed master of Sidney Sussex College in 1610 and remained at that post until his death thirty-three years later; he also served in the university as Lady Margaret Professor

3. Prynne is the youngest of the ten. We refer throughout to that period in his life before 1640. For Prynne "life began at forty," in the sense that after that time he manifested those dominant—and lamentable—characteristics by which he is chiefly remembered. After 1640 his intolerance and arrogance greatly increased (although they were pronounced enough in his youth) and, more damaging from our point of view, he became a "Puritan Erastian" in Parliament. In his earlier life, however, he stands as a fair example of the kind of Puritanism dealt with here.

of Divinity.[4] The Cambridge divine was an English representative at the Synod of Dort in Holland. Episcopius, one of the opposing Remonstrant leaders, called Ward the most learned member of the synod. Holdsworth, too, ministered in Cambridge University where he was a beloved tutor, professor of divinity in Gresham College, master of Emmanuel College, and finally vice-chancellor of the university.

Many others, including anonymous writers, acted in supporting roles to the above ten. All these Puritans made a telling impact upon the political life of the time. Preston was almost more politician than preacher—at least it can be said, as his critics did say, that he busied himself with the body politic as well as with the body of Christ. The effectiveness of the divines was increased by their willingness, almost eagerness, to suffer for their convictions. Sibbes was deprived of a professorship and a lectureship by the High Commission and later reprimanded by the commission for continuing offenses. Baynes' preaching was silenced and his lectureship at Cambridge was "put down." Bradshaw was restricted by the crown and placed under surveillance. Prynne was fined, imprisoned in the Tower, stripped of his university degree, expelled from Lincoln's Inn, and had his ears cut off in the pillory. Scott fled the country and finished his ministry in Holland, where he was stabbed to death by an English soldier at the door of his church in Utrecht. Theirs was a persuasive and unrelenting witness. It is small wonder that James and Charles considered the Puritans to be redoubtable opponents.

THE MINOR POINT OF CHURCH POLITY

The early seventeenth-century Puritans had diverse convictions about the organization of the church. At least three major positions can be discerned. There were some who supported the established church in its present form, some who argued for the adoption of Presbyterianism, and others who proposed that the Church of England become a loose federation of independent parishes. The first

4. *DNB* errs on some of the events in Ward's later life. The error understandably results from the existence of two Samuel Wards, both of whom were Puritan clergymen, authors, and associated with Sidney Sussex College. The other Samuel Ward was a stepson of Richard Rogers, the Puritan divine of considerable influence in the very early years of the century. The record is only partly corrected in *DNB*, Errata, p. 275. Consult Marshall M. Knappen, *Two Elizabethan Puritan Diaries* (Chicago, American Society of Church History, 1933), pp. 37 ff., for accurate biographical details on the Samuel Ward referred to here.

group can be called Anglican as well as Puritan, for it approved the episcopal structure of the Tudor church settlement. The Presbyterians, on the other hand, were incensed over the prelatical system of the established church, and urged the adoption of a church polity modeled on Geneva and Scotland. The third group argued that any form of ecclesiastical supervision other than that arising from within each individual parish was contrary to the true government of the church.

In terms of numbers and influence, the Presbyterians were the least important. Such a statement could scarcely be made about the late sixteenth century for, in the reign of Elizabeth, Presbyterianism had been nearly synonymous with Puritanism. By the 1590's, however, Presbyterian vigor had greatly declined. The queen and Archbishop Whitgift trampled on the growing shoots so carefully nurtured by Cartwright and Travers. Still, at the Hampton Court conference of 1604, the Presbyterians were bold enough to make a bid for the new king's support. James would have none of their arguments which urged, among other reforms, the substitution of a Presbyterian form of church government for the established episcopacy. This formal and severe rebuke of the first Stuart was a blow to the Presbyterian party. The strictly enforced conformity policy of Archbishop Bancroft provided an additional barrier to any reorganization of the church along Genevan and Scottish lines. The leaders of the movement were generally content to suffer under episcopacy during the early part of the century. The Presbyterian surge was only temporarily stopped, however; in the 1630's and 1640's rapid growth was resumed. The writings of Dr. Alexander Leighton and Henry Burton and the work of the Westminster Assembly displayed the Presbyterian revival in full swing.

The most numerous and influential of the crown's ecclesiastical opponents were the Puritan Anglicans. These folk consisted of those who wholeheartedly affirmed the historic polity of the Church of England and those who gave it momentary, tongue-in-cheek support. Preston, Sibbes, Scott, Prynne, Baynes, Ward, and Holdsworth were divines whose conviction bade them favor the current episcopacy. Other Puritan Anglicans supported the established church because they felt a bitter struggle with king and archbishop over church polity was simply not worth while in the present circumstances. Gouge and Gataker were good examples of the latter position. They asserted the current necessity of the establishment without applauding it. Later on in the 1640's, both Gouge and Gataker became rabid

Presbyterians, but in the pre-1630 period they and many others felt that episcopacy merited temporary support. Devotees of prelacy and latent Presbyterians were joined together in Puritan Anglicanism.

The prewar Independents, or what Perry Miller [5] and others call the "nonseparating Congregationalists," represented the third major position on the organization of the church. From the point of numbers, these divines ranked somewhere between the Presbyterians and the Puritan Anglicans as a party for the crown to reckon with in the ranks of early seventeenth-century Puritanism. With Ramist logic and strained casuistry, the Independents called for an established church and yet insisted on the autonomy of the local parish. Because of the latter point, they were pursued by Archbishop Laud in his militant campaign to enforce "Thorough" conformity to prelacy. Many Independent leaders left England for Holland and America, for instance William Ames (1576–1633),[6] John Cotton (1584–1652), Thomas Hooker (1586?–1647), John Winthrop (1588–1649), and John Davenport (1597–1670). William Bradshaw was one of the few Independents able to withstand partial containment and still minister effectively at his post in England.

We use the word "prewar" to distinguish early seventeenth-century Independency from other movements with which it was partly allied.

5. See *Orthodoxy in Massachusetts, 1630–1650. A Genetic Study*, Cambridge, Harvard University Press, 1933.

6. Ames is called by William Haller one of the two "intellectual fathers" of Independency; Bradshaw is cited as the other. See *The Rise of Puritanism. Or, the Way to the New Jerusalem as Set Forth in Pulpit and Press from Thomas Cartwright to John Lilburne and John Milton, 1570–1643* (New York, Columbia University Press, 1938), p. 79.

Ames was not selected as a leading Puritan figure for this study because his influence was far greater in Holland and in the New World than in his native England. After he was forbidden to preach in his first parish in Colchester, he transferred to Holland where he spent the large part of his mature life, dying there in 1633. In his Dutch pastorates and in his teaching at the University of Franeker, Ames was more concerned with the continental Arminians and the problem of conscience than with the politico-ecclesiastical issues raging in his homeland. It was in America that he made his greatest impact. On Ames' interest in New World Puritanism, see George L. Kittredge, "A Note on Dr. William Ames," *Publications of the Colonial Society of Massachusetts, 13* (1910–11), 60-9. The influence of Cotton, a towering Puritan figure, was likewise more pervasive outside England, and his lifework was also oriented around New World problems rather than those of the land of his birth. On the other hand Thomas Scott, who went to Holland in 1623, spent only three years across the Channel. Throughout his brief exile, Scott was passionately concerned with problems of church and state in his native land. He remained very much an English Puritan.

Bradshaw and his colleagues were quite different from the Independents of the 1640's and later. The latter—so provocatively studied by A. S. P. Woodhouse [7]—represented a political liberalism not shared by Independents of the prewar period. The two groups were primarily divided over religious toleration and resistance to magistrates. The later Independent, Hugh Peters (1598–1660), who was executed as a regicide upon his return to England from America, stood in sharp relief to Bradshaw and the earlier Independents on the matter of resistance to kings. For Bradshaw, obedience to political authority was the command of God.[8] The prewar Independents made little contribution to the idea of religious toleration. Expediency might require toleration, but the concept was not a first principle of religious and ecclesiastical life.

Even in matters of church polity, the earlier group differed from the later. Thomas Goodwin (1600–80) and Philip Nye (1596?–1672), for instance, the two most influential of the five independent "dissenting brethren" at the Westminster Assembly, displayed separatist leanings. The idea of separating from the established church was anathema to Bradshaw and his associates. They likewise stood apart from the American Independents, such as Cotton, Hooker, and Davenport, who finally asserted the necessity of separating from the Church of England. The prewar Independents were also distinct from contemporary English separatists, or the "orthodox Congregationalists" or Baptists, the savagely persecuted followers of Greenwood, Barrow, and Browne. On many counts, then, prewar Independency was a distinctive group in seventeenth-century Puritanism.

To describe the Puritanism of this period solely in terms of ecclasiastical organization, or polity, is to paint a confusing and unreal

7. *Puritanism and Liberty. Being the Army Debates (1647–9) from the Clarke Manuscripts with Supplementary Documents,* 2d ed. Chicago, University of Chicago Press, 1951. Consult the 100-page introduction.

8. All the Puritans joined with Bradshaw and the prewar Independents in condemning resistance to kings, even resistance to an evil Stuart. John Preston preached: "that which is said of *David,* he is *a man after Gods own heart,* may bee said of every King and Governour; they doe what *God* would have them to doe (though it bee for evill, as Davids was for good), they are men *after Gods owne heart . . ." Life Eternall. Or a Treatise of the Knowledge of the Divine Essence and Attributes* (3d ed. London, 1632), p. 151 (2d pagination).

One of the major shifts in 17th-century Puritanism came in the 1640's when the rampant Independents not only encouraged resistance to the crown but clamored for the king's head. See Roland H. Bainton, "Congregationalism: From the Just War to the Crusade in the Puritan Revolution," *Andover Newton Theological School Bulletin, 35,* No. 3 (April 1943).

picture. The lines between Puritan Anglican, Independent, and Presbyterian were never drawn definitively. Presbyterians sought refuge
and found reasonable comfort within Puritan Anglicanism. Once devoted to episcopacy, the Puritan Anglicans deserted it under Laud's
administration to join the Independents in flight to America. Indeed,
the three Puritan groups were more united than divided over church
organization, at least in its English fundamentals. Nearly all Puritans
subscribed to the Thirty-Nine Articles and the Book of Common
Prayer, although some wanted certain articles changed and sections
of the prayer book modified. The differences among them were minor
and did not produce factional strife. Most important, the three groups
agreed that England should have a church established and maintained
by the crown. They might disagree as to whether the Church of England should be episcopal, independent, or presbyterian, but again the
disagreement was not divisive. They stood together in upholding the
essential idea of the Tudor establishment, namely, that in England
there must be a union of church and state. By wholehearted support
of the established church, the Puritans betrayed their love for an
institution that was "peculiarly English." There was something about
the Church of England, they felt, that gave their land its special
characteristics, that made it a true national community. If the established church ceased to exist, the very spirit of the nation would
languish.

At this point, the Puritans displayed an essential Anglicanism
which compels one to be wary of any facile separation of Anglicanism
and Puritanism in the early 1600's. There was, for example, an affinity
between "that learned and judicious divine, Mr. Richard Hooker"
and the Puritans. The early seventeenth-century Puritans stood a
great deal closer to Hooker, the great Anglican apologist, than many
authorities have placed them. In *Of the Laws of Ecclesiastical Polity*,
written at the end of the sixteenth century, Hooker insisted that the
English crown and the Church of England were indispensable institutions of the nation and that to bifurcate them, or to eradicate either
one, would destroy the English commonwealth. The early seventeenth-
century Puritans carried on this theme of a national community
formed by the union of English church and state. One astute historian
has commented on the psychological and political importance of
such like-minded Anglicans and Puritans. Mr. Woodhouse writes that
they contributed "the habits of thought and feeling on which democracy must necessarily rely, and in whose absence it would inevitably
break down: a sense of the oneness of, and the individual's oneness

with, the community, an overriding loyalty to the community and a habit of steady obedience to the decrees of government. These things supply, not the principles, but the matrix of English democracy . . . they determine its temper." [9] Both groups held that the established church played a major role in the creation and preservation of the English nation.

Nor can one easily separate Puritanism and Anglicanism in regard to other ecclesiastical matters. Comparing the Puritans again with Richard Hooker and those who stood in the laudable *via media* of Anglicanism, similarity rather than dissimilarity is seen. Neither Hooker nor the early seventeenth-century Puritans made a claim for the divine right, or the *jus divinum,* of whatever polity they advocated for the Church of England. Hooker argued in the *Laws* that "there are at this day in the church of England no other than the same degrees of ecclesiastical order . . . which had their beginning from Christ and his beloved Apostles themselves." [10] But he did not say that episcopacy was a *sine qua non* for the church and that such a structure had been decreed by God in an irrevocable sense. He was quite different from Neile, Laud, and other members of the Anglican hierarchy who later asserted unequivocally the divine right status of episcopacy. Like Hooker, most Puritans of the early 1600's argued that a prelatical, independent, or presbyterian form of the church— whichever one they exposed—accorded with the ecclesiastical organization which they felt Christ and the apostles had decreed. But they were loath to place the one-and-for-all divine imprimatur upon their choice.

Preston, Sibbes, Gataker, and their colleagues were one with Hooker against the late sixteenth-century Puritans Cartwright and Travers, who claimed that Presbyterianism represented the absolute will of God. And they were distinct, by and large, from the Puritans of the 1630's and after, such as Henry Burton and the Westminster Assembly leaders, who again asserted that the Church of England organized along presbyterian lines was *jure divino.* Both Hooker and the Puritans were willing to argue among themselves about the polity of the church, but neither was confident that God sided completely with

9. Arthur S. P. Woodhouse, "Religion and Some Foundations of English Democracy," *Philosophical Review, 61,* No. 4 (Oct. 1952), 510.

10. Bk. V, ch. 78, sec. 12, in *The Works of . . . Richard Hooker,* ed. John Keble (3d ed. Oxford, The University Press, 1845) *2,* 482. See also James T. Addison, "Early Anglican Thought, 1559–1667," *Historical Magazine of the Protestant Episcopal Church, 22,* No. 3 (Sept. 1953), 335 ff.

a particular position. John Preston, preaching before King James, warned of confusing the present order of the church with the eternal will of God: "where God intendes to give the end, he alwaies gives the meanes to effect and bring that end to passe; but he gives *not to the Church the meanes of infallibilitie*, as perfect knowledge of the truth, sincere love of it, right ordered zeale for it . . ." [11] The Anglicans of Hooker's stamp and the early seventeenth-century Puritans were on common ground in refusing to claim divine favor for Episcopacy, Independency, or Presbyterianism.

The similarity between Puritanism and Anglicanism in the early seventeenth century manifested itself in still another way. Traditionally the Puritans have been thought of as a "church purification" party, while the Anglicans have been considered supporters of a corrupt *status quo*. Most Puritans did have purifying ideas about ritual and ceremony, innovations which were not shared by their Anglican colleagues. However, in respect to cleansing the church of glaring institutional disorders, the two groups were united. Both were concerned about the evils of plural benefices and nonresidency of the clergy, unjustified practices whereby clergymen were assigned parishes which they seldom visited, let alone ministered unto. Both groups were aroused over the unlearned clergy. Paul Baynes, Samuel Ward, and Richard Holdsworth stood out as Puritans who were dedicated to correct such evils. On the Anglican side, the most conspicuous example was Archbishop Bancroft (1604–10), who busied himself with curing the major ills of the church. [12] Here again, it is difficult to draw a line between Puritanism and Anglicanism.

What is it, then, that makes English Puritanism distinctive in the early 1600's? Certainly it is not the matter of church polity or issues related to the organization of the church. Nor can it be said that many of the divines were conspicuous for venturing beyond the superstructure of polity to formulate a doctrine of the church. Their American successors were to surpass them in this important respect. The importance of early seventeenth-century Puritanism does not lie in ecclesiology, doctrinal or organizational. We must look to theology and belief and the attendant pattern of life in order to assess the significance and the meaning of the movement. As William Haller

11. "The Pillar and Ground of Truth," in *Sermons Preached before His Maiestie* (London, 1630), pp. 9–10, italics supplied.

12. Roland G. Usher, in *The Reconstruction of the English Church* (2 vols. New York, Appleton, 1910), brings out clearly the role of Bancroft as a church reformer.

says, "It was the Puritan spirit as set in motion by the Puritan epic and the Puritan code . . . which in the long run chiefly mattered." [13]

THE ESSENTIAL CALVINIST CORE

GENERAL ASPECTS

The English Puritans of the early seventeenth century were Calvinists. The fruits by which they were known consisted of a steady insistence from pulpit and press on the efficacy of divine grace, the place of works, the necessity of religious experience, and the authority of the Bible. A perpetual affirmation of these and other tenets knit them together so conspicuously that there was little doubt as to who was within and who was without the Puritan camp. To be sure, the Puritans added their own interpretations and elaborations to basic Calvinist themes. This was especially true in the use of the doctrine of divine sovereignty and the idea of institutional independence, matters which were of crucial political significance. But, in their embellishments upon the work of the Genevan reformer, they radiated out from a hard core of Calvinist doctrine. They never sought an essentially different center of orientation.

The Puritans of the early 1600's also looked for authority to other continental reformers. The Marian exiles who returned in the 1560's came back citing the practices of Zurich, Basel, and Strassburg as well as those of Geneva. Zwingli, Jud, Bullinger, Oecolampadius, Capito, Bucer, and Martyr were held in high regard by the late sixteenth- and early seventeenth-century Puritans. Many of the Rhineland leaders visited England, where they became effective spokesmen in church and university for their particular variety of Reformation thought. The Rhinelanders unquestionably exerted an influence on English Puritanism.[14] Still, John Calvin and his immediate associates in Geneva were considered by the Puritans to be their foremost spiritual fathers.

The Latin edition of Calvin's *Institutes of the Christian Religion* appeared in England in 1576, whereupon it was immediately translated and went through several printings. Theodore Beza (1519– 1605), Calvin's successor at Geneva, was held in higher repute toward the end of the century than any other Reformed scholar and theologian. In the 1580's his polyglot version of the Pentateuch and his

13. Haller, *Puritanism,* p. 192.
14. See Leonard J. Trinterud, "The Origins of Puritanism," *Church History, 20,* No. 1 (March 1951).

Codex Bezae were presented to and gratefully received by the library of Cambridge University. Anthony Wingfield, public orator at Cambridge, spoke for Puritan England when he said that Calvin and Beza were held to be next in authority to scripture itself.[15] The nine Lambeth Articles of 1595, designed to correct the Calvinist deficiency of the Thirty-Nine Articles, showed striking and unashamed agreement with the *Institutes* on predestination, election, man's will, and the perseverance of the saints. John Calvin was a specter constantly at work among the Puritans of the early 1600's, directing nearly all matters of faith and order.

Calvinism was never fully espoused by Anglican leaders, although parts of it were well received. In the *Laws*, Richard Hooker acknowledged his admiration for the man Calvin and aspects of the reformer's thought. George Abbot, long-time archbishop of Canterbury (1611–33) between Bancroft and Laud, was sympathetic to the theology of the Puritans he was supposedly persecuting. James Ussher (1581–1656), head of the theological faculty at the University of Dublin, later archbishop of Armagh in Ireland, and correspondent of Preston, Sibbes, Gataker, and Ward, helped to lay Genevan thought at the very foundations of the 1615 Irish Articles of Religion. Indeed, Archbishop Ussher, a confirmed and consistent Calvinist, can even be called a Puritan. But he was an exception among the church's hierarchy. By and large, the chief principles of Anglicanism, as stated by Hooker at the beginning of the early seventeenth-century period and restated by Chillingworth (1602–44) at its close, tended to stand apart from the full-fledged Calvinism of the Puritans.

A fundamental difference between Puritanism and Anglicanism appeared in convictions about divine grace. The Puritans preached and wrote that God's grace was irresistible, all-powerful, and immutable. The grace of God, often called the mercy of God, was never the object of precise Puritan theologizing. It was a root term referring, in a comprehensive way, to God's act in the drama of man's salvation. Grace was held to be self-sufficiently efficacious and irrevocable in the Puritan scheme of soteriology. Upon this foundation were constructed the more elaborate theories of predestination,[16] man's de-

---

15. See J. Bass Mullinger, *The University of Cambridge* (Cambridge, The University Press, 1873–1911), *2*, 325–30, for Wingfield's oration and for the general importance of Calvin and Beza in the Puritanism of the late 16th and early 17th centuries.

16. Instead of Calvin's definitive election-or-damnation scheme, the Puritans

pravity, and the holy community. The chief point in the primacy of grace was the explicit, elemental insistence on the action of God. Again and again, the emphasis was laid squarely on God's will, choice, and maintenance, and on man's inability either to begin or continue the pathway to blessedness. Gataker spoke for all Puritans when he preached, "Let who will, therefore *trust* to merit: let us *fly to*, let us *rely upon mercie*." [17] It lies beyond our task to discuss the Puritan concept of God's relation to man, but suffice it to say that the Puritans preached a determinism which their Anglican contemporaries eschewed. The labels of "Arian," "Pelagian," and especially "Arminian" were pinned on the Anglicans. These terms of opprobrium were used indiscriminately and had little significance apart from their application in specific instances. It was true, however, that the Anglicans were generally unwilling to base human salvation solely on God's action and were not above saying that man could do much to save himself.[18] The Puritans considered such doctrine an affront to the grace of God.

The Puritans also agreed with Calvin on the place of works. Although works could never earn salvation, a believer who had experienced the operation of grace in his life was bound to display his

occasionally spoke of the outpouring of God's grace in predestination as extending to a particular people or, very rarely, to all mankind. Preston preached that "*Christ* be offered, and freely given to all, yet *God* intends him onely to the Elect" (*The Breast-Plate of Faith and Love* [5th ed. London, 1634], p. 9). Most Puritans seldom discussed the condemning action of God or the state of the damned. However welcome such modification of Calvinist doctrine might be, these divines labored under many an inconsistency which the Genevan reformer avoided, at least in the last edition of the *Institutes*.

Certainly it must be said that unabashed and unqualified preaching of universal, "free" grace brought criticism. The dominant factor in the equation of grace was still God's will. The Puritans were quick to ostracize even those of their own number who set about to deny God's arbitrary, secret choice in election. Such Puritan *personae non gratae* were John Goodwin, who was John Davenport's successor at St. Stephen's in London, and John Saltmarsh, pamphlet opponent of Thomas Gataker. These two belonged to the post-1630 period and represented a further modification of Calvinism.

17. *Iacob's Thankfulnesse to God* (London, 1624), p. 72.

18. This view was prevalent in the Anglican preaching and writing of the period, e. g., Launcelot Andrewes, Richard Hooker, and John Cosins. Consult Eustace M. W. Tillyard, *The Elizabethan World Picture,* London, Chatto & Windus, 1943, and Herbert J. McLachlan, *Socinianism in Seventeenth-Century England,* London, Oxford University Press, 1951. Not all Anglicans, however, preached humanistic optimism. John Donne, for example, was a leading figure in the English "Counter-Renaissance" and close in many ways to the Puritans. See Hiram Haydn, *The Counter-Renaissance* (New York, Scribners, 1950), *passim,* especially pp. 160 ff.

good fortune in his works. It made sense to the Puritans, as it did to
John Calvin, that those who had been elected to salvation should
glorify God in earthly labors. Indeed, as John Preston urged in his
sermons on works, the oft-degraded Epistle of James was not to be
considered a pillar of straw.[19]

The divines showed forth their own election by preaching and writing, and they urged parishioners to glorify God in their own fields
of endeavor. The Puritan clergy's concern and tremendous capacity
for pastoral works demonstrated the "conversionist" attitude of militant Calvinism. The divines of the early 1600's were out to evangelize
England, the Continent, America, and anyone who would listen.
Like John Wesley in the next century—possibly in a more determined
sense—they took the whole world for their parish. Although the
Puritan ministers were first of all concerned with the national established church, they fought in the pulpit and in Parliament for the
cause of international Calvinism. They rallied to the support of the
German Palatinates and of the orthodox Dutch party at the Synod
of Dort. When separated into New and Old World groups, they
corresponded with one another feverishly. They worked everywhere
for the propagation of the "true gospel" and the conversion of mankind.

The Puritan emphasis on works and evangelism came about not
only from a desire to glorify God. It resulted from a "spirit" which
so thoroughly possessed the believer that he could do no other than
lead an activist life. As with Luther, the confession "Here I stand, so
help me God" spoke to their condition. They had experienced God's
grace, knew it for a fact, and were now utterly incapable of sup-
pressing their enthusiasm.[20] If a man had the proper spirit, he had all;
he need not concern himself over the complexities of Calvinist theology.

The topics of religious experience and personal conversion occupied

19. *Breast-Plate.* The subtitle of this collection of 18 sermons is *A Treatise,
wherein the Ground and Exercise of Faith and Love, as They Are . . . Expressed
in Good Works, Is Explained.* The title page bears the texts 1 Thess. 5:8 and
James 2:14, both strong "works" passages. Preston and other Puritan divines
tried to maintain steadfastly that works were of no avail, indeed impossible, apart
from the initiating grace of God. The Puritans insisted so strongly on works,
however, that one has a right to wonder if they did not half believe that a good
life sometimes induced God's mercy. At any rate, they illustrated the old proverb
that most ministers are Calvinists when they pray but Arminians when they
preach.

20. See Alan Simpson, *Puritanism in Old and New England* (Chicago, Unversity
of Chicago Press, 1955), ch. 1: "The Puritan Thrust," where religious experience
is depicted as the "root of the matter."

the preachers far more than the themes of predestination and election, or the intricacies of faith versus works. Consequently a great proportion of the sermons dealt with the means of obtaining the spirit. How to be converted was as favorite a theme as how to convert others. Frequently the spirit was identified with the Pauline conception of the indwelling Christ: "I am crucified with Christ, but I live, yet not I any more, but Christ liveth in me" (Gal. 2: 20a). Paul Baynes, one of the more subdued university Puritans, urged his readers to "get C H R I S T, know Him, and thou knowest all." [21] The second person of the Trinity alone is incarnate, argued Baynes, and because Christ is partly like us a "getting" of him is a real possibility. Once gotten, Christ provided the *élan* which both guided and dominated a believer's life. Nowhere in the Anglican preaching and writing of the early seventeenth century was there a comparable emphasis on personal religious experience. Nor did the Anglicans manifest the activism which the infixed spirit irresistibly produced.

A concern for morality was an additional mark of the Calvinist core. Sermons preached on the "good life" vied for top popularity with those on experience and conversion. Together they far outnumbered those dealing with the organization of the church or political topics. The Puritan divines saw life as a savage battle with demonic principalities and powers. Each believer with God's help could achieve victory, however, by "watching," "exact walking," and "mortification"—a common Puritan term for the turning of the heart from sin to grace. A favorite theme of Puritan moralists was self-limitation. Thomas Gataker, preaching on Psalm 13:1, urged his hearers to search within themselves to see if their excesses of body and spirit were responsible for their estrangement from God.[22] The feeling of spiritual lostness was attributed more often to inadequate restriction of desire than to God's wrath.

Puritan moralism was perhaps most vividly expressed in Sabbatarianism. An enlarged edition of Nicholas Bownd's *The Doctrine of the Sabbath* was released in 1606. Bownd's book, originally published in 1595, was an amplification of *A Treatise of the Sabbath* written by his father-in-law, Richard Greenham, in 1592. Each successive edition of this Puritan textbook laid down stricter rules than the last for the observance of both Sabbath and weekday life. Neither

21. *A Commentarie upon the First and Second Chapters of Saint Paul to the Colossians* . . . (London, 1634), p. 77.

22. *David's Remembrancer . . . A Sermon at Serjeants Inne in Fleet Street,* London, 1637.

Israel nor Geneva had lived under such an uncompromising set of proscriptions.

The Puritans did not fail to warn their political allies, the common lawyers, about the proper observance of God's holy day. Gataker noted that many Lincoln's Inn barristers conducted business with their clients on Sunday mornings. In the chapel services of the inn he spoke against the practice, and craftily moved his 7:00 A.M. Sabbath lecture to a later hour in the morning and his Wednesday lecture to Sunday afternoon.[23] The lawyers complied with the changes; Sabbath scrambles for legal fees gave way to Puritan strictures. It was even said that Gataker's popularity at the inn increased rather than diminished. Sabbatarianism and strict morality were issues between the Puritans and Anglicans and further served to differentiate the two groups.

The Calvinist core was seen once again in Puritan thought on the authority of the Bible. In the commandments of scripture, the Puritans found answers to questions on church polity, theology, and the good life. They applied the old epithet "antinomian" to their brethren, both Anglicans and dissenters, who refused to give the Bible its due authority in all aspects of Christian faith. William Bradshaw spoke for all his fellow believers in the opening sentence of his *English Puritanisme*: "*Im primis*, They [the Puritans] hold and maintain That the Word of God contained in the writings of the Prophets and Apostles, is of absolute perfection, given by Christ and head of the Church, to be unto the same, the sole Canon and rule of all matters of Religion, and the worship and service of God whatsoever." [24]

The biblicism of the early seventeenth-century Puritans differed from that of their Presbyterian forerunners in the preceding century. Preston, Gouge, Gataker, Bradshaw, and their associates did not use the Bible as a collection of scattered proof-texts for support of various polity and theological positions, as did Cartwright and Travers. Of course, the Bible did have definite things to say about belief, morality, and the organization of the church, but the Jacobean Puritans warned their congregations not to seize hastily upon a particular text as the embodiment of the whole scriptural truth. John Preston, preaching before James on the means of achieving the good life, said: "First, looke to the whole rule, he that lookes but to a part

23. Thomas Gataker, *A Discours Apologetical* (London, 1654), pp. 16–17.
24. In *Several Treatises of Worship & Ceremonies* (Cambridge, 1660), p. 35. *English Puritanisme* was first published in 1604; it was translated into Latin by William Ames in 1610 for circulation on the Continent.

shall never do a business exactly . . . you must have respect to all
the commandments, to all the precepts that runne thorow the booke
of God." [25] The advice to seek the "whole rule" of the Bible was frequently given. The biblical standards for such complex matters as
church polity and the good life could only be found after long and
soul-searching study. The Bible had an unquestioned authority as
God's word, but a special knowledge born out of continual wrestling
with scripture in its entirety was required before biblical authority
could be known and declared. The Anglicans did not, as a rule, ascribe
such authority to the Bible, nor did they show signs of having grap-
pled with the problem of scriptural interpretation.

These were the marks of English Puritanism in the early seventeenth century. The adoption of a hard core of Calvinist doctrine
was, of course, accompanied by the continuous process of innovation and modification. The warm devotionalism of the Puritans in
particular was a full step removed from the somewhat stony piety
of John Calvin. John Preston and others preached again and again
that God revealed himself to men as not only perfect, unchangeable,
almighty, and eternal but also kind, patient, and abundant in mercy
and truth.[26] Here was a God who could be known intimately in the
personal experience of believers. Perhaps the most significant transformation of Calvinist doctrine came in matters of political importance: the Puritan use of the doctrine of divine sovereignty and
the idea of institutional independence. These topics deserve and will
receive special consideration in the remainder of the chapter. No matter what changes were wrought, however, early seventeenth-century
Puritanism never seriously departed from its Calvinist heritage.

DIVINE SOVEREIGNTY

The Puritans believed God to be the absolute and final ruler of the
world and all that lay therein. God's rule extended everywhere; it
could not be divided or qualified. All things acknowledged the sway
of the sovereign Lord. The early seventeenth-century Puritans were
not to be confused with their successors in the 1640's, who made a distinction between the realms of grace and nature. The later Inde-

25. "Exact Walking," p. 109, in *Sermons*.
26. E.g., see his *Life Eternall*, pp. 119 ff. (1st pagination). Such devotionalism
was not as far removed from Calvin as the thought of later Puritan mysticism,
with which early 17th-century Puritanism is not to be confused. Under the rubric
of later Puritan mysticism would come the Seekers, Happy Finders (particularly
John Saltmarsh), Ranters, and Quakers.

pendents, in quasi-alliance with the Levellers and sectaries, saw "nature" through a wide-angle lens. The term referred both to the physical world and, more significantly, to man's whole social and political life. The word "grace," on the other hand, had narrower confines and related primarily to personal belief and the life of the church. The expedient idea spread among the mid-century Puritans that while God had created the state of nature, he left its governance and direction to man, who was at liberty to follow human reason, common sense, and natural law. Religious toleration and democratic equality were held to be possible and necessary in the state of nature. Toleration and equality in nature were compatible with one true faith and divine election which still held in the God-directed state of grace.[27] For these Civil War Puritans, nature displayed an indirection in God's rule, whereas grace showed full divine sovereignty.

There was no such division in the world for John Calvin, the spiritual father of the early seventeenth-century Puritans. The Genevan reformer did entertain a certain dualism when he spoke of the realms of God's redemption and of God's wrath, and the realms where God ruled directly and where he ruled by covenant. Still, no matter what the dualism, Calvin maintained that God ruled both parts with plenary power. Divine sovereignty was not delegated, divided, qualified, or reduced simply because there were joints and sections in the structure of the world. Like Calvin, the Puritans asserted the singular, comprehensive, forthright power of God, who held the helm of the universe in his hands.

The idea of an all-embracing divine sovereignty was not the sole property of the Calvinist tradition. The concept had found expression in medieval Roman Catholic thought and, more indigenously, in John Wyclif, the proto-reformer of the late fourteenth century. John Calvin gave the idea of God's rule a new vividness, however; the English Puritans carried on where Calvin had left the matter. The Marian exiles returned with translated Genevan Bibles bearing an abundance of printed marginal notes which elaborated the point of God's transcendent sway.[28] A favorite text of both sixteenth- and

27. See Woodhouse, *Army Debates*, intro.

28. The English translation of the Genevan Bible was the standard text for English Protestants, both Puritan and Anglican, in the late 16th and early 17th centuries. Not until the mid-17th century did the King James Version supplant the Genevan. Biblical quotations in this book are taken from *The Bible. That Is, the Holy Scriptures Conteined in the Old and New Testament . . . with Most Profitable Annotations upon All Hard Places, and Other Things of Great Importance,* London, Barker, 1608. This is one of the nearly 200 editions of the original English Genevan Bible (1560) printed by 1640. The Genevan Bible is

seventeenth-century Puritanism was Exodus 3:12–15: "And God answered Moses, I AM THAT I AM. Also he sayd, Thus shalt thou say unto the children of Israel, I AM hath sent me unto you" (v. 14). The passage was used again and again to show both the finality and the absoluteness of God's rule.[29]

The Puritans were quick to single out for approval any thinkers who supported their understanding of divine sovereignty. William Prynne cited Martin Bucer, the Rhineland reformer, as a learned, authoritative non-Arminian who bespoke the true doctrine of God.[30] Bucer came to England in later life and held a divinity professorship at Cambridge from 1548 until his death in 1551. Throughout the late sixteenth and early seventeenth centuries, the Puritans steadily commended him for his concept of the "reign of Christ," to which they felt indebted for illumination of divine sovereignty.[31]

Thomas Gataker was attracted to Marcus Aurelius and Roman Stoicism because he saw, even in the works of a "Heathen Emperor, under whose reign the Christians suffered persecution," the clear emphasis on God's rule and providence. In Gataker's preface to an edition of Aurelius' maxims, the divine paraphrased Stoic thought as follows: "THE DIVINE PROVIDENCE takes care of human affairs; and not of the universe only, in general; but, of each single man, and each single matter: Is present in all the affairs of man . . . God is, therefore, above all to be . . . acknowledged . . . To him alone, we ought, in singleness of heart, to yield a willing obedience in all we do." [32] For the Puritans, it was an inescapable fact that God ruled everywhere and in everything.

---

often called the "Breeches" Bible because of the rendering of Gen. 3:7b. "And they sewed figge tree leaves together, and made themselves breeches," rather than "aprons."

The 1611 King James Version cannot be disassociated from Puritanism, particularly in its manner of depicting God's sovereignty. John Rainolds, or Reynolds, and other Puritan leaders at the Hampton Court conference in 1604 were the chief ones who urged the king to authorize the translation. Work on the new Bible was conducted at three centers, two of which were the universities, where Puritan sentiment was strong. Samuel Ward of Cambridge was in charge of the committee responsible for the Apocrypha.

29. E.g., see Preston, *Life Eternall*. Thirteen of the 18 sermons in this collection were preached on Exodus 3:13–15.

30. See Prynne, *Anti-Arminianisme. Or the Church of Englands Old Antithesis to New Arminianisme* (2d ed. London, 1630), pp. 80 ff., 139.

31. Consult Wilhelm Pauck, *Das Reich Gottes auf Erden: Utopie und Wirklichkeit. Eine Untersuchung zu Butzers "De Regno Christi" und zur englischen Staatskirche des 16. Jahrhunderts,* Berlin, de Gruyter, 1928.

32. *The Meditations of the Emperor Marcus Aurelius Antoninus,* trans. James

It is often said that English Puritanism modified the Calvinist doctrine of God by the use of covenant or "federal" theology. This theology, which elaborated on the meaning of the word *foedus*, held that man and God had entered into a testament, an agreement, or a league with one another.[33] Such doctrine canceled out the austerity and remoteness of Calvin's supreme being and made God more approachable. God entered into a compact with man, as he had with Abraham and other Old Testament figures, whereby he promised salvation and protection in return for man's faithfulness. Covenant thought, it is maintained, was not only important for God-man relations, but had important implications for social and political development. People covenanted among themselves to form a church, a family, a commonwealth, or a state. They also covenanted with God as a third partner, who became the guarantor of the terms of the arrangement. The political mutations of the covenant theme were numerous; various meanings of the compact between God, ruler, and people were seen. Many historians have pointed to the versatility and provocativeness of covenant thought in English Puritanism and have found there the basis for the secular political contract of Hobbes, Locke, Rousseau, and others.

Federal theology was present in Puritanism and undoubtedly exerted an influence upon the development of political thought. The Puritans saw all kinds of covenants. There were covenants between man and God, God and Christ, Christ and man, and covenants of works, of grace, of nature, and of creation.

So much so good. It should be made clear, however, that covenant thought as it existed in English Puritanism of the early 1600's was a subordinate point under the major heading of divine sovereignty. The

Moor and Francis Hutcheson (Glasgow, Foulis, 1742), pp. 296–9. Certain sections of Gataker's heavily annotated edition of the *Meditations* have been translated by Moor and Hutcheson and placed at the end of their book. The divine's work originally appeared as a Latin translation of Aurelius' Greek in Thomae Gatakeri, *Opera Critica*, Trajecti ad Rhenum, 1697–98.

33. Consult Champlin Burrage, *The Church Covenant Idea. Its Origin and Its Development*, Philadelphia, Baptist Publication Society, 1904; Samuel E. Morison, *The Puritan Pronoas*, New York, New York University Press, 1936; and Trinterud, "Origins." In ascribing uniqueness to English covenant theology, it must be remembered that covenant thought was prevalent on the continent; see Everett H. Emerson, "Calvin and Covenant Theology," *Church History, 25*, No. 2 (June 1956), and the unpublished dissertation (Yale, 1956) by Charles S. McCoy, "The Covenant Theology of Johannes Cocceius [1603–69]." Indeed the idea of covenant, being a dominant biblical motif, has been in evidence throughout the history of Christian thought.

granting of a compact or covenant was always an exercise of God's sway and power. If the idea of covenant could be used to exemplify divine sovereignty, it was so employed, but it had no place apart from the overriding concept of God's rule of the world. In fact, some divines of the early seventeenth century were loath to use the concept because it implied that God needed an intermediary between himself and what he had created. If God compacted or covenanted, did not this mean that he ruled indirectly? John Preston, who preached of covenant but who scarcely can be hailed as a great expounder of federal theology, was always careful to put first things first. Since God does things "immediately by the presence of his essence, hence we gather; first, that he governs the world immediately. . . . he guides immediately, and being everywhere present, hee needeth no Deputies." [34] William Whitaker, Richard Rogers, Paul Baynes, Samuel Ward, and William Twisse in all their extant tracts and sermons were pointedly against covenant. William Prynne made only passing references to the concept. To be sure, Richard Sibbes and a few other Jacobean Puritans were on fire with the idea and helped to develop federal theology, but always as an exemplification of divine sovereignty.

The connection of covenant theology with divine sovereignty can be more precisely established by a clarification of terminology. Use of the word "contract" in describing covenant thought accomplishes a great injustice. Any *quid pro quo* arrangement between God and man, wherein God and man bargain with each other over their respective rights and responsibilities, was simply not found in the federal theology of the seventeenth century. Such unrefined covenant thought had appeared, however, in the Puritanism and Anglicanism of the previous century. When man was a child of righteousness, God favored him and, conversely, when man lived in iniquity, God chastised him. Queen Mary was held by many sixteenth-century Protes-

---

34. *Life Eternall*, p. 150 (2d pagination). Preston's so-called "covenant theology" is thought to be found chiefly in 18 collected sermons entitled *The New Covenant: Or the Saints Portion*, 5th ed. London, 1630. Preston's principal use of covenant in these sermons is to explain the Puritan concept of election. God covenants or promises to preserve and direct the elect. The divine act is not, however, an arrangement into which man enters freely and knowingly with God. God's covenant is not fully known to man, for election is secret; nor can man, or God, revoke the terms of the covenant, for election is immutable. Preston advances 15 "doctrines" in these sermons. Fourteen deal with God's qualities and man's condition, and only one with the idea of covenant. The subtitle of the work is *A Treatise Upholding the All-Sufficiency of God.*

tants to be a punishment for the sins of Englishmen, whereas Queen
Elizabeth was considered a reward for uprightness. Elizabeth was
frequently called Deborah, sometimes Jael, the deliverer whom God
had sent as a manifestation of his pleasure over man's good conduct.
The defeat of the Spanish Armada was held to be another sign of
God's pleasure over the righteousness of his children. God's favor to
man largely depended on whether man had fulfilled his part of a contract.

This kind of thinking was conspicuously absent in the seventeenth
century. The main point of emphasis in the 1600's was not man's part
in a contract with God, but God's promise to man that he would faithfully protect and redeem. Man's response, of course, was a rigid
moral life. The response came about, however, because of a Jeremiah-
like new law planted by God in the human heart, not because of man's
fulfillment of a Mosaic set of conditions as part of a bargain made
for God's care. It is important to note that man does not wring anything from God, nor is he capable of initiating the covenant relationship. Never a mechanical debit-credit system, covenant thought was
ultimately a doctrine of comfort and assurance.[35] God had sworn
to save and he could not fail. As Preston put it, God's promise "is
an *everlasting covenant* and the fruits are *sure mercies* . . ." [36] God
bestowed his blessings on those whom he had chosen as an exercise of
his beneficent rule and power. Variations on this basic idea produced
the concept which was so crucial for both ecclesiology and political
theory.

The point of this discussion for our study is that covenant thought
—in any of its forms, even as a doctrine of comfort—was not prevalent in early seventeenth-century English Puritanism. Neither the
Lambeth Articles of 1595 nor the Canons of the Synod of Dort in
1618–19 contained a clear reference to the concept. The Irish Articles of 1615 used the word "covenant" in the sixth heading of the
text, but none of the 104 articles explicitly developed the concept. It
was the Westminster Confession of 1647 which rendered the first
working out of the concept; all of chapter 7, "Of God's Covenant
with Man," was devoted to a statement of covenant thought. The
period 1603–30 was seedtime for the blossoming of the federal theology that was to bedeck the Puritanism of the 1630's and 40's. Cove-

35. See the unpublished dissertation (Yale, 1948) by William W. McKee, "The
Idea of Covenant in Early English Puritanism (1580–1643)."

36. *Life Eternall,* p. 87 (2d pagination).

nant as comfort and assurance was the message of those who flour-
ished chiefly in the post-1630 period, such as William Ames, John
Davenport, John Cotton, and Thomas Hooker. Indeed, federal theology had its greatest flowering in mid-century America, where a
new social, ecclesiastical, and intellectual environment largely accounted for its growth. Whatever amount of covenant thought existed among the early seventeenth-century Puritans, it was hardly a
signal alteration of the Calvinist doctrine of God. When these Puritans resorted to federal theology, they did so to corroborate their
inheritance of divine sovereignty. Their modification of Calvinist
doctrine is more correctly seen as an intensification of the fundamental idea of God's rule.

All major characteristics of Stuart Puritanism depended on the
reality of this rule. The Puritan concept of divine grace was incon-
ceivable unless God was the sole originator and sustainer in the
process of salvation. The saints' evangelical program of works was
an automatic response to God's rule. The Puritan code of morality
was required of all, but especially of the believers who thereby bore
witness to the divine sway in their own lives.[37] And, of course, the
Bible contained the record and laws of God's rule. Even religious
experience and personal conversion were connected with divine sovereignty. The "spirit" came to a person because the Almighty had
sent it. God suddenly overwhelmed the human heart and accomplished
what no amount of Aristotelian *contemplatio* had been able to do.
There was simply no substitute for the divine action. Preston preached
a sermon on Paul's conversion and entitled it "The Right Way to
Be Saved." [38] God's power in conversion was so great that he could
overcome whatever obstacles the individual believer set in the divine
path. In fact, God's rushing in was frequently painful. Each Christian was "bruised" or left "smoking," much as the Apostle had been
left blind on the road to Damascus.[39] The Puritans preached that a
man could die to his old ways and live in the spirit only because God
had sent the Redeemer who was able to enter the heart despite the

37. See Thomas Gataker, *God's Eye on His Israel* (London, 1645), for the
continuing importance of a strict moral code for those who were thoroughly regenerate. Believers showed forth God's rule by living upright lives.

38. In *Remaines of That Reverend and Learned Divine, John Preston*, 2d ed.
London, 1637.

39. As the foremost "personal religion" preacher of the age, Richard Sibbes
emphasized time and again the turmoils of conversion and the struggles of the

forces arrayed by sin and the devil. Divine sovereignty was the scarlet thread that knit together all parts of the Calvinist core.

INDEPENDENCE: THE CHURCH AND THE UNIVERSITIES

A final characteristic of the early seventeenth-century Puritans was their insistence on institutional independence. This trait was of moment in Stuart England, for the divines pressed for the independence of the crucial institutions of church and university. In the early 1600's, these two institutions were without doubt the principal arenas for Puritan proclamations. The divines maintained that both must be unfettered, if they were to be effective places for propagating the true message. The Puritans' demand that the church and the universities be free to perform certain functions took on political significance when it became clear that James and Charles sought to control not only matters of state but also matters ecclesiastical and educational.

The Puritans were one with Lutheran, Zwinglian, and Calvinist continental reformers of the sixteenth century in describing the church as that institution in which the word was preached and the sacraments were administered. Along with these Protestant essentials, the Puritans embraced the particularly Calvinist emphasis that the church must also be a place of edification. The church was "an example of life" which served as instruction for individual believers in their glorification of and service to God.[40] The edifying role of the church was seen also in its disciplinary function, by which adherence to the Puritan way of life was encouraged and enforced. Out of the Calvinist-Puritan concept of the church came several theories on the relationship of church and state.

The principal church-state positions can be illustrated by varying answers given to a fundamental question: Granted that both church and civil government are required in society, should the church be the senior partner? If the answer was yes, a theocracy re-

---

inner religious life. A typical sermon title was "The Bruised Reed and Smoking Flax," preached on Matt. 12:20, in *The Complete Works of Richard Sibbes,* ed. Alexander B. Grosart (Edinburgh, Nichol, 1862), *1,* 33–101. On the motif of combat in Christian maturation, see William Gouge's sermons "Of Arming a Christian Soldier" and "Of the Meanes to Use Spirituall Armour Aright," in *The Workes of William Gouge* (London, 1627), Vol. *2.*

40. See "Calvin's Programme for a Puritan State in Geneva, 1536–1541," in *Collected Papers of Herbert D. Foster* ([New York] priv. print., 1929), p. 39.

sulted in which the normal functions of civil government were either taken over directly or controlled by the church. This was the answer given, with modifications, by John Knox in Scotland and by some of the seventeenth-century American Puritans. If the answer was an emphatic no—but the conversionist zeal remained—a kind of Puritan Erastianism resulted. Civil government was held to be senior to the church, but the holy mission of the church was given to the state. The program advanced by certain Puritan leaders of the 1640's stands as the best example of this answer. William Prynne, lawyer as well as Puritan, angered by the demands of the orthodox Presbyterians during the Civil War, proposed that Parliament assume full direction of ecclesiastical matters. Convinced that Parliament could faithfully respond to the calling of the church as well as to new political responsibilities, Prynne joined with non-Puritan Erastians in urging secular control of the church.[41]

There was a third answer to the question, an answer which fell between yes and no. It was exemplified by the majority of the early seventeenth-century Puritans. No theocratic schemes of church-state relations were put forward by the divines of the early 1600's. Such proposals were not advanced in England until Presbyterianism rose militantly in the 1640's. Nor did Preston, Gataker, Gouge, Bradshaw, and their colleagues suggest that Parliament—or any other branch of the civil government—assume the control, let alone the function, of the church. Any form of Erastianism was banned. The early seventeenth-century Puritan leaders considered the church and the state to be independent institutions, each with its own personnel and responsibilities. The two were close cooperators, for each was charged with maintaining God's glory and truth in unadulterated form. What church and state had in common, though, did not obliterate the lines that separated them. John Preston reminded King James on his birthday that "Ministers are the vines that bring

---

41. Prynne's post-1630 Erastianism was not to be confused with that of other lawyers who were the usual secular Erastians, e.g., John Selden (1584–1654). Prynne assumed that Parliament had enough rightly oriented Puritan members to direct the holy mission of the church. He thus proposed to take ecclesiastical administration out of the hands of the radical, naive, bickering Presbyterian clergy. Parliamentarians, not church officials, were to be the cooperators with God in bringing in the kingdom. The secular Erastians had no religious motive other than to effect ecclesiastical peace. J. H. Hexter, "The Problem of the Presbyterian Independents," *American Historical Review, 44,* No. 1 (Oct. 1938), discusses Erastianism based on genuine religious motives in the post-1630 period.

forth grapes, yet Magistrates are the elemes that underprop and hold up the vines." [42] Although ostensibly a sermon of praise for the current establishment, Preston's deliverance made it clear that the crown must support and defend the church but never interfere with the church's own functions. Similar points, qualifying the maintenance of the church by the crown, were made by other divines, especially Gataker and Gouge. The church had spiritual duties over which the state had no control, just as the state had civil functions over which the church had no sway.

The Puritans again betrayed their Calvinist lineage in refusing to answer yes or no to the question of whether the church should be senior to the state. Calvin's chapters in the *Institutes* dealing with the church and civil government and his occasional references in biblical commentaries to church-state relations make it clear that he upheld the coordinate functions of church and state. At the very least it can be said that no carte blanche was given to a program which advocated the subordination of the civil to the spiritual.[43] The desirability of the contrary Erastian arrangement was not even discussed.

Genevan Calvinists, French Huguenots, Scottish Presbyterians, English Puritans, and American Independents all proposed different solutions to the problem of church and state, depending on the political, ecclesiastical, and ideological climate of their *loci operandi*. The closest agreement between these groups was found in the case of Genevan Calvinists and English Puritans of the early 1600's. The Puritans continued in the tradition which stressed the coordinate relation of church and state. Whether or not one wishes to trace a line from mid-sixteenth-century Geneva to early seventeenth-century England, it cannot be denied that the Puritans had a recognizable position which separated them from their Anglican brethren in the matter of church and state. As we shall see, the Anglicans conformed to James' and Charles' Erastian demands, whereas the Puritans contended with the Stuarts over the crown's tampering with the church.

As in the church, so it was in the universities. The Puritans, who represented a sizable and vocal element in the university life of seventeenth-century England, steadfastly resisted the crown's attempted manipulation. Their strength was largely centered in Cam-

42. "The Pillar and Ground of Truth," in *Sermons*, p. 20.
43. On the independence of church and state in Calvin, see H. Richard Niebuhr, *The Kingdom of God in America* (Chicago, Willett, Clark, 1937), p. 39, and Foster, "Calvin's Programme," pp. 38–41.

bridge University, although Oxford educated many Puritan critics of the crown, such as John Rainolds (or Reynolds), William Prynne, and John Pym. Freer matriculation oaths, proximity to Puritan-dominated London and the eastern counties, and a long tradition of furnishing leaders for the church made Cambridge the university stronghold. Nine of the ten divines selected for close study in this book were educated at Cambridge.

During the late sixteenth and early seventeenth centuries, Emmanuel College was probably the leading Puritan entrenchment in the universities. Emmanuel had been founded by the influential Puritan sympathizer, Sir Walter Mildmay, who secured a charter for its organization from Queen Elizabeth in 1584. Mildmay and his associates clearly intended the college to be a seminary for the ministry. Consequently the usual fellowships or appointments were not available in medicine and civil law, the other two recognized areas of professional training. The first master of the college was the highly respected divine Lawrence Chaderton. Following Chaderton's thirty-six-year administration, later masters in the early seventeenth century included John Preston and Richard Holdsworth. Bradshaw, Ward, Yates, and many other vigorous Puritan divines were members of Emmanuel during undergraduate days. Some of them were appointed as fellows for teaching and further study in the college.

Emmanuel educated the leaders of American as well as English Puritanism in the 1600's. Nathaniel Ward, Thomas Hooker, Samuel Whiting, Nathaniel Rogers, John Cotton, Thomas Shepard, Samuel Stone, and Francis Higginson received all or part of their education within its halls. So rapidly did Emmanuel grow that in the early seventeenth century it had the second largest combined total of fellows and undergraduates and the largest number of undergraduates of any college in the university.[44] Mildmay's famous remark of the 1580's that he had "set an acorn, which when it becomes an oak, God alone knows what will be the fruit thereof" [45] took on special relevance in the seventeenth century.

Other colleges at Cambridge joined in the nurturing of Puritanism. Sidney Sussex, founded in 1596, St. John's, Christ's, Trinity, King's, and Queen's all afforded an opportunity for Puritan indoctrination. A final indication of the role which Cambridge University played in the Puritanism of the early seventeenth century was that five of the

44. Mullinger, Cambridge, 2, 472.

45. Evelyn S. Shuckburgh, Emmanuel College (London, F. E. Robinson, 1904), p. 22.

six British delegates to the Calvinist Synod of Dort, including the one alternate, were Cambridge men.

The connection between the universities and Puritanism was mutually beneficial in the early 1600's. Cambridge and Oxford educated the clergy and bolstered the Puritan cause, and the divines supported, by and large, the total educational program of the universities. Cambridge and Oxford were welcomed not only as seminaries for training in theology, biblical studies, and holy orders but also as places for the advancement of secular knowledge and general learning.

In the late sixteenth and early seventeenth centuries, both Cambridge and Oxford were escaping from a narrow scholastic curriculum. The universities began to offer genuinely new courses of study in the liberal arts and sciences.[46] The study of logic, long held as a prerequisite for scholastic theology, was given a lesser role, whereas that given to rhetoric was expanded. Under the latter rubric, a whole survey of classical literature was offered with new readings selected for basic texts. Rhetoric was no longer just a division in the scholastic curriculum dealing with the fine art of expression. Moreover, contemporaneousness was added to university life by studies in modern languages, modern history, new philosophical concepts, and current developments in mathematics and science. Finally, the system of instruction shifted away from formal university-wide lectures to the personal direction of students by college tutors, a change which permitted flexibility and individual attention.

Cambridge and Oxford were thus in the process of winning an educational independence from the dead weight of scholastic tradition. This did not mean that theological instruction and religious life vanished from the universities. Professorships of divinity maintained their high prestige. Conformity with the doctrine and ritual of the established church was still imposed on the universities. The unorganized, informal religious devotion of students, fellows, and faculty continued and probably increased. No longer, however, was theology the queen, with the ancient trivium and the quadrivium serving as obeisant courtiers.

The early seventeenth-century Puritans were sympathetic to the transition. Many of them played a part in the change, spending their ministries as fellows, tutors, and masters in the colleges. The scholarly

46. See the unpublished dissertation (Yale, 1952) by Mark H. Curtis, "Oxford and Cambridge in Transition. An Essay on Changing Relations between the English Universities and English Society, 1558–1642," *passim*. I have depended on this excellent study for much of the above section on the universities.

interests of the divines both before and after the receipt of degrees showed their interest in the new range of subjects. Gataker was excited by some of the heretofore neglected thinkers in classical thought, particularly the Roman Stoics. As a student in Christ's College, Ward became intensely interested in geometry and later in natural science. Preston began with philosophy, shifted to medicine, and finally turned to divinity. Gouge was a philosopher of repute and highly regarded for his expertness in Ramist logic. Nathaniel Carpenter, a B.A. and B.D. graduate of Oxford and later protégé of Archbishop Ussher in Ireland, was a noted geographer, poet, mathematician, and philosopher. One university divine, Richard Holdsworth, associated with both St. John's and Emmanuel Colleges, busied himself studying the role of the student in the changing curriculum. In "Directions for a Student in the Universitie," Holdsworth carefully described the best ways for an undergraduate to imbibe the new education.[47]

The Puritans of the early 1600's gave more than passive approval to the transition under way in the universities: they were caught up in the prevailing enthusiasm for the renovated arts and sciences. As master of Emmanuel College and vice-chancellor of Cambridge, Holdsworth bespoke the Puritan love for the new Cambridge and Oxford: "The Universities are not only seminaries for the Church, but eyes for the Kingdom; not only the homes of the Prophets, but fountains for civil society, giving forth healthful waters. They are places where the finest minds prepare for the governance of all of life . . . whatever harm is sustained by the Universities, to the same degree, the whole land is necessarily jeopardized." [48]

The Puritan concern was expressed in wholehearted support of the universities' traditional autonomy. From early medieval times, Cambridge and Oxford had enjoyed a minimum of interference with their freedom. Even when the universities were essentially arms of the church in the pre-Reformation period, they were entitled to certain exemptions from episcopal and archiepiscopal control. Before assuming ecclesiastical administration of the land, Henry VIII was

47. Mr. Curtis assigns probable authorship of this MS to Holdsworth when the divine was either a fellow of St. John's College, 1613–20, or master of Emmanuel, 1637–43 ("Oxford and Cambridge," pp. 246–8).

48. "Oratio . . . in Vesperiis Comitiorum, apud Cantabrigienses," in *Praelectiones Theologicae,* ed. Rich. Pearson (Londini, 1661), p. 735, my translation of a section in Holdsworth's Latin oration delivered at the Cambridge commencement of July 1641, just before the outbreak of hostilities. See the combined translation and paraphrase of the whole address in Mullinger, *Cambridge, 3,* 215 ff.

careful to guarantee the independence of the two institutions in a
charter of 1523. Throughout the Tudor period successive charters
and statutes confirmed and enlarged university privileges. In 1571
Queen Elizabeth granted Cambridge and Oxford a "Magna Carta"
which, among other things, bestowed official names, the status of incorporation, and the right to sue and be sued; guaranteed all existing properties and rights thereto; and "ratyfied stablished and confirmed" all previous liberties and exemptions—"any Statute lawe
usage custom contruccion or other thing to the contrary in any
wyse notwithstanding." [49] "This blessed act of parliament," to use
the words of Sir Edward Coke,[50] gave Cambridge and Oxford a definitive, legal independence.

An important freedom reconfirmed for the universities by the 1571
statute, one which had been abrogated in the earlier Tudor period,
was exemption from jurisdiction of the king's courts. Cambridge and
Oxford each had a "chancellor's court" where the vice-chancellor sat
as judge to handle cases in which academic persons were involved.
Originally designed to keep students from legal involvement in distant courts, the arrangement allowed the universities to conduct a
large part of their legal affairs under a procedure quite distinct from
that which prevailed elsewhere in the country. Blackstone later
termed it "a course much conformed to the civil law." [51] This situation, unique in a land dominated by the common law, was typical of
the autonomy which the universities had long enjoyed.

In the Stuart era, the independence of the universities continued
to be at least superficially guaranteed. James granted a charter in
1605 which once again confirmed the ancient liberties. But James
and Charles actually sought to control the universities and took
steps to implement their aim. The Puritan divines lamented the interferences of the Stuart crown. As master of Sidney Sussex College,
Samuel Ward deplored the king's act in imposing a scholar upon the
fellowship of Christ's College, a sister Puritan society. He wrote in
his diary under entry of November 8, 1609, "Woe is me for Christ's
College. Now is one imposed upon [it] who will be the utter ruin and
destruction of that College. . . . Lord, my God take some pity and

49. *Enactments in Parliament Specially concerning the Universities of Oxford
and Cambridge,* ed. John Griffiths (Oxford, Clarendon Press, 1869), p. 31.
50. *The Fourth Part of the Institutes of the Laws of England* (London, 1797),
sec. xliv, p. 227.
51. William Blackstone, *Commentaries on the Laws of England* (11th ed. London,
1791), *3,* 84.

compassion upon that poor college. In the multitude of thy mercies do not utterly forsake it. . . . O Lord, have mercy, mercy, mercy." [52]

As we shall see, the divines attacked the king for interference not only in the matter of appointments but also in the broader issues of educational policy and university religious life. Unless Cambridge and Oxford continued to enjoy their ancient independent existence, they could not be effective "homes of the Prophets" and "fountains for civil society." The Puritans' support of university independence became another mark of differentiation from the high churchmen. The Anglicans generally acceded to the crown's demands for greater control over the life of Cambridge and Oxford. Baynes, Ward, and Holdsworth, on the other hand, safeguarded not only their churches, or their places of worship and preaching, but also their beloved places of learning.

The Puritan confirmation of the universities' autonomy was perhaps specially English, yet it was connected with the Calvinist insistence on the independence of institutions. John Calvin had employed afresh the medieval conviction that church, empire, and university (*sacerdotium, imperium,* and *studium*) were at once separate and at the same time bound together as the very foundation of Christian society. The Genevan beheld the church, the magistracy, and the academy as free from each other and yet joined to one another in a single base for the new Protestant *corpus Christianum.* Characteristically, Calvin used the offices of Christ as priest, king, and prophet (or teacher) to demonstrate the different functions of and the free relations between ministers, magistrates, and masters.[53] The early seventeenth-century divines were true to their religious heritage in pronouncing that university, as well as church and state, should be independent and unfettered in order to perform particular tasks in the English community.

These Puritans whom King James called "pestes in the Church and Common-weale" were, above all else, religious men. They were known by their beliefs and their practices. They were not an ecclesiastical faction, for the matter of church polity was by no means agreed upon, nor was it a matter of great moment among them. The Puritans were identified by a theology which was rooted in sixteenth-

52. Knappen, *Diaries,* pp. 130–1, from Ward's MS "Adversaria."
53. See George H. Williams, "An Excursus. Church, Commonwealth, and College. The Religious Sources of the Idea of a University," in *The Harvard Divinity School. Its Place in Harvard University and in American Culture,* ed. George H. Williams (Boston, Beacon Press, 1954), pp. 342 ff.

century Calvinism. The early seventeenth-century divines constantly forced changes upon the fundamental doctrine. It was still Calvinism, however, which set them apart from their Anglican colleagues, who were beginning to espouse liberal, Arminian tendencies. Although men of a religious calling, the Puritans had a high political potential. Once prodded by royal absolutism, the potential became actuality in the early 1600's. The Puritans proved to be a plague on Stuart kingship, and James' excoriation of them rang true.

2 THE COMMON LAWYERS: MEDDLERS WITH THE KING'S PREROGATIVE

IN SOME WAYS, the crown's legal adversaries can be identified more readily than its religious opponents. The "popular sort of lawyers who most affrontedly" trampled on the prerogative were, first of all, dedicated to the practice of law. They argued the law of the land in courts, interpreted it as judges on the bench, and commented on it in treatises and reports. They had been called to the bar. Law was their profession and their life.

The lawyers considered here are not to be confused with those whose careers had a tangential connection with the law of the land, but whose major pursuits lay elsewhere. Some who were skilled in the ways of English law, for instance, considered the furtherance of Parliament to be their primary calling. Stalwarts of the House of Commons like John Eliot and John Pym belong in this group. Although Eliot, the great idealist leader of Parliament in the late 1620's, resided at an inn of court, there is no record of his being called to the bar. He never served as a judge or acted as counsel in the chief cases of the early 1600's. Pym, Eliot's fiery successor in the leadership of the house in the 1640's, was likewise not called to the bar, nor was his career essentially a legal one. Of course, the parliamentary cause was a concern of the professional lawyers, but they were fighting by and large for genuine legal concerns in the halls of Westminster. For them, Parliament was more a means than an end.

The lawyers of our study should also be distinguished from the common law "antiquarians" of the period, such as Henry Finch, Robert Bruce Cotton, Henry and John Spelman, Michael Dalton, and others. These men were collectors, editors, and writers, whose work has proved to be invaluable for the later understanding and interpretation of English law. Some of the lawyers studied here were, to be sure, legal writers, but their primary task was never that of collecting manuscripts and founding libraries. They were more active. As justices of the common law bench, counsel in leading cases, and members of Parliament, the professional lawyers were more in the thick of things.

Their activity was directed against the whole governmental program of the Stuart crown. They were out to block the absolutist policies of James and Charles. This characteristic further distinguished them from other lawyers, also actively dedicated to the practice of law, who supported the Stuart regime. The crown generally found dependable support in the first part of the century from such lawyers as John Doddridge (or Doderidge), Francis Bacon, Robert Heath, John Finch, and David Jenkins. Bacon, of course, was the leading royal protagonist of the early seventeenth century. Then there were the less dependable lawyers, from the crown's point of view, who sometimes did and sometimes did not side with the king. Among such wavering supporters of the throne were Robert Phelips, Henry Yelverton, William Noye (or Noy), and Edward Littleton. The common lawyers with whom we are concerned were not only dedicated to and active in the practice of law but implacable and consistent in their opposition to the Stuarts.

Without question the leader of these lawyers was *Sir Edward Coke* (1552–1634).[1] Coke was probably the man most feared by James and Charles. A person of great acumen, he has rightly been called the intellectual leader of the opposition to the crown.[2] In 1606 Coke became chief justice of the Court of Common Pleas, in which capacity he stoutly opposed the Stuart exercise of royal prerogative. In an effort to mollify his opposition, possibly to win him over, James made him chief justice of the King's Bench in 1613. The great lawyer's trenchant criticism of the crown's policies continued, however, and in 1616 James summarily dismissed him from high judicial office. Thereafter Coke continued his fight against the crown in Parliament. Probably his greatest contribution to the common law was his compilation of legal reports and the writing of *The Institutes of the Laws of England*. These works were instrumental in saving the common law from burial with medieval relics; Coke is frequently cited as

1. *DNB* generally provides accurate biographical data for the lawyers. G.P. Macdonell's article on Coke is first-rate. Catherine Drinker Bowen, *The Lion and the Throne. The Life and Times of Sir Edward Coke, 1552–1634* (Boston, Little, Brown, 1957), is by far the best full-length biography of the great jurist.

2. Wallace Notestein, "The Stuart Period: Unsolved Problems," *Annual Report of the American Historical Association for the Year 1916, 1,* 392.

the one most responsible for the adaptation of England's ancient law to the modern period. Although the bulk of the *Institutes* and *Reports* was concerned with private law (e.g., torts, contract, and agency) and the jurisdiction of the courts, Coke found ample room in such realms to carry out his attack on the Stuart crown.[3] His commentary in the *Institutes* and *Reports* on the so-called "constitutional cases" displayed an unmistakably antiroyalist persuasion. His power also lay in the prestige and influence which he enjoyed among the people. When Coke's death appeared imminent in 1631, Charles ordered the jurist's papers destroyed because their publication would augment popular resentment of the crown.

Coke's personal life and habits do not win unreserved admiration. He practiced law for the love of it, but also for the money. He had an abundance of the latter because of high legal fees, although he never became involved in bribery as did so many of his colleagues and contemporaries. His two marriages were shrewdly calculated for their benefit to his career, and by nature he was narrow-minded, conservative, and frequently vitriolic. Nonetheless, on the basis of a brilliant and forceful legal career, Coke deserved the position of leadership which he indisputably held among the common lawyers of the early seventeenth century.

Three others stand out as common law principals in the struggle against the king. *William Hakewell* (1574–1655), *Sir James Whitelocke* (1570–1632), and *John Selden* (1584–1654) were, like Coke, professionally and actively concerned with the law, and steadily defended it against the crown. Hakewill and Whitelocke were influential leaders of the opposition in the impositions issue, which centered around the right of the king to lay direct financial levies on his subjects. Selden was conspicuous in many battles with the crown. He was particularly important for his telling arguments on behalf of habeas corpus in the Case of the Five Knights, or Darnel's Case, which grew out of the impositions struggle. Others, less prominent in their leadership, played supporting roles. *Nicholas Fuller* (fl. 1604–14) espoused the Puritans' and the lawyers' cause against the ex officio oath administered in the Court of High Commission. *Sir*

---

3. The *Institutes* were written in four Parts: (1) "A Commentary upon Littleton [the authoritative 15th-century jurist] not the Name of a Lawyer only, but the Law Itself"; (2) "Containing the Exposition of Many Ancient, and Other Statutes"; (3) "Concerning High Treason, and Other Pleas of the Crown, and Criminall Causes"; and (4) "Concerning the Jurisdiction of Courts." The *Reports* summarized and commented upon leading cases from 1572 through 1616.

Ranulphe Crew, or Randolph Crewe (1558–1646), was stripped of his chief justiceship on the King's Bench for refusing to affirm the legality of the crown's forced loans. The above six were joined by many more who upheld the ancient law of the land when it was challenged by the crown. Like the Puritans, these common lawyers were considered by James and Charles to be mortal enemies of Stuart kingly rule.

The judges and lawyers who stood against the king are finally identified by a legal ideology which set them apart from others in the profession. Coke and his colleagues insisted on the primacy of fundamental law and the independence of institutions. A close examination of these intricate concepts as understood by the lawyers is in order.

FUNDAMENTAL LAW

In England the term "fundamental law" was not employed in a political sense until the early seventeenth century. The standard historian of the period, Samuel R. Gardiner, holds that the concept originated among the courtiers of Queen Henrietta Maria, the wife of Charles I, and first came into political use during the ship money controversy of the mid-1630's.[4] Mr. McIlwain cites earlier uses of the term at the beginning of the century.[5] The present writer has found fundamental law prominently employed in many areas of political concern in the early 1600's, particularly in the debates of the first decade over the king's right to levy impositions. Early seventeenth-century England, however, cannot be considered the birthplace of the concept. The idea of a law "fundamental" to governing authority was a common motif in the Middle Ages and found expression in the ancient idea of the "supremacy of law." In France the words "fundamental" and "law" were conjoined in political usage before the period of this study.[6] Yet it was in Stuart England for the first time that

4. *History of England from the Accession of James I to the Outbreak of the Civil War, 1603–42* (London, Longmans, 1884), *8*, 84–5. Gardiner usually speaks of the term in the plural—fundamental law*s*.

5. Charles H. McIlwain, *The High Court of Parliament and Its Supremacy. An Historical Essay on the Boundaries between Legislation and Adjudication in England* (New Haven, Yale University Press, 1910), pp. 75 ff. Anyone dealing with fundamental law stands indebted to the work of Mr. McIlwain; the present author is no exception. The debate over the meaning of fundamental law in the 17th century and later is expertly brought up-to-date in John W. Gough, *Fundamental Law in English Constitutional History*, Oxford, Clarendon Press, 1955.

6. See Francis D. Wormuth, *The Royal Prerogative, 1603–1649. A Study in*

fundamental law began to fill the air. It entered freely and master-fully into common law courts, the halls of Parliament, the chambers of the king, and even the pulpits.

So strident were the cries of fundamental law that any definite sense of the term is hard to grasp. Mr. Allen rightly speaks of the confusion and ambiguity caused by the uproar in the England of the 1600's: "The meaning of the . . . peculiarly elusive term varied with the point of view of those who used it. Coke might mean one thing by it, and James I quite another. It might indeed be said that the whole controversy turned on just this question: What is the fundamental law of the English constitution? So it was that in using the term each side begged the question." [7] Coke spoke out impetu-ously in the 1628 Parliament that the word "fundamental" was "a word I understand not." [8] There were others who found the vague-ness intolerable and likewise reached the saturation point.

Fundamental law certainly did lack the precision in the early seventeenth century which it acquired in later times. In America to-day the term usually applies to the Constitution, with special ref-erence to the limitation of the legislative and executive branches of the government and to the implied right of judicial review. No such exactitude was possible in Stuart England. Not only James and the royalists, Coke and the lawyers, but nearly every identifiable political group seized upon the term for their own purposes. At least four in-terpretations of fundamental law were current in the early years of the century.

There was first the conception of the Stuart kings and their allies. It was carefully set forth by James at the beginning of his reign when he defended his succession to the throne. In a speech before Parlia-ment the new monarch stated that fundamental law maintains "the King's descent . . . and the heritage of the succession and Mon-archie." Having secured and guaranteed a prince his throne, funda-mental law also becomes the rule of a "free Monarchie," or a govern-

---

English Political and Constitutional Ideas (Ithaca, N.Y., Cornell University Press, 1939), pp. 32–3.

7. *English Political Thought, 1, 3.*

8. Referring to "fundamental property" and "fundamental liberty" (Gough, *Fundamental Law,* n. P, p. 218). Coke's words appear in the Grosvenor Diary MS. See also Margaret A. Judson, *The Crisis of the Constitution. An Essay in Con-stitutional and Political Thought, 1603–1645* (New Brunswick, N. J., Rutgers University Press, 1949), p. 247.

ment that is unfettered and limitless. "Fundamentall Lawes" [9] are the particular laws enacted by the king for the implementation of a free monarchy.

James' concept of fundamental law was elaborated by Charles and the associates of the second Stuart. A royalist judge, David Jenkins, writing during his imprisonment in the Civil War, placed fundamental law, as the law of the king's government, above all other forms of law. "The law of this Land hath three Grounds: First, *Custom.* Secondly, *Judicial Records.* Thirdly, *Acts* of *Parliament.* The two latter are but declarations of the *Common Law* and *Custom* of the Realm, touching *Royal Government.* And this law of *Royal Government* is a *Law Fundamental.*" [10] Oliver Cromwell, speaking something like a king, later made a similar appeal to the fundamental law of his Protectorate, a law which could not be set aside by parliamentarians, republicans, or any other disruptive faction.[11]

The term "fundamental law" was also found useful by those who passionately supported the cause of Parliament in the early 1600's. Many such folk argued that, since Parliament was that body wherein king and realm acted together to make statutes for the governing of the land, the laws which prescribed the role of Parliament were fundamental. The particulars of the law were found in ancient precedents, such as Magna Carta, which decreed that statutes should be written and promulgated only in Parliament. When the crown departed from the principle of making law with Parliament—from the king-in-Parliament theory of legislation—fundamental law was breached. The fundamental law also protected the members of Parliament; by it they were granted freedom of speech in both houses and the right to determine such intramural matters as disputed elections. Whenever the king interfered in parliamentary privileges, fundamental law was also at stake. Toward the end of the 1603–30

9. James' words in this paragraph are from "A Speach to Both the Houses of Parliament, Delivered in the Great Chamber at White-Hall, the Last Day of March 1607," in McIlwain, *James' Works,* p. 300.

10. *Jenkinsius Redivivus. Or the Works of . . . Judge Jenkins, Whilst a Prisoner in the Tower* (London, 1681), p. 1. The above are the opening words of the tract entitled *Lex Terrae* (1647). Later in the same work (p. 3) Jenkins substantiated his interpretation of fundamental law with the famous words of Bracton, the mid-13th-century legal authority: " 'Everyone is under the King, and he is under no one except God; he is not inferior to his subjects, and he has no equal in his Realm [my translation]': This shews where the supream power is." See also McIlwain, *High Court,* pp. 85–6.

11. McIlwain, *High Court,* pp. 86–7.

period and certainly by the outbreak of hostilities, some parliamentarians were making demands in the name of fundamental law which would give the House of Commons a new and startling plenitude of power. Eliot, Prynne, and Pym employed fundamental law to such an end.

A third use of the term appeared among the Levellers and republicans of the 1630's and 1640's. Dissatisfied with forms of existing fundamental law, whether seen in royal government, statutory procedure, parliamentary privilege, common law, or even Magna Carta, these people would make a new fundamental law for England. John Lilburne and John Wildman decried the common law's "yoke" and the "bondage" of Magna Carta; they proposed that a document be drawn to incorporate republican principles. Such a document would be based on what they considered to be "natural law" for political society. The Levellers and their fellow republicans were among the first in England to propose explicitly a written constitution which would then become fundamental law for the land.

A fourth understanding of the term was held by the common lawyers studied here. Judges and barristers like Coke, Whitelocke, Hakewill, and Selden believed that fundamental law was found in the customs, common law rules, and statutes which made up the law of the land. These components were often referred to as the "common law tradition," or simply "the common law," or sometimes just "the law." The common law was not liege to the fundamental law proclaimed by king or that upheld by the radical parliamentarians, nor could it be set aside by any new comprehensive document. For all its apparent specificity, the fundamental law of the lawyers was an intricate conception. The other interpretations of fundamental law had dealt with one kind of law, but that of the lawyers was composed of parts whose relationship was unclear. The judges and barristers had to answer a delicate intralegal question: In the case of a conflict between custom, common law rule, and statute, which was fundamental? The overriding issue for the lawyers was the relation between common law rules—in which custom was held to be the chief ingredient—and statutes. Did a statute, duly written and promulgated in Parliament, have precedence over a common law rule? The answer given by the early seventeenth-century lawyers displays their complex understanding of fundamental law.

The theory of Coke and his colleagues on the relationship of the parts of fundamental law was considerably different from that held by their counterparts in previous centuries. The difference arose largely out of the growing importance of statutes in the transition from medieval to modern times. In the thirteenth and fourteenth centuries when statutes were few in number, no compulsion existed on the part of judges to follow a statute strictly. The common law rules were held to be supreme. If a statute was inadequate for a particular litigation, its meaning was extended on the basis of the common law. Or, if it contradicted a common law rule or the common sense of the matter, the statute was simply set aside.

In the fifteenth, sixteenth, and early seventeenth centuries it became increasingly difficult to treat statutes in this cavalier fashion. Parliament was developing from a high court into a supreme legislative body; its enactments had to be taken more seriously. The problem of statutory interpretation slowly emerged as a dominant issue. During Elizabeth's reign, Sir Thomas Egerton, later Lord Ellesmere, edited a discourse on the interpretation of statutes, which was the first formal indication of the problem's seriousness. Not only did the work give elaborate rules for the proper interpretation of statutes, but it implied that the parliamentary enactments could no longer be set aside because of a conflict with common law or the common sense of a particular case. An appeal must be made to a higher principle, such as the law of "reason" or "nature," if a common law judge were to render judgment against the plain meaning of a statute.[12]

The importance of statutes continued to grow. During the late eighteenth- and early nineteenth-century era of Blackstone and Bentham, statutes became unquestionably supreme. Under no circumstances could a statute of Parliament be set aside because of some prior principle or law, for there was nothing of higher or more fundamental nature.

The early seventeenth-century lawyers and judges stood at a crucial point in this development. They were in the dilemma of recon-

12. The above analysis of statutory interpretation adheres to that advanced by Samuel E. Thorne in a 100-page introduction to *A Discourse upon the Exposicion & Understandinge of Statutes. With Sir Thomas Egerton's Additions,* San Marino, Calif., Huntington Library, 1942. The introduction reviews the problem of statutory interpretation from the 14th to the 17th century. Mr. Thorne criticizes the traditional position which held that statutory interpretation had existed in the Middle Ages; he claims the problem did not arise until the 16th century. For the other view, consult the early writings of Theodore F. T. Plucknett, primarily *Statutes & Their Interpretation in the First Half of the Fourteenth Century,* Cambridge, The University Press, 1922. For additional consideration of the problem see Gough, *Fundamental Law.*

ciling the traditional authority of common law rules with that of the increasing authority of Parliament's statutes. In a sense, they wanted to uphold both, for both were part of the common law tradition or the fundamental law. The attempted resolution of the dilemma will be treated in Chapter 7 when the lawyers' contribution to the idea of parliamentary supremacy is discussed. Here it is important to note that fundamental law for the common lawyers consisted of two ingredients, common law rules and statutes, whose relationship was in a process of transition.

Although in doubt about the relationship of its parts, the lawyers were convinced that their fundamental law taken as a whole was indispensable to English life. Legal customs, ancient rules, and acts of Parliament settled legal differences, determined the administration of justice, ordered the powers of government, and generally bequeathed an orderliness to the affairs of men. The English nation was blessed by the pervasiveness of the common law tradition. The lawyers waxed ecstatic over their fundamental law, saying that it was reason personified—a special kind of English reason, to be sure, for no other land enjoyed the advantages of this law. Sir William Dugdale (1605–86), citing Plowden and Coke as authorities, wrote: "That which we call the *Common Law* is, out of question, no less antient than the beginning of differences betwixt man and man, after the first Peopleing of this Land; *it being no other than pure and tryed Reason;* (as the late great Lawyer Mr. *Plowden* expresseth) *or the absolute perfection of Reason,* as Sir *Edward Coke* affirmeth . . ." [13] For the lawyers the common law tradition, being the perfection of reason, could rightly be called fundamental.

At this point a final complexity is seen in the common lawyers' interpretation. Fundamental law was composed of a set of specific legal entities—customs, rules, and enactments—but it also incorporated an ideal, an ultimate criterion, that stood above the particulars. The ideological structure of fundamental law will be discussed in Chapter 6. Here we would call attention to a wavering between the legal norms and the legal principle, between fundamental laws and *the* fundamental law, or the concrete and the abstract in the lawyers' understanding. But whatever the intricacy of fundamental law, this much was sure: it had created the unique English community and was to be honored and revered by all subjects of the land.

13. *Origines Juridiciales. Or, Historical Memorials of the English Laws, Courts of Justice . . . Innes of Court and Chancery* (2d ed. London, 1671), p. 3.

Independence: The Courts and the Inns of Court

The judges and lawyers of our study were finally known by an unrelenting fight for the common law courts and the inns of court, two institutions very dear to the legal profession. The strongest defender of the courts was Chief Justice Coke. The great jurist maintained that justice for England depended on the freedom of the common law bench to interpret and apply the ancient law of the land. Coke was joined by legal associates who forcefully opposed the interferences of James and Charles in the function of the courts. The judges and barristers argued that the Stuart kings were prohibited, as former kings had been, from tampering with legal procedures and jurisdictional lines which for centuries had determined the operation of the common law bench. The great courts of Common Pleas, the Exchequer, and King's Bench had a near sacred aura in the early seventeenth century. James' charge that the lawyers were "meddlers" was hurled back at him in the matter of the autonomy of these courts.

The barristers and judges can rightly be accused of reading the past with a bias when they held that the independence of the courts was an inviolate tradition of English legal history. Data abounds to prove that former English monarchs had interfered with the common law bench, even in the blessed Tudor era. The point, however, is that James and Charles were exceptional interferers. The concern of the common lawyers, if not their historical interpretation, was justified.

The inns of court were likewise precious things in the eyes of the barristers and judges. Throughout his life each lawyer was known as a member of the inn where he had received instruction in the law of the land. His closest associates in the profession were frequently those with whom he had studied. In some cases a lawyer continued to live at his inn after being admitted to the bar. The four inns of Lincoln's, Gray's, and the Middle and Inner Temples, plus the preparatory inns of chancery, actually comprised a "third university" in the realm. Allegiance to one's inn was as great as that accorded to Cambridge or Oxford.

The strength and prestige of the institutions lay in the fact that they alone offered training in the law of the land. To be a common lawyer one must have studied at an inn; Cambridge and Oxford offered legal training only in civil and canon law. If a student of a university wished to embark upon a legal career, he must later take up residence at an inn, although some lawyers-to-be were able to combine university and common law education. In general, the program was more rigorous than that encountered at the universities. Before one could be called to the bar, at least six years, and sometimes as many as eight, must have been spent in study at an inn. The length of study was regularized in 1596 at which time a seven-year limit was established. Not only academic endurance but an all-consuming love for the common law was demanded. Even in the moments of respite between reading, listening to arguments and the exposition of statutes, and participation in "moots," a student was expected to steep himself in the common law. He must "talk law," "put cases," and generally show that he had competence in *ars bablativa*, the "bablative art" of the common lawyer.[14] As Mr. Notestein remarks, "It was a long training and men who had gone through with attention and purpose must have been as thoroughly trained as anyone in England." [15]

No one knows when the first inn of court was established. The records of Lincoln's Inn known as the *Black Books*, which are the earliest official documents of any inn, go back to 1422. There are indications, however, that Lincoln's Inn as well as the others came into being before the early fifteenth century. Probably societies or associations of *apprenticii ad legem*, similar to the later inns of court, were functioning in the fourteenth century. It is likely that legal scholars may discover traces of such legal societies at the end of the thirteenth century in the reign of Edward I, the "English Justinian," at which time laymen began to replace clerics among the king's judges. The shift from cleric to lay would logically require that specific places be established for the training of nonecclesiastical judges.[16]

The common law system of legal education, evolving from unknown medieval beginnings, reached the height of its development in the sixteenth century. The inns were well suited to a growing corpus of law which was taught by informal methods at a time when the literature was small and printed books were rare. The system was maintained down to the Great Rebellion, but suffered a damaging col-

14. William S. Holdsworth, *A History of English Law* (London, Methuen, 1924), *6*, 497.

15. *English People*, p. 89. The above discussion is indebted to Mr. Notestein's ch. 8, "The Inns of Court and the Lawyers."

16. For a brief summary of the many theories on the origin of the inns, see John Hutchinson, "The Middle Temple. Its Origin and Early History," in Charles H. Hopwood and Charles T. Martin, eds., *Middle Temple Records, 1501–1703* (London, Butterworth, 1904) *1*, 1–16.

lapse in the disruption of the Civil War and the Commonwealth.[17]
The decline continued in the eighteenth century. Instruction in the
law of the land at the inns rapidly became farcical, and most apprentice lawyers deserted the societies to read law in the chambers of some
older experienced lawyer. In the middle of the eighteenth century,
Charles Viner provided for a chair in English law at Oxford University. During the last hundred years the universities have assumed
the burden of education for the legal profession, although residence
at a society in the form of dining in the hall is still technically required.
The old chestnut of "eating one's way to the bar" retains its point.
The present system of legal training is administered by the Council
of Legal Education, which sets standards and coordinates the work
of the universities and the inns. Thus the ancient societies are today
playing a vestigial role in the profession. In the early 1600's, however,
they were still virile, necessary institutions with specific responsibilities.

Throughout their golden age in the sixteenth and early seventeenth centuries, the inns of court enjoyed almost complete self-
government. They were noncorporate societies directing their affairs
by means of hoary medieval precedents and customs. Each inn had its
own governing body, such as the Benchers, or Pensioners, or a Parliament. These bodies were self-perpetuating; they determined the
course of the society in all matters, be it finance, lodging, instruction, or deportment. The government of the societies has provoked the
oft-heard generalization that the inns of court carried on the independent guild life of the Middle Ages long after it had ceased to exist
in other trades and professions.

The inns were technically beholden to the judges who had unde-
fined visitatorial powers. The judiciary was circumspect and hesitant
in the exercise of visitation; instructions and orders were usually
issued only after the accord of the individual governing bodies had
been obtained.[18] The men on the bench were, on the whole, sympathetic
guardians rather than oppressors of the independence of the inns.
The king's Privy Council likewise had vague duties of supervision,
but such responsibilities were again usually exercised after consultation with the inns. An order of the council and the judges issued in
1574 showed the high respect in which the autonomy of the societies

---

17. Holdsworth, *English Law, 6,* 481 ff.

18. See Reginald J. Fletcher, ed., *The Pension Book of Gray's Inn (Records of
the Honourable Society), 1569–1800* (London, Stevens & Haynes, 1901–10), *1,*
xli, 103, 120, 212.

was held. The order related to the reformation of the subsidiary inns of chancery, a much discussed legal issue in the 1570's. The judges and councilors declared that "The Reformacon & order of the Innes of Chauncerye is refered to the consideracon of the Benches of the Houses of Courte wherto they ar belongeng . . ." The order was repeated in 1584, and a similar decree was issued in 1630.[19]

Even the crown showed reluctance to interfere in the ancient autonomous life of the inns. From the very beginning English kings had given the societies written guarantees of rights and privileges. The inns jealously guarded all charters, patents, and grants which they had received from the throne. The 1608 patent granted to the Inner and Middle Temples was kept in an iron box, locked with two padlocks, deposited under the communion table in the Temple church, and periodically inspected. The treasured document guaranteed all "Jurisdictions, Franchises, Liberties, Privileges, Immunities and Exemptions, such and which and as fully freely and entirely and in as ample a manner and form as the late Priors and brothers of the said late priory of S John of Jerusalem, in England, or any of them, or any other or others . . . at any time had held or enjoyed . . ."[20]

The lawyers were unable to contain their pride over the close-knit, autonomous life of the inns of court. "Now all these inns of *court* and *chancery* . . . not far distant from one another . . . do make the most famous profession of the law that is in the world . . ."[21] For Coke, Hakewill, Whitelocke, and their colleagues, it was the independence which in large part made the societies unique.

In one sense the lawyers have been easier to describe than their clerical allies. The term "common lawyer" does not cry out for differentiation as does the word Puritan. But this ease is only superficial, for as one probes into the lives of the early seventeenth-century barristers one discovers complex problems of identification. The lawyers with whom we are concerned were consistent in their opposition to the crown, yet they were consciously in association with others in the profession who supported the Stuarts. A common pursuit of the law brought all lawyers together. The line between Puritan and high Anglican was drawn more sharply, despite a seeming unity in the min-

19. *Ibid.,* pp. xli, 62, and 295.
20. Frederick A. Inderwick, ed., *A Calendar of the Inner Temple Records, 1505-1714* (London, Stevens & Haynes, 1898), *2*, xvi. See pp. 337-43 for the complete Latin text of the patent issued to the Inner and Middle Temples.
21. William Herbert, *Antiquities of the Inns of Court and Chancery* (London, Vernor and Hood, 1804), p. 180, quoting Dugdale, *Origines.*

istry of the church. The things that finally divided the lawyers grew out of particular cases, as did the law which they all professed. Specific conflicts over fundamental law, the courts, and the inns of court allowed Coke, Hakewill, Whitelocke, Selden, Fuller, and Crew to show their true colors. It was then that James I and Charles I came to know their devastating "sharpe edge."

3 THE NATURE OF PURITAN AND COMMON LAW OPPOSITION

GERMANE CONCERNS AT STAKE

THE POLITICAL CONTRIBUTION of the early seventeenth-century Puritans and lawyers is not immediately apparent. Neither group directly augmented the growth of democratic or "liberal" political ideas. The divines did not insist on the semiconstitutionalism of Genevan Calvinism, the self-government of the Baptists, the individual freedom of the Independents and Levellers, or the political federalism of the covenant thinkers. Even in the matter of resistance to an evil prince, the Puritans of the early 1600's were conservatives rather than innovators.

The lawyers also failed to take patent leadership in the development of new political thought. To be sure, the barristers and judges sought to preserve the law of the land against the excesses of the crown, but they also preserved the inequity and political antiquity of the ancient law. Coke was a leading antagonist of equity, the system of law which mollified the harshness of the common law, and of the Court of Chancery where suits in equity were heard. Any reform which did not find sanction in the old customary law was unthinkable. The common lawyers of the early seventeenth century were very different from those of the late eighteenth and nineteenth centuries such as Jeremy Bentham, who would have Parliament reform the law of the land because of its social inadequacy. For Coke and his associates, the authority of the ancient law must not be undermined by legislative tampering.

Here were two groups whose contribution to political history was indirect and subtle rather than forthright. The Puritans and the lawyers were occupied with the church and the law. Political activity as such was a secondary concern. They became involved in the affairs of state according to the physical axiom of action and reaction. In the estimate of the Stuart throne the Puritans might be pests and the lawyers meddlers, but they became so only after they had been meddled with and pestered. The political activity of the divines and barristers came out of an opposition to Stuart interference with their own proper concerns.

The counterattack was directed in its most comprehensive sense against the Stuart theory of the divine right of kings. James I was by no means the initiator of the divine right concept, although he and his royalist associates cemented its pieces into a formidable political structure. By the time of James' accession, the theory had the following main points: (1) a king has an individual right, derived from God, to his throne; (2) this right is hereditary; (3) a king is responsible to God alone; (4) a king's prerogative—or right to rule —is of a higher order than the ordinary law of the land.[1] The first Stuart set forth his views on kingship in *The Trew Law of Free Monarchies* published while he was James VI of Scotland, in *A Defence of the Right of Kings* (1616), and in several other writings. Although his political thought was often ambiguous and wavering, James developed a high level of consistency in the realm of practice. It became apparent to Englishmen of the early 1600's that their new king conceived himself to be God's sole appointed ruler in all realms of national life. What James started, Charles was to continue. The second Stuart had an even higher regard for unlimited kingship, and he demonstrated early in his reign that he would surpass James in the exercise of royal prerogative.[2]

The Puritans and the lawyers soon found that Stuart kingly rule extended to their particular interests. University, church, inn of court, and common law court were subject to the comprehensive royal sway. Moreover, divine sovereignty and fundamental law became liege to the divine right of kings.

In the case of the universities, there was an unmistakable disregard on the part of the throne for the traditional autonomy cherished by Cambridge and Oxford. To be sure, James and Charles did assert what they considered to be a precedent for interference. In 1534 Henry VIII had obtained the passage of an act which gave the crown the right to "visit" Cambridge and Oxford. "Colleges, Hospitals, &c."— i.e., all ecclesiastical places formerly exempt from the jurisdiction of the Roman episcopacy—were confronted with a king who was given "full power and authority from time to time to visit, repress, redress,

1. McIlwain, *James' Works*, intro., pp. xxxiii–xxxiv.
2. See Allen, *English Political Thought, 1*, 8–10.

reform, order, correct, restrain and amend all . . . offences, contempts and enormities, whatsoever they be . . ." [3] Despite the strong words of the enactment, visitation by the crown was not widely practiced in the sixteenth century. The right to visit was granted only to an official commission which operated in a prescribed way under appointment by the crown. Henry, Edward, and Elizabeth usually demanded little of their university commissions, and the independence of Cambridge and Oxford remained substantially intact during the Tudor period. With the Stuarts, however, the situation became one of constant meddling. [4]

The visitation rights of the crown were widely conceived by James and Charles. Acts of the Privy Council relating to the universities increased. The two Stuarts personally interfered with injunctions, ordinances, and letters to Cambridge and Oxford officials. There was royal interference with the granting of degrees, the appointment of fellows, and the election of masters. Even the individual colleges were subject to the demands of the king. In 1629 Charles sent "Injunctions, Orders, and Directions to the Vice-Chancellor and Heads of Houses in the University of Cambridge for the better government of the same University," [5] in which the royal supremacy over the colleges was unmistakably set forth. The tampering of the king became most flagrant in the years just before the Civil War. In 1636 Charles declared with the advice of his Privy Council that it was "the undoubted right of the Crown to visit the said Universities, whensoever his Majesty pleaseth." [6]

An even more injurious exercise of the royal prerogative from the Puritan standpoint was the crown's interference in the life of the church. The Stuarts considered direction of the church to be an absolute essential of kingship. James stated on numerous occasions that his responsibility to God included maintenance of the body of Christ and that the proper nurture of the church was a chief point of earthly glory for kings. The instructions of the first Stuart to his son declared

3. George E. Corrie, *Brief Historical Notices of the Interference of the Crown with the Affairs of the English Universities* (Cambridge, The University Press, 1839), pp. 1–2; see also p. 59. The only copies of this book in the United States and Canada known to the author are in the New York Public Library and the University of Toronto Library.

4. Consult D. Harris Willson, *King James VI and I* (New York, Holt, 1956), pp. 292 ff.

5. Corrie, *Interference*, p. 51.

6. *Ibid.*, p. 55. See also John Rushworth, *Historical Collections* (London, 1680), Pt. 2, pp. 324–32.

that a prince must not only be a loving father to the church but must exercise great care over its doctrine and discipline.[7]

James' theory of church-state relations grew out of personal experience in his homeland where he had had grievous dealings with Scottish Presbyterians. Although in favor of Scotland's break with Rome, he argued that the Reformation had begun the wrong way north of the Tweed. The correction of the church had proceded from "a popular tumult and rebellion, of such as blindly were doing the worke of God, but clogged with their owne passions and particular respects," rather than from the prince's sagacious order. The techniques of Reformation in England, Denmark, and parts of Germany were much to be preferred. Throughout the remainder of the sixteenth century, the leaders of the Scottish movement continued to play havoc with royal authority. They spoke against James just "because I was a King, which they thought the highest euill."[8] It is small wonder that the first Stuart stated at the Hampton Court conference in 1604 that Presbyterianism agreed with monarchy as God with the devil.[9] James consistently failed to understand, let alone appreciate, the church-state theory of English Puritanism. Equating it with Scottish Presbyterianism,[10] he proclaimed on the basis of his experience with the latter that any scheme short of a church controlled by the crown was inimical to his rule.

The situation worsened as the Jacobean period gave way to the Caroline. The second Stuart took his father's instructions to heart, and showed that he would more easily tolerate interference with his prerogative than with the royal direction of the church.[11] The accession of Laud to the bishopric of London in 1628 and to the see of Canterbury in 1633 gave Charles a resourceful and compliant churchman eager to implement the policy of royal supremacy in church affairs. The combination of king and archbishop was singularly effective against the Puritans.

The particular concerns of the lawyers were likewise subject to the interference of the Stuart crown. The inns of court continued to retain, by and large, their traditional independence, but even these guild-like societies were acquainted with the meddling of James and Charles.

7. "Basilikon Doron," in McIlwain, *James' Works*, pp. 22–4.

8. *Ibid.*, p. 23, for both quotations in this paragraph.

9. J. R. Tanner, *Constitutional Documents of the Reign of James I, A. D. 1603–1625. With an Historical Commentary* (Cambridge, The University Press, 1930), p. 67.

10. Willson, *King James*, p. 202.

11. Consult Holdsworth, *English Law, 6,* 131.

Occasionally the record book of an inn tells of an appointment or an elevation in status accomplished by royal intervention.[12] The religious services of the inns proved fair game for Stuart tampering in the early Caroline period. Charles and Archbishop Laud conspired to lay down instructions for the observance of Lent and other events in the church year. They eventually issued elaborate orders for the conduct of all chapel services. In many other intrasociety matters, as Mr. Holdsworth writes, "the earlier Stuarts did not hesitate to interfere with the Inns of Court if they thought interference necessary . . ."[13]

From the lawyers' point of view, the common law courts received the brunt of the Stuart drive toward divine right monarchy. James and Charles knew that implementation of an absolutist government depended in large part on nullification of the common law's claim to be the final authority in all disputes. The claim was as strong as the judges who sat on the bench to interpret the law. The Stuarts wisely did not suggest that the law of the land be supplanted by another kind of law more conducive to absolutism. When fellow royalists proposed such a radical change, the crown was politic enough to rebuke them.[14] If the king could bend the common law judges to his will, however, he would possess the power of interpretation and application of the existing law.

James consciously sought to intimidate the judges. "As Kings borrow their power from God, so Iudges from Kings: And as Kings are to accompt to God, so Iudges vnto God and Kings . . ." The first two Stuarts were confident that the crown was the source of earthly justice. The existence of another source opposing the King was unthinkable. "Kings are properly Iudges, and Iudgement properly belongs to them from GOD: for Kings sit in the Throne of God, and thence all Iudgement is deriued. . . . Iudgement is deferred from the King to his subordinate Magistrates . . ."[15] The Stuart position had no better spokesman than Francis Bacon, who reminded the judges going on summer circuits in 1617: "First, you that are Judges of Circuits are as it were the planets of the Kingdom (I do you no dishonour in giving you that name), and no doubt you have a great stroke in the frame of this government, as the other have in the great

12. See *Pension Book, 1,* xliii, 182–3.

13. *English Law, 4,* 269. Mr. Holdsworth believes that the Tudors interfered as much as the Stuarts in the affairs of the inns.

14. See Tanner, *Documents,* p. 14.

15. This and the previous quotations are from "A Speech in the Starre-Chamber," in McIlwain, *James' Works,* pp. 327, 326.

frame of the world. Do therefore as they do: move always and be carried with the motion of your first mover, which is your Sovereign."[16] Against this, the greater part of the common law judiciary rebelled.

The judges and lawyers were also brought into conflict with the crown because of Stuart disregard for the letter and the spirit of fundamental law. James and Charles believed that the authority by which they governed was of a higher order than the ordinary law of the land. Nothing except the law of God stood above the law of royal government. Consequently a king had a right to break the ordinary law whenever he deemed such a course necessary. It was precisely the right to "break the law," held the crown, which marked the practical manifestation of royal power.[17] The lawyers dissented vigorously, as we shall see. Nothing must be allowed to fracture the ultimate authority of the fundamental law based on statutes, customs, and ancient rules.

Focus on Parliament

Opposition by the Puritans and the common lawyers to the crown was connected with the ascendancy of Parliament—the most important political development of the early seventeenth century. Every skirmish in the struggle with the king had its climax in the House of Commons.

In the case of the lawyers parliamentary leadership can be readily established. The chief issues of the time were debated in terms of law and precedent, and the knowledge and skill of the lawyers proved essential for the parliamentary cause. Not only did Parliament need lawyers, but the lawyers came to depend on Parliament for the protection of their own interests. Beginning approximately with Coke's removal from the bench in 1616, the struggle for fundamental law, the common law courts, and the inns of court was carried to the halls of Westminster. The former chief justice bespoke the lawyers' high regard for the House of Commons when he cried out in the 1621 Parliament, "We are here for thousands and ten thousands."[18] The alliance between the common lawyers and Parliament against the

16. Tanner, *Documents,* p. 198.

17. On the crown's claim to break law as the crucial political issue of the early 1600's, see Allen, *English Political Thought, 1,* 12.

18. As quoted by Charles H. McIlwain, *Constitutionalism. Ancient and Modern* (Ithaca, N.Y., Cornell University Press, 1947), p. 130.

king became tighter in each session of Commons in the early seventeenth century.[19]

The role of the Puritans in Parliament is more difficult to assess. If one takes the word Puritan in its broadest sense, one can agree with the then popular saying that three parts of the lower house were Puritan at the beginning of James' reign.[20] The Puritans studied here were chiefly clergymen, however, dedicated to service in the church. Preston, Sibbes, Gataker, Gouge, Scott, and the others were not members of Parliament, yet they and their ideas were represented there.

At least two reasons exist for the influence of early seventeenth-century Puritanism in the House of Commons. The first relates to the pervasiveness of Puritanism in the early 1600's and the second to the attitude of the movement toward Parliament. Whereas Puritanism had been primarily a clerical movement in the sixteenth century, it began in the seventeenth to reach deep into the ranks of the laity.[21] Members of Parliament flocked to the divines' influential London churches. Law students, who were to be future leaders in Parliament, listened attentively to Puritan sermons in the chapels of the inns of court. Puritanism burst its ministerial bonds in the opening years of the century and gained important supporters who were to carry its ideas to Stuart Parliaments.

Secondly, the Puritan clergymen looked upon Parliament as the only possible ally in the defense of their concerns. The hierarchy of the church was on the other side. With Coke's dismissal from the bench the common law courts had capitulated to the crown's dictation. Sorely pressed by the king, the Puritans espoused the idea of lawful resistance by magistrates.[22] The Stuart kings had commanded what was contrary to God's word and thereby could rightfully be resisted by proper authorities. These authorities were none other than the duly elected members of Parliament. Thomas Scott openly congratulated the 1621 Parliament on its demand for redress of grievances and on its petitions to the crown. In sharp criticism of James'

---

19. See Holdsworth, *English Law, 6,* 101–2.

20. Gardiner, *History, 1,* 178.

21. Marshall M. Knappen, *Tudor Puritanism. A Chapter in the History of Idealism* (Chicago, University of Chicago Press, 1939), p. v.

22. See "The Political Theories of Calvinists before the Puritan Exodus to America," in *Collected Papers of Herbert D. Foster* ([New York], priv. print., 1929), pp. 78 ff.

policies, Scott set forth the prevailing Puritan view that parliamentary opposition proceeded with divine sanction.[23]

The leaders of Parliament reciprocated the Puritan support. There was no end of encouragement from the House of Commons for the spread of "true religion" conceived in Puritan terms. Sir Benjamin Rudyard, or Ruddierd, speaking in 1628, uttered the sentiments of the majority of his fellow members:

> although Christianity and Religion be established generally throughout this Kingdom, yet untill it be planted more particularly I shall scarce think this a Christian Common-wealth, seeing it hath been moved and stirred in Parliament, it will lye heavy upon Parliaments, untill it be effected. Let us do something for God here of our own, and no doubt God will bless our proceedings in this place the better hereafter.[24]

The stimulation of religious awakening was unquestionably a goal of the House of Commons in the early 1600's. John Preston struck a responsive chord when he preached in the halls of Westminster: "Are not Religion And Zeale the two which hold all up? Are they not the pillars that beare up the Church and Common-wealth? Are not they the rescues that deliver the Citie?" [25] Parliament's unanimity with the Puritans on the necessity of religion was exemplified in Sir Walter Erle's outcry in the 1629 session: "Take away my Religion, you take away my life; and not only mine, but the life of the whole State and Kingdom." [26]

There was ample opportunity in the early 1600's for the lower house to act on behalf of the Puritan cause. The crown's repeated enforcement of new ceremonial rules in the church unfailingly elicited protests from Commons. In 1614 Parliament as a body refused to attend communion at Westminster Abbey, preferring St. Margaret's

23. "Vox Regis," in *The Workes of the Most Famous and Reverend Divine Mr. Thomas Scot* (Utrick [Utrecht], 1624), pp. 37 ff. This rare collection of Scott's complete works is located in the Houghton Library of Harvard University. Additional reasons for Puritan support of Parliament are listed by Williston Walker, *Ten New England Leaders* (New York, Silver, 1901), p. 52.

24. Thomas Fuller, ed., *The Soveraigns Prerogative and the Subjects Priviledge* (London, 1658), pp. 179–80.

25. *A Sermon Preached at a Generall Fast before the Commons-House of Parliament* [July 1625] (London, 1633), p. 286.

26. Wallace Notestein and Frances H. Relf, eds., *Commons Debates for 1629 Critically Edited with an Introduction* . . . (Minneapolis [University of Minnesota Press], 1921), p. 19.

where they would not be subjected to distasteful rites.[27] Parliament also supported the Puritan concern for the fate of international Calvinism. In 1621 Edward Floyd, a Roman Catholic lawyer, was sentenced to a fine and the pillory for deprecation of Frederick, the Elector Palatine and militant Calvinist, who had married James' daughter. The lower house clearly exceeded its jurisdiction in the imposition of such a harsh sentence on a nonmember. The House of Lords interfered momentarily, but in the end the upper house gave an even more severe punishment to Floyd.[28] Both houses were likely to unleash their strength against anyone who did not support what they considered to be God's cause in the religious wars of the Continent. In March 1628 when the fortune of the continental Calvinists was very low, Lords and Commons petitioned the king that one or more days be set apart for fasting and praying. The request was made "upon a tender and passionate sense of the extream Calamities of the Reformed *Churches* abroad." [29]

The common lawyers and the representatives of the Puritans were thus prominent in the leadership of the early seventeenth-century Parliaments. As a result, the special interests of Puritanism and common law became parliamentary concerns. The divines and the barristers brought more than their grievances to the House of Commons: they came with a common understanding of authority. The Puritan–common law conception of institutional authority became a guiding principle for the body that was to control the government of England.

27. *Journals of the House of Commons* ([London], 1803), *1*, 463. The fragmentary record for April 13, 1614 reads: "The Communion to be received at the Parish Church: Not at the *Abbey*, but at the Parish Church.—That, in the *Abbey*, they administer not with common Bread, contrary 20th Canon, and the Book of Common Prayer."

28. Tanner, *Documents*, pp. 319–21.

29. Fuller, *Prerogative*, p. 31.

4 PURITAN DIVINES VERSUS STUART KINGS

THE UNIVERSITIES

EARLY in the century the Puritans began to speak against the crown's interference with their interests. One of the first outcries resulted from new ceremonies and ritual which James prescribed for use in the universities shortly after his accession. At first the divines found it difficult to believe that the king had sanctioned changes in the religious life of Cambridge and Oxford. Samuel Ward, fellow of Emmanuel College, future master of Sidney Sussex College, and Lady Margaret Professor of Divinity, wrote in his diary: "Remember on Wednesday, January 18th [1605], was the day when the surplice was first urged by the ArchBishop to be brought into Emmanuel College. God grant that other worse things do not follow the so strict urging of this indifferent ceremony. Alass, we little expected that King James would have been the first permitter of it to be brought into our college . . ."[1] As the ceremonial interferences mounted, the Puritans changed their tactics from private lament to public proclamation. William Prynne maligned Peterhouse's new altar "to which the Master, Fellowes, Schollers bowed, & were enjoyned to bow . . . there were Basons, Candlesticks, Tapers standing on it and a great Crucifix hanging over it."[2] In this and other widely disseminated pamphlets, Prynne and his associates charged that the king and his ecclesiastical ministers had exceeded their jurisdiction over Cambridge and Oxford.

The Puritans also criticized the crown for its interference with preaching and teaching in the universities. Great St. Mary's and the chapel of Trinity Church, two main channels of expression for

1. Knappen, *Diaries*, p. 130, from Ward's MS "Adversaria."
2. *Canterburie's Doome* (London, 1646), pp. 73–4.

the divines at Cambridge, were closed to Puritan exhortations. John Preston and others were denied the right to preach in many other college chapels and parish churches at Cambridge and Oxford. The Puritans vigorously attacked this restriction on their freedom to speak from university pulpits, but James and Charles had efficient machinery for implementing compliance and the divines were usually forced to capitulate. In the matter of teaching appointments in the colleges, circumvention of the king's order was more successful. A nomination from the crown was occasionally met with the shrewd reply that the post in question was a supernumerary one and that it would lapse when vacant.[3]

The most violent Puritan reaction to the crown's interference with the universities resulted from Stuart insistence on subscription to the infamous Three Articles. The articles required unqualified acceptance of the royal supremacy in ecclesiastical and temporal matters, of the revised Book of Common Prayer, and of the Thirty-Nine Articles. James was fond of the capsule-like qualities of these norms and referred to them as his "three darling articles." The crown first required subscription from all ministers who would preach before a university congregation. Formal affirmation of the articles was then demanded of all those admitted to the B.D. degree and to the doctorate in any faculty. Finally in 1616 subscription was required for all university degrees. The Puritans, joined by other defenders of Cambridge and Oxford, severely criticized this unwarranted tampering with university life, particularly with the academic matter of granting degrees.[4]

The visit of King James to Cambridge in 1615 typified the reaction of the Puritans to the crown. James had not visited Cambridge since coming to the throne, although he had visited the more loyal Oxford in 1605 and 1614. Most of the colleges at Cambridge bedecked themselves gaily for the occasion; masques, debates, receptions, and other special events were planned. The Puritan colleges, however, made scant preparation for the king. John Preston refused one of his pupils the opportunity of playing an important role in a comedy to be given at Queen's College before the royal party. Emmanuel, as one might expect, was singularly aloof from the proceedings. A poet of the time wrote:

3. The material of this paragraph is drawn largely from Mullinger, *Cambridge,* *3,* 98–102.
4. See Willson, *King James,* pp. 294 ff.

> But the pure House of *Emmanuel*
> Would not be like proud *Jesabel*,
> Nor shew herself before the King
> An hypocrite, or *painted* thing:
> But, that the ways might all prove fair,
> Conceiv'd a tedious mile of prayer.

Puritan morality was involved in the refusal to participate, for the visit would surely turn out to be a debauchery, as had all previous visits of the crown to the universities. But more than the Puritan ethical code was at stake in the cool reception given the king by the university divines. The aloofness registered a long-felt disapproval over the crown's meddling with the independence of the universities. The poem quoted above continued:

> I wonder what your Grace doth here,
> Who have expected been twelve year,
> And this your son, fair *Carolus*
> That is so *Jacobissimus*.[5]

The Puritans did more than wonder about the presence of the king in the universities. They questioned and challenged his right to interfere with the historic autonomy of Cambridge and Oxford.

The crown's meddling with the universities strengthened the ties between the Puritans and Parliament. The issue of ceremonial changes in the college chapels was treated as a pressing grievance by the lower house. John Yates, a parish minister in Ipswich and former fellow of Emmanuel College, complained to Commons about Richard Montagu, a fellow of King's College.[6] Montagu was a high churchman, openly favored by the crown, who was attempting to introduce "popish" doctrine and ritual into both the universities and the established church. As usual the House of Commons took up the Puritan cry. We shall hear more of the Commoners' treatment of Montagu in the next section when we deal with the church.

In the 1629 Parliament, the lower house attempted in a specific way to protect the universities from royal interference. An act was brought in "to prevent Corruption in Presentations and Collations to Benefices and in Elections to Headships, Fellowships, and Schol-

5. "A Certain Poem," in *The Poems of Richard Corbet,* ed. Octavius Gilchrist (4th ed. London, Longmans, 1807), pp. 14–15, 17. Corbet (1582–1635), an Oxford wit, later became bishop of Oxford and then Norwich.
6. Mullinger, *Cambridge, 3,* 30.

ars places, in Colleges and Halls." [7] The act was read twice, referred to a committee, and would probably have become law were it not for the dissolution of Parliament in March of that year. The next session of the house was not until 1640, at which time the attack on the king's tampering with the universities was resumed.

THE CHURCH

The crown's interference with the church engendered full Puritan fury against Stuart rule. The divines considered here stood in sharp contrast to the high Anglican clergy, who generally condoned, if not encouraged, the trespasses of the crown. The canons of the 1606 convocation, for example, referred to the Old Testament emphasis on the direction of ecclesiastical affairs by secular rulers, and explicitly stated that God had charged kings and rulers to direct and control the church.[8] These enactments were disavowed by most Puritans. The Anglican position naturally followed from the hierarchy's support of the whole Stuart theory of kingship. The first canon passed by convocation in 1640 stated: "The most high and sacred order of kings is of divine right, being the ordinance of God himself . . ." [9] Such blatant, unqualified affirmations of the divine right of kings were not found in Puritan pronouncements.

The Anglicans not only gave unreserved support to the "free monarchy" of the Stuarts but rallied to the defense of the crown in particular crises. Archbishop Abbot responded to the crown's plea for augmented income by authorizing the "clerical loan" of 1614 and the "benevolence" of 1622.[10] Throughout the early 1600's, the Puritan clergy were in no mood to furnish the king money, or in any other way to help the Stuart cause.

THE 1604 CANONS

A major target for the Puritan attack on the crown was the ecclesiastical legislation promulgated early in James' reign. The new laws for the church, in the usual form of canons, became the first complete codification of English ecclesiastical life. They were passed

7. As quoted in *ibid.,* p. 99.

8. See canons 18–22 in *The Convocation-Book of MDCVI. Commonly Called Bishop Overall's Convocation Book* (Oxford, Parker, 1844), pp. 27–36.

9. Edward Cardwell, ed., *Synodalia. A Collection of Articles of Religion, Canons, and Proceedings of Convocation in the Province of Canterbury . . . 1547 to . . . 1717* (Oxford, The University Press, 1842), *1,* 389.

10. See Tanner, *Documents,* pp. 362–3, 370–3.

by convocation in June 1604, and received confirmation from the crown the following September. One scholar of the period treats the 1604 canons, which stressed matters of administration rather than of belief, as the heart of the early seventeenth-century "reconstruction" of the English church.[11]

The legislation displayed in both genesis and scope the power of the Stuart crown over the church. The laws were prepared under royal license and were immediately approved by the king's letters patent. *Ipso facto* excommunication by the governor of the church, i.e., by the king, was decreed for any refusal to comply with the legislation. The 1604 canons made it clear that the legislative power of the bishops in convocation had been severely curtailed, if not usurped by the crown. More than ever before, decisions in convocation were now seen to survive or perish as they agreed or disagreed with the royal command.

In 1606 additional canons dealing with doctrine and biblical interpretation were drawn up by convocation. These canons, as mentioned above, corroborated the king's direction of the church. James did not, however, grant assent to these laws because, as he expressed in a letter to Archbishop Abbot, sanction of the crown's proposal to aid the Dutch against their Spanish overlords was implicitly withheld.[12] Despite convocation's unquestioned approval of the 1606 canons, they never became official church law or doctrine.

Charles carried out his father's policy of dictation to the bishops in convocation. In 1628 the second Stuart wrote, "the Clergy in their Convocation is to order and settle them [disputes], having first obtained leave under our broad seal so to do: and we approving their said ordinances and constitutions . . ." Charles revealingly continued: "Out of our princely care . . . churchmen may do the work which is proper to them . . ."[13] As the Stuart regime advanced, it was established that convocation would supervise minor matters, such as ordination proceedings and conflicts in diocesan jurisdiction, whereas the king would be primarily responsible for the major concerns of ritual, creed, and ecclesiastical organization. The extensive

11. Usher, *Reconstruction, 1*, 7. Mr. Usher divides the reconstruction into three parts: (1) 1583–1603, preparation; (2) 1603–05, active reconstruction; (3) 1605–10, defense of the settlement.

12. *Bishop Overall's Book*, pp. 7–8.

13. Samuel R. Gardiner, *The Constitutional Documents of the Puritan Revolution, 1625–1660* (3d ed. Oxford, Clarendon Press, 1906), p. 75, for both quotations, which are taken from the declaration prefixed to the 1628 edition of the Articles of Religion.

reconstruction canons of 1604 set the pattern and provided the authority for Stuart Erastianism.

The Puritans had long clamored for a standardization of church law. In fact, clarification of the ambiguities in the Tudor settlement was pressed for at the Hampton Court conference of 1604. The new legislation, however, contained an evil far greater than that which it sought to remedy. The canons were founded on a presumption which, to the Puritans, would destroy the church rather than gather it together. A small book written by an anonymous Puritan and dedicated to the Privy Council helped to launch the attack on the new church laws. The book was a sharp reminder to the king that what he had enjoined in convocation must not stand. The Privy Council was asked to

> bee petitioners unto his Maiestie, that by his Regale and Supreame power, there might bee an healing of the former errour, and uncharitableness of the Diocesans and other ordinaries. For it can not be denied but that by their manner of proceedings, they have sinned against God; in this, that they have equaled, nay rather in some things preferred their owne Canons & Decrees, before the commandment of God.[14]

The basic evil in the new legislation was the conviction of the king that a complete, immutable law could be made for the church by an earthly authority. James never questioned that the church should have such a law and that he could provide it. The Puritans, as we have seen, were convinced that man-made laws governing church organization and practice could never be absolute. To be sure, there must be ecclesiastical laws if the church was to be a properly constituted institution of society. Some of the necessary laws were provided in the Bible and consequently were of divine, unchangeable nature. Preaching before James, John Preston spoke to this point when he warned his sovereign that there was only one "infallible judge, and that is the holy Ghost, speaking in the Scriptures, which are therefore called the word of God." [15] But the majority of church laws had to be made by men, and were subject to review and modification as were any human fabrications. James' conception of himself as an infallible ecclesiastical lawgiver was never accepted by the

14. *Certaine Considerations Drawne from the Canons of the Last Sinod. And Other the Kings Ecclesiasticall and Statute Law* ([London], 1605), dedicatory epistle, pp. 4–5.
15. "The Pillar and Ground of Truth," in *Sermons,* p. 12.

Puritan divines. They attacked not only the specific decrees but the arrogance of the new legislation.

In the early 1600's the Puritans fought against the crown's control in three general realms of church life. The 1604 canons established efficient machinery for the peremptory deprivation of ministers who failed to comply with the new church regulations. The drastic exercise of the king's power over the ministry of the church became the first point of dispute between the Puritans and the crown. Soon followed a second struggle over the king's attempt to determine the worship of the church by the imposition of new ceremonies and the restriction of preaching. Thirdly, the Puritans attacked the efforts of the crown to control the church's doctrine and moral teaching.

DEPRIVATIONS

The new laws for the church were put to effective and immediate use. No Tudor drive for ecclesiastical conformity had ever removed so many clergy from their parishes as the deprivations of 1604–05.[16] The dismissals continued in the remainder of Archbishop Bancroft's administration which ended in 1610. The ejection of ministers from their posts was less frequent during Archbishop Abbot's time (1611–33), but Abbot's administration was just a lull before the furious storm set off by William Laud. This archenemy of the Puritans, who became bishop of London in 1628 and archbishop of Canterbury in 1633, revived the earlier age of deprival known under Bancroft.

The divines never doubted that the Stuart crown was responsible for the dismissal proceedings. The standards of conformity had been established by the 1604 canons. The king's council set in motion the machinery for proceeding against nonconformist ministers. The council's letter of instruction to the archbishop warned the obstinate clergy that "his Majesty is well pleased to have it known that he is as far from alteration of his purpose to work an uniformity as they are importunate in their unjust desire of innovation . . ." Those who persisted in their ways were declared "guilty of disobedience to his Majesty." [17]

The Puritan counterattack was based on an appeal to the terms

16. The actual number of Puritan clergy deprived of their parishes in 1604–05 is debatable. Mr. Gardiner sets the figure at approximately 300; see *History, 1,* 197–8. Mr. Usher believes that about 60 were actually deprived and around 100 more were suspended and admonished; see *Reconstruction, 2,* 3 ff.

17. Tanner, *Documents,* p. 74.

of the original Tudor settlement. The previous legislation of the church had been designed to ensure a broad-gauged uniformity on doctrine, sacraments, and church organization. On these points the Puritans were willing to conform. Any doctrinal revision of the Thirty-Nine Articles by radicals usually met with a Puritan cry for uniformity. The present canons, however, had so reinterpreted the historic regulations of the church that conformity was now required in detail far greater than that stipulated by the laws of Henry VIII, Edward VI, and Elizabeth I.

Parliament supported the Puritan demand for a conformity based on the essentials of the original establishment. The opening session of James' first Parliament urged the clergy to subscribe only to the norms set forth in the key Elizabethan statute of 1570. In 1610 the lower house reminded the king in a petition that the only legal subscription provided by the 1570 statute was "confession of the true Christian Faith and the doctrine of the Sacraments." [18] The speeches of members as well as the formal pronouncements of the house upheld the cause of the ejected clergy. Yelverton, Fuller, and Morrice stated boldly in the 1605 session that the king's power as governor of the church did not include arbitrary control of the ministry.[19] In 1606 the members of Parliament endorsed the arguments and the recommended steps of resistance put forth in a Puritan "manifesto" against the dismissals.[20]

The divines wrote numerous pamphlets giving thanks to God for the support of Parliament and praising the Commoners for harkening to divine guidance. The alliance between the Puritans and the lower house was cemented in a more practical way when the divines pointed out that James had usurped powers that legally belonged to Parliament. Tudor legislation for the Church of England had consisted primarily of statutes. The Jacobean regulations and interpretations which qualified and changed these statutes, argued the Puritans, represented a new kind of authority. The divines accused the king of bypassing Parliament in setting new standards of conformity by means of which he and his ministers deprived clergy of their parishes. As one Puritan critic put it:

> the intent of the Parliament, not beeing so much to binde the Minister to such an exact and precise observation . . . it

18. *Ibid.*, p. 78.
19. See Usher, *Reconstruction, 2,* 118 ff.
20. *Ibid., 1,* 406–7.

seemeth very unreasonable, and much derogatorie to the authori-
tie of that Parliament that . . . extentions, constructions, and
interpretations . . . invert the playne meaning of the Parliament, and that, *ea qua sunt destinata in unum finem*, should . . .
bee converted to another end.[21]

CEREMONY AND PREACHING

The ecclesiastical legislation of 1604 provided King James with
definitive standards for ceremonial conformity. The canons prescribed new ritual for the church and set forth rigid enforcement
proceedings. The hierarchy of the church was enjoined by the laws
not only to carry out the new ceremonies but also to enforce those
of the Tudor age which had been neglected. No longer could the Puritans depend on the laxity of the crown's ecclesiastical ministers in
such matters as the wearing of the surplice, the use of the cross in
baptism, and kneeling in communion.

The year 1604 also witnessed a substantial revision of the Book
of Common Prayer. Conformity to the new prayer book became
another means of controlling the worship of the church. The 1604
revision was ostensibly designed to meet the demands expressed in the
Millenary Petition and the Hampton Court conference of 1603–04.
But, as happened in nearly every act of the king, the result agitated
rather than placated the Puritans. The Jacobean revision of the
prayer book did not meet a single major demand of the Puritan party.

What angered the divines even more than those things left undone
was the way James did what he did. The revision was accomplished
with brash arbitrariness. One authority has this description of
James' method: "The alterations . . . were not submitted either to
the parliament or even to the convocations of the clergy. The king
required his metropolitan and others of his commissioners for causes
ecclesiastical to make declaration of the changes agreed upon, and
then issued his letters patent to ratify their act . . . He certainly
believed that he possessed ample authority under the broad shield of
his prerogative . . ."[22] When the Puritans questioned the new Book
of Common Prayer, James interpreted their query as disobedience

---

21. *Certaine Considerations*, p. 26. See also William Bradshaw, *A Myld and
Iust Defense of Certeyne Arguments at the Last Session of Parliament . . .
in Behalf of the Ministers Suspended and Deprived* [London], 1606.

22. Edward Cardwell, *A History of Conferences and Other Proceedings Connected with the Book of Common Prayer . . . 1558 to . . . 1690* (3d ed. Oxford,
The University Press, 1849), p. 143.

of his authority. "I charge you," he said, "never speak more to that point, how far you are to obey orders of the church." [23]

The Stuart efforts to control the worship of the church did not stop with the issuance of new canons and revision of the Book of Common Prayer. Both James and Charles bestowed royal favor on those clergy who were willing to inaugurate forms of worship which the Puritans called Arminian or "popish." Probably the most flagrant use of the crown's influence occurred in the reign of Charles. In February 1627 there appeared a book which had been written upon royal commission by one John Cosin. The author had been the recipient of appointments from the king which had markedly advanced his career. Cosin's book, popularly called *Private Devotions* or *The Hours of Prayer*, provided a new manual of private prayer for the English church. It was supposedly founded on the simple Elizabethan primer of 1560, but in reality it introduced a form of worship and devotion quite foreign to the Church of England. Elaborate prayers and litanies were provided for the first, third, sixth, and ninth hours as well as for vespers and compline. Holy days, confession, and absolution were given more emphasis than they received in the current practice of the Church of England. A final bit of obnoxiousness to the Puritans was a prayer for the king which upheld Charles' absolute and divine right over all temporal and spiritual matters. Cosin rapidly became one of the most controversial figures of the late 1620's.[24]

William Bradshaw, Samuel Ward, William Prynne, and several anonymous writers served as Puritan critics of the crown's ceremonial impositions. The divines began with the premise that ecclesiastical problems must be solved within the framework of the established church. No matter how despicable the king's commands concerning matters of worship, the crown was still acknowledged to have supremacy in spiritual matters.[25] The actual plenitude of royal power depended, however, on the qualifications which the Puritans attached to the king's power as governor of the church.

23. As quoted in *ibid.,* p. 145.

24. The outlines of Cosin's career can be found in *DNB* and in Gardiner, *History*. Cosin (1594–1672) was a personal friend of other influential high churchmen, e.g., Neile, Laud, and Montagu, who were also supported by the crown; he was at one time chaplain to the royal family. Cosin later became master of Peterhouse at Cambridge, vice-chancellor of Cambridge University, dean of Peterborough, and (in the Restoration) bishop of Durham.

25. See William Bradshaw, "A Protestation of the Kings Supremacy [1605]," in *Treatises,* especially pp. 90 ff.

The qualifications were numerous and severe. Ceremonies and rites must accord with the natural and unfeigned religious needs of men; if a ritual contained artifice and was forcefully imposed on man, it served no good purpose. "Nature only frameth them [ceremonies] well, so if it shall appear they proceed from her, and are not forced and wrung from men (*invita minerva*), she putteth into them such a light, that any of ordinary conceit may in the sign see the thing signified." [26] The Puritans cited the worship of other reformed churches as an additional standard by which the king must abide in his innovations. Although the divines served the Church of England, their connection with international Calvinism was never forgotten. "We refuse Obedience . . . to such Canons as require the performance of such Acts, and Rites of Religion, as are rejected and abandoned of all other Reformed Churches . . ." [27]

No restriction of the king's ecclesiastical authority was as serious as the biblical. The Puritans amassed text after text to show that the Bible spoke against the crown's newly contrived ceremonies. In some instances, biblical standards were cited as clear and unequivocable prohibitions of certain ritual. The second of the ten commandments (Exodus 20: 4–6) was sufficient to refute the sign of the cross in baptism [28] and kneeling in communion. When scripture "flew at" the Jacobean rites, the king and his spiritual advisers stood convicted of ignoring the authority of God. In such cases the Puritans were quick to predict that divine wrath would descend on the king and his ecclesiastical ministers. Sometimes the word of God required considerable interpretation before it would produce the sought-after prohibition. After elaborate and painful exegesis Deuteronomy 12: 30a, for instance, was cited as a denunciation of present-day ceremonies and a warning to those who indulged in them.[29] "Beware, lest thou be taken in a snare after them, after that they be destroyed before thee, and lest thou aske after their gods . . ."

The divines were ready to claim that the word of God in the Bible had positive authority as well as negative. Scripture was held to be the guide and norm for the invention and use of ceremony. The

26. William Bradshaw, "A Treatise of Divine Worship [1604]," in *Treatises*, p. 4.

27. Bradshaw, *Protestation*, p. 90.

28. See Anon., *Certaine Demandes with Their Grounds, Drawne out of Holy Writ, and Propounded in Foro Conscientiae by Some Religious Gentl. unto . . . Richard* [Bancroft] *Archbishop of Canterbury* (London, 1605), pp. 31 ff.

29. *Ibid.*, pp. 22 ff.

frequent employment of Isaiah 8:20 was typical.[30] All rites should be referred "To the Law, and to the testimonie, if they speak not according to this word: it is because there is no light in them." According to the Puritans, James and Charles had more often than not ignored the guidance of the Bible. As Bradshaw put it, Stuart direction of the church was guilty of "Will-Worship."[31] The kingly governors of the church instituted ceremonies which proceeded from their own will and desire rather than from God's will known in the scriptures.

As in previous instances of Puritan opposition to the control of the church, the support of Parliament was everywhere apparent. Indeed, Parliament rapidly became the most effective channel for the denunciation of ceremonial impositions. Whereas the crown was able to silence individual divines, it was singularly unsuccessful in stifling the leaders of Commons. Various resolutions drawn up by the subcommittee on religion in the 1620's were pointedly concerned with the new ritual of the church. Individual members bemoaned the spread of popery occasioned by the imposed ceremonies; they asked for stricter punishment of those who engaged in "superstitious" practices. The lower house even pressed for new laws which would redefine the worship of the church within established Tudor patterns.[32] Prynne, the vocal Puritan lawyer, caught the prevailing mood of the House of Commons with a dedicatory epistle to his fellow members in a book against Cosin. "Go on therefore, you Christian Heroes, and valiant worthies of the Lord, to vindicate the cause, and Doctrines of our Church, against those *Cozening*, treacherous and rebellious Sons (if Sons) of hers, who have betrayed her with a kisse and *wounded her with one hand, whiles they seemingly imbrace her with the other:* and the God of heaven shall be with you."[33]

The crown's interference with preaching was of even greater consequence to the Puritans than the inauguration and enforcement of ceremony. The divines had long insisted on the primacy of the spoken word in the services of the established church. On the other hand, the Anglican clergy of Elizabethan and especially Stuart times

30. E.g., *ibid.,* biblical reference on title page.

31. William Bradshaw, "Twelve General Arguments [1605]," in *Treatises,* pp. 53–4.

32. Consult Gardiner, *Documents,* pp. 79 ff.

33. William Prynne, *A Briefe Survay and Censure of Mr. Cozens His Couzening Devotions. Proving Both the Forme and the Matter . . . to Differ frome the Private Prayers Authorized by Queen Elizabeth, 1560* (London, 1628), dedicatory epistle, pp. 7–8.

emphasized the ritual of the church. James and Charles sided with the Anglicans. At the Hampton Court conference James had a ready answer to the Puritan insistence on preaching. The king attacked "the hipocrisy of our times which placeth all religion in the ear, through which there is an easy passage . . ." [34] He agreed with the bishop of London who stated that preaching was not essential in a church long established. If pastoral exhortation was needed, James declared that the reading of approved homilies might better serve.

James' attitude toward the spoken word became law in the 1604 canons. Canon 14 unmistakably placed the emphasis in divine worship on the rites and ceremonies of the prayer book; preaching was not to interfere with the matter or form of these elements. [35] The first two Stuarts were opposed to preaching on grounds of expediency as well as principle. James was especially fearful of the political implications of Puritan preaching. In his 1622 "Directions to Preachers" the king declared that no minister "shall presume in any auditory within this kingdom to declare, limit, or bound out by way of positive doctrine in any lecture or sermon the power, prerogative, and jurisdiction, authority, or duty of Sovereign Princes . . ." [36] Charles also knew the power of the preachers. Writing to his wife while in captivity during the Civil War, he remarked that the militia could afford small comfort if the pulpits failed to preach obedience. [37]

In an effort to control the preachers, James saw fit to proscribe the treatment of certain topics from the pulpits. The "Directions to Preachers" stipulated that no sermon should deal with a topic which was not "comprehended and warranted, in essence, substance, effect, or natural inference, within some one of the Articles of Religion . . . or in some of the Homilies . . ." The Sunday and holy day afternoon lectures were further restricted: they must be based on the catechism, ten commandments, or Lord's Prayer. Particularly antagonistic to the Puritans was the king's arbitrary ruling on certain themes of the Reformed tradition. No preacher except those of high office might "preach in any popular auditory the deep points of predestination, election, reprobation, or of the universality, efficacy, resistability or irresistibility of God's grace . . ." [38]

---

34. Tanner, *Documents*, p. 65.
35. Cardwell, *Synodalia*, *1*, 253–4.
36. Tanner, *Documents*, p. 81.
37. Godfrey Davies, "English Political Sermons, 1603–1640," *Huntington Library Quarterly*, *3*, No. 1 (Oct. 1939), 22.
38. The two quotations in this paragraph are from Tanner, *Documents*, p. 81.

The evangelical command "Goe thou and preach the kingdome of God" (Luke 9:60b) was, to the Puritans, incapable of being fulfilled in the early 1600's. The king's decrees struck at the very heart of the movement, for successful propagation of the Puritan message depended in large measure on the power of the pulpit. All parts of the embellished Calvinist core found their most forceful expression through this medium. The preacher, felt the Puritans, must be free to speak the word as he knew it in the light of experience and conscience.

Parliament once again came to the aid of the divines. Early in the century the lower house manifested its concern with preaching; Parliament's 1604 Articles of Religion clearly stressed the importance of the spoken word in the services of the church. Commons even set standards for the determination of preaching ability, in case a divine's record and performance were not immediately demonstrative of such ability.[39] Parliament's interest in preaching continued throughout the early seventeenth century and was perhaps at its height in the early 1640's. There were few issues that provoked a more immediate reaction from the parliamentarians on behalf of the Puritan clergy than the crown's interference with the freedom of the pulpit.

DOCTRINE AND MORALS

Early in his reign King James gave notice of a supposed competence in doctrinal matters. He frequently recalled that his education had included studies in theology, church history, and the scriptures. James loved to boast of his dialectical skill in religious debate, as indicated by his words after the Hampton Court conference: "We have kept such a revel with the Puritans here these two days as we never heard the like, where I have peppered them . . . They fled me so from argument to argument without ever answering me directly . . ."[40] Unlike Elizabeth, who sensibly abstained from theological disputes, the first Stuart was always willing to fight it out with his adversaries. No quarter was given or expected, but if the day was ever in danger of being lost, James would end the fray by asserting his authority as governor of the church. On several occasions during the conference, he angrily concluded matters by stating that the church's polity and belief were to be decided by the crown.

39. See *ibid.,* pp. 69–70.
40. *Ibid.,* p. 51.

James' 1622 "Directions to Preachers" displayed the Stuart attempt to control the doctrine of the church. The decrees against preaching on grace and election might have been the prudent move of an impartial king to end a malignant quarrel in the church, but James had indicated by this time that he had another motive. The proclamation was an implicit statement of the crown's right to decide theological issues. Charles also issued decrees pertaining to the doctrine of the church. Aiming principally at Calvin's doctrine of predestination, the second Stuart stated "That therefore in these both curious and unhappy differences, which have for so many hundred years, in different times and places, exercised the Church of Christ, we will, that all further curious search be laid aside, and these disputes [be] shut up in God's promises . . ." [41] James and Charles claimed the right to determine the content and set the bounds of church doctrine.

The Stuarts again wielded personal influence so that clergy favoring the crown's views were given important posts. Representatives of high church theology were made royal chaplains, deans, lecturers, bishops, and archbishops. A brief survey of the careers of Richard Neile, John Buckeridge, William Laud, and George Montaigne validates the Puritan charge of royal favoritism for the Arminian party. The crown's patent support of the high church group caused the greatest furor in the case of Richard Montagu, influential bishop and author.[42] Montagu was attacked with a vehemence which even exceeded that vented on John Cosin. If not the most lucid of the high Anglicans, Montagu was one of the most conspicuous because of his prolific and controversial writings. His first important book, *A Gagg for the New Gospell? No: A New Gagg for an Old Goose*, while attempting to defend the Protestant or Anglican position against the Roman Catholic Matthew Kellison, ended with a denial of Calvinism. His *Immediate Addresse unto God Alone* occasioned Puritan scorn because of its insistence on saint worship and other "superstitious" elements. Montagu's last controversial book, *Appello Caesarem*, which gave support to the Stuart theory of kingship, further convinced the Puritans that the writer stood unalterably opposed to them.

The divines were not long in rising to attack this opponent of

41. From the declaration prefixed to the 1628 edition of the Articles of Religion, Gardiner, *Documents*, p. 76.

42. Biographical details on Montagu (1577–1641) and other high churchmen can be found in *DNB* and Gardiner, *History*.

Calvinist doctrine. William Prynne, the Ipswich ministers Samuel Ward and John Yates, John Preston, Anthony Wotton, Daniel Featley, and George Carleton (Montagu's successor in his first bishopric) roundly condemned the high churchman in sermons and tracts. Montagu, argued the Puritans, challenged the inevitability of God's decree in predestination, denied the causal effect of Adam's fall on the loss of free will, affirmed man's role in salvation, and held for the transmission of divine forgiveness through priestly mediators.[43] Worst of all, Montagu proudly renounced the historic tradition which the Puritans held dear: "I am none, I professe, of that Fraternity, no *Calvinist*, no *Lutheran* . . ."[44]

Despite the sharp criticism of Montagu, James and Charles consistently supported the high churchman's views and furthered his career. He was given a fellowship at King's College in 1597 and continued to hold it, by special act of the crown, along with a canonry, two livings, an archdeaconry, and a royal chaplaincy. James made it clear that Montagu's doctrinal position agreed with that espoused by the crown. After reading the high churchman's *Immediate Addresse* and conferring with the author, the first Stuart was so favorably inclined that he remarked, "If that is to be a Papist, so am I a Papist."[45] During Charles' reign, support for Montagu was elicited by the crown from his fellow bishops, several of whom held a conference at which approval of his writings was expressly declared. When Commons joined in the Puritan clamor against Montagu, the king made him chaplain to the royal family, a move which theoretically immunized him from any attacks. In June 1626 Charles forthwith commanded Commons' silence on the whole matter by a royal decree. In July 1628, when the controversy of the midtwenties had somewhat subsided, Montagu was rewarded by appointment to the bishopric of Chichester. An even higher post was given him when he was made bishop of Norwich in 1639. The latter appointment was particularly opprobrious to his opponents in the church because the diocese was a Puritan stronghold. Throughout Montagu's career the Puritans saw the blessings of the crown bestowed on a figure who, in their estimation, was undermining the true doctrine of the church.

Montagu and his colleagues were considered enemies not only be-

43. These and other points found their clearest statement in *Appello Caesarem*, London, 1625.
44. *Ibid.*, p. 45.
45. *DNB, 38,* 267.

cause of their Arminian doctrine. The Puritans saw an even more fundamental evil in the high churchman: the citation of incorrect authorities for theological innovation. In nearly all of his writings, Montagu criticized the Puritan view that the Bible was the foundation of the church's belief. The opening sections of the *Gagg* declared that the scriptures were not clear, that contradictions abounded, and that therefore the authority of the Bible must be questioned. Numerous passages were cited to illustrate the inadequacy of a biblical foundation for the belief of the church. In place of the Bible as a supreme authority, Montagu would put the judgment of the present church and her ministers, that is, those ministers who represented his own party in the Church of England. The current high church doctrine was correct and inerrant, maintained the author, because it precisely represented the theology found in the first five hundred years of the church.

The Puritans found Montagu's reasoning absurd and obnoxious. The Bible, they held, was in some places obscure, but this hardly detracted from its ultimate authority. The Puritan view was that the interpretive difficulties of the Bible did not undermine its validity as God's word, but rather reflected on man's finite, sinful nature and his incomplete powers of comprehension. Even the most obtuse passages contained the word of God; would that man had the perspicacity to understand their full meaning. Furthermore, the complexity of the Bible was overbalanced by the abundance of passages with definite, unambiguous meaning. Montagu's nearly wholesale rejection of the Bible because of its admitted difficulties cast out the specific commandments in which God spoke clearly and for all to hear. The Puritans agreed that the church should supplement scriptural authority. But Montagu's ecclesiastical authorities were not those of the first rank. The Puritans held that the proper doctrine was not found in the first five hundred years of the church, during which time superstitious elements appeared, but in the early church of the New Testament.

Montagu committed further error, held his opponents, by a citation of unsound contemporary authorities. The Puritans scored his rejection of the doctrinal statements of the Reformed Church. The Synod of Dort, argued the high churchman in chapters 7 and 11 of *Appello*, was of no authority in the Church of England. In chapter 10, Montagu stated that the Council of Trent was not to be condemned and might even serve as a foundation in matters of belief. In the

denial of authority to the Reformed tradition, Montagu was casti-
gated by many Puritan writers, chief of whom was William Prynne
in his tract *Anti-Arminianisme*.

Faced with an intense attack, Montagu and his fellow Arminians
found it necessary to cite a supreme authority for their doctrine.
The answer to the Puritans was always a reference to the crown's
ecclesiastical power. It is not clear whether Montagu argued as a
point of theory that the king should make the church's doctrine, but
it is patent that the crown's authority in matters of belief was cited
as a practical means of quelling the Puritan criticism. The Puritans
interpreted Montagu's appeal as part of the high church capitula-
tion to the Stuart theory of church-state relations. Bishops Buckeridge, Howson, and Laud, writing to Buckingham in defense of
Montagu in 1625, corroborated the Puritan view. The letter stated
that the deciding authority in any doctrinal quarrel was the judgment of the king and bishops in convocation. Since convocations had
become channels through which royal control of the church was
exercised, the ascription of authority to convocation deceived no
one. Moreover the letter, in language similar to that later used by
Charles, maintained that the king must initiate doctrinal decisions:
"the King first giving leave, under his Broad Seal, to handle the
points in difference." [46]

Montagu's dependence on the authority of the crown was to be
seen throughout his own writings. In view of the Puritan attack on
his first two books, Montagu's third had the revealing title *Appello
Caesarem*. Whatever authorities the Puritans cited for the church's
doctrine, Montagu always had his royal trump card. In *Appello*
there was found the familiar theme of the crown's power to decide
matters of doctrine. The book invoked the king's authority in still
another way. Those who propagated the Arminian doctrine, went the
argument, should be protected by the king from Puritan attack. In
return Montagu promised to defend the king. "I . . . prostrate
upon bended knees . . . humbly craving the *Royall* Protection
which sometime William Ockham did of Lewes of *Baviere* the *Emperor; Domine Imperator, Defende Me Gladio, Et Ego Te Defendam
Calamo* [Lord and master, defend me with the sword and I will defend
you with the pen]." [47]

The Puritan revolt against the imposed theology found natural

46. As quoted by Gardiner, *History, 5,* 402.
47. *Appello,* pp. 321-2. These are the concluding words of the book.

support in Commons. Charges of "Arminian" and "papist" were leveled against all the leading high churchmen of the 1620's. The sermons and writings of Bishops Neile and Montagu were analyzed and scored in the name of Reformed theology.[48] The parliamentary criticism was also directed against the authority which sanctioned and encouraged the theological innovations. The 1629 resolutions of the subcommittee on religion and the subsequent protestation of the session maintained that the king had denied the authority of Parliament in the suppression of the true doctrine established by statute in 1570.

Further evidence of the crown's tampering with the church was found by the divines in royal pronouncements relating to Puritan morality. The despised *Book of Sports*, published first in 1618 and then again in 1633, became a primary grievance of the Puritans. In this document the crown encouraged a host of specific acts which the Puritan saints eschewed—Sabbath sports, May games, ale drinking, bear baiting. James and Charles even forbade the clergy to preach against these pursuits. Ministers who refused to abide by the decrees were to be prosecuted.

The reaction to these promulgations was violent. The divines held them to be a rejection of the exhortations so frequently uttered from Puritan pulpits. The insistence on "exact walking," self-denial, and "mortification" were now countermanded by order of the king. The Stuarts claimed the law of the land and the canons of the church as authority for the proclamations. But the claims were never substantiated, and it is improbable that corroborative precedents could be found. Another authority *was* explicit in the declarations: that of the Stuart kings themselves. Never once citing a statute or canon, James spoke of "our express pleasure" as the authority by which the pronouncements were set forth. Charles, echoing his father's threat of prosecution for those who did not conform, called the obstinate ones "contemners of our authority and adversaries of our Church." [49] The Puritans were quick to cite the counter-authority of

48. See Thomas B. Howell [William Cobbett], ed., *A Complete Collection of State Trials . . . from the Earliest Period to the Year 1783* (London, Longmans, 1816–26), *2*, 1258–67, for a nearly complete account of the 1625 proceedings in Commons against Montagu. In February 1629 Oliver Cromwell made his first speaking appearance in Parliament via an attack on Bishop Neile; Gardiner, *History, 7,* 55.

49. Gardiner, *Documents,* p. 101.

the Bible, which contained the specific provisions of the Calvinist moral code.[50]

Parliament was once again ready to defend the Puritan cause. The first bill to pass the lower house in the 1614 Parliament was "an act for the keepinge of the Saboathe, to restrayne morisdance, beare baytinge on the said daye." [51] The Puritan members of Parliament were extremely harsh on the minority who deprecated Calvinist morality. In the 1621 session, an incident occurred which raised the question of the proper authority in the moral teachings of the church. A certain Thomas Shepherd violently dissented from the prevailing Puritan faction which was urging a new Sabbath act to combat James' 1618 *Book of Sports*. Strongly incensed, the lower house expelled Shepherd [52] from his seat. James was displeased over the censure of one of his few allies in Parliament and upbraided Commons for its act. He warned the body not to proceed with any bill contrary to his 1618 pronouncement.[53] In the speeches on the Shepherd case, the Puritan members referred freely to the authority of the Bible. Although Shepherd was denounced on many grounds,[54] a common parliamentary complaint was that "He spoke with a great deal of petulaunce and prophaning the holy scriptures . . ." [55]

The Commoners were sure of their authority in pressing for a rigid Sabbath observance and a strict moral code. So great was their cofidence that a new "act for punishing divers abuses on the Sabbath day" [56] was passed less than a month after Shepherd's seques-

50. E.g., Thomas Gataker, *David's Instructer* (London, 1620), defending Puritan "godliness." William Prynne, *Healthes: Sicknesse . . . Proving the Drinking and Pledging of Healthes to Be Sinfull* (London, 1628), and *The Unlovelinesse of Love-Lockes* (London, 1628), display an even more lavish biblicism.

51. Wallace Notestein, Frances H. Relf, and Hartley Simpson, eds., *Commons Debates 1621* (New Haven, Yale University Press, 1935), 7, 643–4. The quotation is from a MS diary of the 1614 Parliament.

52. Not to be confused with Thomas Shepard (1605–49), exiled Puritan and famous first minister of the First Church at Newtown, or Cambridge, in New England. Shepard was every bit a Sabbatarian; he wrote *Theses Sabbaticae. Or the Doctrine of the Sabbath,* London, 1649.

53. *Commons 1621, 2,* 104.

54. John Pym is believed to have made his first speech in Parliament on the Shepherd case. He emphasized Shepherd's divisiveness, i.e., his attempt to worsen the relations between Parliament and king and to destroy the unity of the House of Commons. See *Commons 1621, 2,* 95, and *4,* 62–5.

55. *Ibid., 5,* 502; see also *4,* 64.

56. *Ibid., 2,* 164.

tration. This legislation specifically forbade ale drinking, dancing, and May games; it was supplemented by a bill "to represse drunkenes, and restraine the inordinate hauntinge of Inns and alehowses." [57] Parliament was, as usual, on the side of the Puritans and willing to act in the face of the king's decrees.

DIVINE SOVEREIGNTY OVER KINGLY RULE

The conflict over university and church had a meaning far more significant than a mere struggle for control of certain institutions. Amid the strident confusion it was clearly seen that James and Charles considered themselves unlimited monarchs. Their practice of the heretofore delicate art of kingship allowed nothing to exist beyond the power of the crown. The Stuarts admitted in theory that God stood above them and that they were responsible to him. But so drastic was the crown's control of precious places of learning and of worship that the Puritans rightly asked whether James and Charles did stand under God. Could it be said that in Stuart England God ruled the institutions of university and church, as indeed he must rule everything? For the Puritans, the root of the trouble was that divine sovereignty had been supplanted by kingly rule.

The divines spoke to the deeper meaning of the early seventeenth-century struggle more effectively in the case of the church than in the university. Paul Baynes put the issue of the crown's dictation in its ultimate perspective when he wrote in his commentary on Colossians, "Let us therefore take heed, that while we set up other heads then [sic] *Christ* over the Churches, we doe not reject this glorious Head Jesus Christ from ruling over us: as the *Israelites* when they refused that Aristocraticall government in which *God* ruled, and would have a King like other Nations; the Lord chargeth them not only to have cast off *Samuell*, but himselfe."

The Cambridge Puritan spoke for all his ministerial brethren when he argued that the national church must be nourished and maintained by the king. Care must be taken, however, to avoid the ever present danger of the crown's unlimited control of the church. The Puritans charged that the king had exceeded his role as administrative, supportive head of the church and was attempting to become the actual head of the body of Christ. This was an affront to him who truly governed the church. "Sooner shall the heaven have two Suns, then [sic] the Church two heads: and though meta-

57. *Ibid.,* 7, 300.

phorically one may be said to be the Head of a Church, for the name of *God* Himself is thus Communicable, yet in proper analogy none can be so termed . . . A double head and a double husband become not the Church . . . Thus much [for] who is over us." [58]

The Stuarts were usurpers of a divine authority. Acquiescence in the actions of the crown, believed the Puritans, was the giving of allegiance to the usurpers. William Bradshaw saw the matter clearly: "To use these Ceremonies in manner and forme prescribed, is to performe a more than civil honour (even a Religious) only to humane Power and Authority . . ." [59] Or, put another way, a surrender to the king meant the glorification of man, albeit a princely man, rather than the glorification of God.[60] This was a serious matter for anyone steeped in Calvinism.

58. Bayne, *Colossians,* p. 98, for both quotations in this paragraph.
59. Bradshaw, *Arguments,* p. 56.
60. See Bradshaw, *Worship,* pp. 1–2.

5 JUDGES AND LAWYERS AGAINST THE CROWN

THE INNS OF COURT

JUDGES AND LAWYERS joined Puritan divines and teachers in criticism of the king's trespasses. The distinctions made in Chapter 2 should be in mind as we examine the legal opposition to the crown, for members of the profession had differing convictions about the power of the king. The inns of court well demonstrated the variance; each legal society was in some ways a house divided against itself on the matter of the crown's authority. The inns harbored a royalist faction that became more vocal as the Great Rebellion approached. In 1641 the crown sympathizers of the four societies made an armed demonstration at Whitehall on behalf of the king.[1] But there were few benchers, even among the royalists, who gave in to the crown's interference with intramural matters. Certainly among the lawyers led by Coke, Hakewill, Whitelocke, and their colleagues there was no evidence of condescension to the meddling of the king in the ancient independent life of the societies.

The matter of appointments displayed the friction between the crown and the governing bodies of the inns. In April 1613 James wrote a letter to the Inner and Middle Temples stating his pleasure that a clerical favorite, the Reverend Alexander Simpson, be appointed lecturer. The treasures of the two societies were commissioned by the benchers to make a reply. With firm and careful reasoning, the treasurers wrote that the would-be appointee was unacceptable on several counts. The next month James replied that he would abide by the decision of the benchers as reported by the treasurers. So great was the elation over the crown's submission that the societies ordered the two letters from the king and the one of the treasurers to

1. Consult *Pension Book, 1,* xlv–xlvi, 317, 325, 346.

be deposited with the original patent from the crown in an iron box under the communion table in the Temple church.[2]

An incident occurred in the beginning of Charles' reign which further illustrated the reluctance of the inns to tolerate the interferences of the crown. In 1628 a certain Anglican divine, Dr. Paul Micklethwaite, succeeded to the post of master of the Temple. As a high churchman, Micklethwaite set about contriving "popish" rites and ceremonies which quickly aroused the Puritan sympathies of the two societies. Disliked by the benchers for many reasons, Micklethwaite was placed on a minimal salary, ordered to refrain from using Temple church funds, and requested to "forbear the hall till he was sent for." At this turn of events Charles, who had been instrumental in effecting Micklethwaite's appointment, came to the aid of his favorite. In 1633 the issue was brought before the lords of the council sitting in the Star Chamber, where the benchers were ordered to make financial settlement with the high churchman on his terms. A few years later, the king ordered that the proposed and partly implemented "reforms" in the Temple church become the regular form of worship in the two inns. The Micklethwaite affair ended in triumph for the crown over the Middle and Inner Temples, but not without the voicing of sharp criticism which was heard before the king's council and repeated with rancor in the halls of the two societies.[3]

There were signs that the interference of the king with the societies would exceed the manipulation of appointments and the imposition of religious ceremonies. James was known to have a penchant for systems of law which favored his theory of kingship, although he was careful to make a public profession of his love for the common law. In 1607 John Cowell, Professor of Civil Law at Cambridge, published a legal work called *The Interpreter,* which roughly approximated a law dictionary. Cowell defined the terms "king," "Parliament," "prerogative," "subsidy," and others in such a way that the absolutist claim of the crown found complete substantiation. In speeches to Parliament and the judges, James spoke against both Cowell's book and the civil law. His criticism, however, was noticeably tepid and halfhearted. Perhaps he really wanted to substitute civil law for common law training—to introduce legal instruction which would favor the Stuart way of government. This is speculation,

2. See Frederick A. Inderwick, ed., *A Calendar of the Inner Temple Records* (London, Sotheran, 1898), *2,* xxxi–xxxii, 73–4.

3. Consult *ibid.,* pp. lxxxi–lxxxvii, 218, for the Micklethwaite affair and the quotation in this paragraph.

for we have no record of James' and Charles' ultimate designs on the teaching in the inns. We do know, however, that the lawyers were on the alert. Cowell's doctrines were thoroughly repudiated in the House of Commons and *The Interpreter* was ordered to be burned by the common hangman.[4] No common lawyer raised his voice in disagreement with the action of the house.

The king was also suspect because of the means at his disposal to influence, if not control, the basic matter of instruction. The seventeenth-century development of the post of king's counsel afforded the crown an important lever upon the educational life of the inns. King's counsel, a rank created in Elizabethan times, was designed to alleviate the growing duties of the king's attorney and solicitor. Many royalist lawyers attained the position of king's counsel, usually upon the nomination of the attorney general and the subsequent appointment of the king. Those raised to the status were automatically made benchers in an inn of court, in which capacity they helped to govern the society. The obvious danger was that the king could effect a kind of infiltration of the inns by appointing favorites as king's counsel. The threat of infiltration did not exist in the case of the serjeants, also royal appointments, who left their society when elevated by the king and became members of Serjeants' Inn. King's counsel, on the other hand, went on in the inns for life. A loud cry against the practice was not raised until the second half of the seventeenth century. Yet the pre-Civil War period witnessed apprehension over the growing number of king's counsel and their presence on the governing boards of the legal societies. As long as the king's appointees sat as benchers, the inauguration of new instruction or any other alteration of the ancient ways of the societies loomed as a threat.[5]

In the early 1600's the common lawyers were aware of both the real and the possible dangers to the inns of court. The barristers and judges spoke against the actual interferences of the king in the matter of appointments and the imposition of religious ceremony. They were also cognizant of the potential evil of the crown's action in issues of even greater significance for the life of the societies.

THE COMMON LAW COURTS

The common law courts were a prize of higher value than the inns of court in the Stuart drive toward political absolutism. Correspondingly, the lawyers' defense of the courts was more vigorous and con-

4. Tanner, *Documents*, pp. 6, 12–15.
5. Holdsworth, *English Law, 6*, 472–81, deals with the rise of king's counsel in the 17th century.

sistent than their defense of the legal societies. With Coke as leader, every effort was made to perpetuate and increase the independence of the courts. Nearly all members of the judiciary sought to contravene Bacon's description of judges as "planets of the Kingdom" revolving about the crown. Four examples have been chosen to illustrate the intensity and significance of the struggle over the common law courts.

WRITS OF PROHIBITION

An early instance of James' threat to the independence of the courts resulted from the crown's alliance with the high church party. In 1605 an old issue over the respective jurisdictions of the ecclesiastical and common law courts flared up again. The conflict was particularly bitter this time because such strong-willed men as Archbishop Bancroft, King James, and Chief Justice Coke were involved. The common law or temporal courts had long followed the practice of issuing writs of prohibition that restrained the ecclesiastical courts from proceeding in certain cases. The writs prevented action by the ecclesiastical courts until the common law judges had decided whether or not the case in question concerned a "spiritual" matter. If it did not, the case was debarred from the ecclesiastical courts.

Since writs of prohibition were binding on the ecclesiastical or spiritual bench, the common law courts possessed a powerful weapon in jurisdictional disputes. The weapon had been frequently misused. The abuse came about for many reasons, chief of which was the harsh, jealous attitude of the common law judges toward the spiritual courts. It must be said, however, that the attitude had some justification. The secular judges could rightly point to many nefarious practices of the ecclesiastical courts. The ex officio oath, for example, in the Court of High Commission was employed to extract a confession to an unspecified crime leveled by an unknown accuser. An ecclesiastical judge, by virtue of his office, could require that a defendant swear to answer any questions put by the High Commission. The accused was not told why he was being questioned or what kind of information was being sought. The oath could thus be used to force a man to incriminate himself in a supposed misdemeanor. With the ascendancy of Edward Coke in the opening years of the century, the common law attitude toward the spiritual courts became consistently inimical. Writs of prohibition were issued in increasing number, and alarm was expressed by the hierarchy of the church that ecclesiastical jurisdiction would be usurped completely.

Archbishop Bancroft appealed to the crown in 1605 soon after

James' accession. His protest to the king was an elaborate enumeration of grievances presented as propositions, which Coke later named *Articuli Cleri* after a similar document in Henry III's reign.[6] Bancroft's petition provoked a favorable response from the crown and a critical reply from the common law judges. Despite the reaction of the crown, the *Articuli* did not restrict—let alone abolish—the issue of writs. The archbishop felt it necessary to renew his complaint in 1607. The king submitted Bancroft's second statement to the common law judges, who were technically the crown's advisers, in order to gain their opinion on the legitimacy of the archbishop's requests. James must have hoped that the judges would either modify their former position or that Bancroft's persuasiveness would win them over. Neither occurred. The second stage of the dispute ended with James and Coke openly defying one another in a conference of crucial importance for English political history.

The writs continued to be used. Bancroft and the ecclesiastical lawyers appealed a third time to the king. The whole matter came to a head in 1609 when James summoned Coke and the other common law judges to Whitehall and there remonstrated with them. So great was the king's wrath that Coke and his colleagues fell on their knees, begging mercy. James postponed final decision on the conflict, but for the present ordered the cessation of prohibitions. The fortunes of the spiritual courts were already on the wane, however, and no efforts of the crown could restore their former power and prestige.[7]

Coke's struggle with the crown and the high church party was important for reasons other than the defense of the courts' independence. Out of the issue came an assertion of the rightful powers of Parliament. Bancroft's first article in his 1605 declaration maintained the power of the crown to reform abuses in the use of writs. The answer of the judges, while not denying the crown's place as the titular source of all justice, emphasized that fundamental statutory procedures were at stake. If there were inequities in the issue of writs, which the judges doubted, the remedy must be effected by parliamentary legislation, not by a decree of the king. The judges

6. The 25 articles of complaint together with the answers of the common law judges can be found in *State Trials, 2*, 131–60, and Coke, *Institutes,* 2d Pt., *2*, 598–638. The latter contains fuller references to the statutes and common law rules which the judiciary arrayed against Bancroft's grievances.

7. For a brief description of this issue, and the three subsequent ones concerning the crown's interference with the courts and the judges, see the commentary in Tanner, *Documents,* pp. 173–7. Also consult Gardiner, *History.*

replied that "what the law doth warrant in cases of prohibitions to keep every jurisdiction in his true limits, is not to be said an abuse, nor can be altered but by parliament." [8] The particulars of the relationship of king and Parliament were not discussed in this case, however, nor was there any reason to assume that the judges were working out a theory of parliamentary sovereignty. There was only the repeated statement that if the law of the land was to be changed, it must be done in the time-honored way.

More frequently debated in the proceedings was the respective jurisdiction of the ecclesiastical and the common law courts. Bancroft represented to James that the crown had the right and the power to decide where the line should be drawn between spiritual and temporal. This could scarcely be doubted, argued Bancroft in the *Articuli*, since all legal jurisdiction was possessed by the king, who for reasons of practical administration had allotted some to the ecclesiastical and some to the common law courts. The archbishop extended his argument in his 1607 complaint to the crown. Since the king had allocated jurisdiction that originally was his, he could withdraw it for any reason that seemed sufficient. If such a withdrawal were made, the king could then decide cases himself as the supreme and unlimited judge of the land. Bancroft had assured James that "this was clear in Divinity, that such authority belongs to the King by the Word of God in the Scripture." [9]

It was characteristic of the common law position in the early 1600's that no frontal attack was made on the authority of the king. To be sure, most of the judges were conscious that the position taken by the crown and the high churchmen represented a new usurpation of power by James. But there was no denial of the king's authority in English procedure. The *raison d'être* of the common law courts was to make available the king's justice; the spiritual courts were to do the same in another area. "No man maketh any question, but that both the jurisdictions are lawfully and justly in his majesty . . ." [10] Indeed, the common law opposition in the prohibitions issue was more an appeal *to* rather than an attack *upon* the rightful exercise of the king's authority.

The judges asked the king to abide by the age-old allocation of jurisdiction. Bancroft had first persuaded the king that the common law courts were trampling on the rights of the ecclesiastical courts.

8. *State Trials, 2,* 134.
9. Tanner, *Documents,* p. 187, from Coke's *Prohibitions del Roy.*
10. *State Trials, 2,* 134.

When James upheld Bancroft's claim, the judges opposed the king and archbishop with an appeal to the traditional distinctions between temporal and spiritual jurisdiction. The answers of the judges to the *Articuli Cleri* and Coke's further elaboration in the *Institutes* illustrated the characteristic detail with which the judges argued their case. The basic distinction which limited the jurisdiction of the crown-supported ecclesiastical courts appeared in Coke's commentary on heading VI of the *Articuli* in the *Institutes*. The jurist wrote: "the spirituall judges preceedings are for the correction of the spirituall inner man, and, *pro salute animae* [for the health of the soul] . . ."[11] Whatever was of a nonspiritual nature, concluded the argument, was outside the province of the ecclesiastical courts.

Coke believed that James and Bancroft, if unrestrained, would give the ecclesiastical courts jurisdiction over matters that lay beyond the allowable correction of the inner man. He cited precedent upon precedent to show that certain issues under given conditions automatically passed from spiritual to temporal jurisdiction. If spiritual goods were sold, they became temporal goods and any resultant altercation must be settled in a common law court. Tithes which were sold, for instance, became chattels, and attendant disputes must be settled in temporal courts. If a parishioner was enjoined to make pecuniary rather than corporal penance, consequent action on the case must be taken in a common law court. Coke skillfully amassed former statutes, rules, and dicta to show that the spiritual courts were confined to a small, definitive area of jurisdiction. Any enlargement of this area was a threat to the common law courts and to the administration of justice.[12]

Bancroft also convinced James that the crown had full power to break, if need be, the established jurisdictional lines. James put the idea to immediate use when he upheld, in the famous 1607 conference with Coke, the king's power to decide any case "in his royal person." Coke, with the full consent of the judges and the barons of the Exchequer, countered: "the King . . . cannot adjudge any case, either criminal, as treason, felony, etc., or betwixt party and party . . . but this ought to be determined and adjudged in some

11. Coke, *Institutes*, 2d Pt., *2*, 622.

12. The legal reasoning used by Coke and his colleagues to refute Bancroft has been called, fairly enough, biased and exaggerated. E.g., see A. V. Dicey, *Introduction to the Study of the Law of the Constitution* (9th ed. London, Macmillan, 1950), p. 18. There may have been distortion in the interpretation of the precedents cited by Coke, but it does not appear that this sin lay any heavier upon the chief justice than upon the archbishop and the king.

court of justice according to the law and custom of England . . ."
James replied that the law of England was founded upon reason
and that he as well as the judges possessed the reason necessary to
interpret it. Coke then made his famed retort that "his Majesty was
not learned in the laws of his realm of England . . . [legal matters]
are not to be decided by natural reason but by the artificial reason
and judgment of law, which law is an act which requires long study
and experience before a man can attain to the cognizance of it . . ."
In this instance the artificial reason required was that knowledge
of the intricacies and subtleties of common law and ecclesiastical jurisdiction. This knowledge, Coke asserted, the king did not possess.

James angrily replied that such an argument deprived the English sovereign of his due power inasmuch as it placed him under the
law. Coke answered by a strategic reference to Bracton, the respected medieval authority on English law: "Bracton saith, *quod Rex
non debet esse sub homine sed sub Deo et lege* [the king is not to
be under any man, but under God and the law]." [13] The chief justice never stated the precise way in which the king was under God,
although he frequently made such an assertion. The king was under
the law, however, in a very definite sense. The crown had bequeathed
jurisdiction to the temporal and ecclesiastical courts. The king was
the source of all justice, to be sure, but the working of the judicial
system depended on the traditional independent operation of each
element within its own sphere. Coke argued consistently in the prohibitions issue that the proper administration of justice depended on
the functional distinctions made in the past. Even the king must
abide by these.

Bancroft intimated in the next to last of the *Articuli* that the
temporal judges were not true to their judicial oaths in resisting the
program advanced by king and archbishop. The judges saw it quite
the other way. In the broad sense their oaths were to administer the
king's justice, and they felt they were doing just that by opposing
the interpretation of prohibitions held by James and Bancroft. "We
are assured that none can justly charge any of us with violating our
oaths . . . what scandall it will be to the justice of the realme to
have so great levity, and so foule an imputation laid upon the judges
as is done in this, is too manifest." [14] If the crown's view were to prevail the judges felt they would no longer be able to interpret the law

13. The quotations from this conference can be found in Tanner, *Documents*,
pp. 186–7.
14. *State Trials, 2,* 156.

of the land; they would rather be forced to abide by the royal will. Such a compliance destroyed their true responsibility and did run counter to their oaths. Coke and his colleagues were convinced that the position of the king and the archbishop threatened their judicial calling as well as jeopardized the independence of the common law courts.

ROYAL PROCLAMATIONS

A second instance of James' attempt to control the judiciary and the courts occurred in the 1610 struggle over the crown's proclamations. Once again James' opponent was Chief Justice Coke, who proved as intransigent here as he had been in the prohibitions issue. During Henry VIII's reign a bill was passed which gave the king's proclamations full equality with the statutes of the realm.[15] Although the act was subsequently repealed in 1547, thus depriving proclamations of the force of law, the Tudors and early Stuarts continued to issue proclamations. A flood of them occurred in the early years of James' reign.

Parliament became alarmed at both the quantity of these documents and the claims which the crown put forward in their behalf. In a 1610 petition, Commons complained that royal proclamations were creating offenses not known in English law, punishing more severely than legally prescribed, and condoning trials and procedures which played havoc with established practices. James decided as before to consult his legal advisers, the common law judges. In Coke's *Reports* there is an account of the conference between the crown's representatives and the judiciary. The king submitted test questions to the judges, covering the main points in dispute. He found to his dismay that the judges were in complete sympathy with the grievances of the lower house. The crown's legal advisers stood unalterably opposed to any extension of the king's authority over the practices of the law of the land as interpreted by the common law bench.

The argument of the judges, presented by Coke in an extrajudicial opinion, did not make a wholesale condemnation of the king's authority. The judges were simply concerned with a point of law and not a sweeping limitation of the king's power. The repeal of the Henrician

15. Selections from the 1539 Statute of Proclamations are located in J. R. Tanner, *Tudor Constitutional Documents, A.D. 1485–1603. With an Historical Commentary* (2d ed. Cambridge, The University Press, 1930), pp. 532–5.

law had taken away the statutory status of proclamations, but these royal documents still had such power as they possessed at common law. Coke did not deny the crown's right to issue proclamations, nor did he deny the limited authority which these statements had in the government of the land. "The king for prevention of offences may by proclamation admonish his subjects that they keep the laws, and do not offend them; upon punishment to be inflicted by the law, &c." [16] But proclamations were not part of the law of the land, which consisted only of common law rules, statutes, and customs.[17] When a proclamation contradicted the law of the land, it must be disallowed. If a proclamation were permitted to stand in opposition to the law, the true authority of the king was undermined. For it would be an anomaly to have a proclamation oppose the common law administered in the king's courts, or the statutes propounded by the king in Parliament, or the customs which had evolved in the king's realm.

The issue moved beyond the logic-chopping stage when Chancellor Ellesmere stated that if a precedent were lacking whereby proclamations were fully empowered, perhaps one should be made now. "Every precedent had first a commencement," as this representative of the crown shrewdly put it. Coke replied that the making of a precedent was not proper legal procedure. Correct decisions rested on an examination of the past, not on present extemporization: "I answered that, precedents were to be seen . . . 'melius est recurrere, quam male currere' [it is better to turn back, than run ahead badly] . . ."

The royal argument then took another and more drastic course. If no precedent existed (since the Henrician statute had been repealed) and if no precedent could now be made, royal proclamations should have the force of law simply because they proceeded from the crown. Coke returned to his original point. He saw the crucial question to be whether proclamations had an authority high enough to contravene the law of the land. Referring to past statutes and Fortescue's treatise on the laws of England, the answer of the chief justice was unmistakable:

> Note, the king by his proclamation, or other ways, cannot change any part of the common law, or statute law, or the customs of the realm . . . the king cannot create any offence by his proclamation, which was not an offence before . . . for

16. *State Trials, 2,* 728.
17. *Ibid.,* p. 727.

'ubi non est lex, ibi non est transgressio' [where there is no law, there is no transgression]: *ergo*, that which cannot be punished without proclamation cannot be punished with it.[18]

The danger of the king's claim, felt the judges, was the assertion that the crown's proclamations could change the law of the land. This was never stated outright by the king's representatives in conference with the judges, but it was the logical end of their argument. Such a claim flew at the authority of England's fundamental law. Coke and his associates stood fast: No proclamations of the crown could interfere with the established laws and legal practices of the land.

PEACHAM'S CASE

The chief justice and king again came into conflict in the notorious Peacham's Case of 1615. Here was perhaps the most blatant effort of the crown to control the judges and to deprive the courts of their independence. The issue began in 1614 when the Reverend Edmond Peacham, a rector in Somerset, was tried in the High Commission for libel against his bishop. While in prison his house was searched and notes were discovered for a sermon which appeared to be of treasonable character. The king and the king's council became especially alarmed when it was found that the notes predicted James would meet a death as violent as that which came to Ananias or Nabal. The king was so upset, we are told, that every night he barricaded his room with feather beds.

The crown pressed for a conviction of treason. Counsel on both sides expressed doubt, however, that the sermon notes constituted an overt act of treason, since Peacham had neither published the notes nor used them in a sermon. In accord with ordinary procedure, representatives of the Privy Council planned a conference with the judges to inquire if the charge would be defensible. The council and the king very much hoped, of course, that the judges would lend assent to the proceedings for treason. To ensure judicial confirmation, James instructed Francis Bacon to consult with the judges individually, rather than collectively as was the custom. Doubtless James feared that Coke's anticipated opposition would prevail with the other judges should a collective consultation be held. If the judges were petitioned singly, the crown's course might be affirmed, espe-

18. The quotations in this and the previous paragraphs are taken from *State Trials*, *2*, 725–6.

cially if it were elucidated by the gifted Bacon. Coke violently denounced the scheme. Finally, however, the chief justice was forced to give his opinion separately, opposing the crown's plan to proceed with a charge of treason against Peacham.

As most commentators indicate, the importance of the case lies not in whether an accusation of treason could be sustained against Peacham, but in Coke's vigorous opposition to the crown's method of conference. If the judges were consulted individually, Coke rightly saw that royal influence could be wielded more effectively than if the standard procedure of group consultation were followed. Bacon reported in his letter to James that Coke "fell upon the same allegation which he had begun at the council-table; that judges were not to give opinion by fractions, but entirely according to the vote whereupon they should settle upon conference: and that this auricular taking of opinions, single and apart, was new and dangerous . . ."

Bacon, a lawyer himself, was perhaps sympathetic toward Coke's position. At least he did not deny that the standard practice was as Coke maintained. But the attorney general was also a convinced royalist. He argued at the end that it made little difference whether the judges were consulted singly or collectively. The king had a clear right to ask their opinion in whatever way he chose. Bacon told Coke, "judges sometimes might make a suit to be spared for their opinion, till they had spoken with their brethren; but if the king upon his princely judgment, for reason of estate, should think it fit to have it otherwise, and should so demand it, there was no declining." [19] Coke, on the other hand, insisted that if consultations were held they must be accomplished in the established way.[20]

James was incensed at the judges' equivocation. To clarify the situation and to convince the bench of its error, he set down in his own handwriting a statement entitled "The True State of the Ques-

19. *State Trials, 2,* 873, for the quotations in this and the previous paragraphs.

20. Despite the custom of group consultation with the judiciary, Coke was wary of any kind of pretrial conference with the judges. Commenting on a late 15th-century case, the jurist wrote:

> And therefore the judges ought not to deliver their opinions before-hand upon a case put, and proofs urged of one side in absence of the party accused . . . For how can they be indifferent, who have delivered their opinions before-hand without hearing of the party, when a small addition, or subtraction may alter the case: And how doth it stand with their oath, who are sworn, That they should well and lawfully serve our lord the king and his people in the office of a justice? and they should do equall law, and execution of right to all his subjects, &c. [*Institutes,* 3d Pt., p. 29.]

tion, Whether Peacham's Case Be Treason or Not." The document was a careful presentation of the case's facts, which, in James' mind, necessitated a conviction. He never once mentioned the crucial issue of the crown's right to consult the judges separately. James assumed the crown had such right and that the reason for the delay was the judges' hesitancy over the legality of a treason charge. This delay, lamented James at the end of the document, could only mean that the judges cared "more for the safety of such a monster, than for the preservation of a crown . . ." [21] The king was right. The judges did care more for the safety of this maligned and tortured preacher than for any illegal preservation of a crown.

Coke was contending for all the future Peachams in the defense of England's legal procedures. The judges whom James hoped to intimidate were more bound to the authority of these procedures than they were to the unrestrained command of their sovereign. Again there was no attack on the authority of the king, for Coke and his colleagues affirmed the crown's right to confer with the judges collectively. Private consultations, however, made it inevitable that the crown's authority in the administration of justice would be exceeded. Under oath to administer the king's justice, the judges combated any attempt to interfere with their appointed tasks.

CASE OF COMMENDAMS

A fourth instance of the judges' opposition to the crown climaxed the struggle between Chief Justice Coke and King James. This 1616 conflict resulted in the dismissal of Coke from the King's Bench, and thereafter his professional life was chiefly spent as a member of Parliament and a legal scholar. The case of commendams began as a dispute over the king's grant of a living to Bishop Neile of Lichfield, one of the high churchmen under attack by the Puritans. The grant, which added to the bishop's income without adding to his clerical responsibilities, was to be in effect as long as Neile held his bishopric. The case grew to such proportions in both vehemence and legal significance that it was heard in the Court of the Exchequer, where all twelve common law judges could render their opinions.

The plaintiffs, who maintained that the presentation was their property and not that of the king, charged that the crown had no right to make the particular grant. They also hinted at the illegality

21. *State Trials, 2,* 880.

of any presentations *in commendam,* or on commendation of the king. Warned that his prerogative was being debated without his presence, James once again directed Attorney General Bacon to consult with the judges. Bacon wrote to Coke and later to all the judges, requesting a delay in the proceedings until the king should confer with them. The resultant controversy continued the dispute begun several months before over the king's right to issue the writ *de non procedendo rege inconsulto* (no proceeding, the king not being consulted) to the common law courts.[22]

The judges at first paid no heed to Bacon. They simply proceeded with the argument of the case. Under Coke's direction, however, they at last wrote a letter to the king defending their refusal to delay justice upon demand of the crown. James replied in a letter which set forth the royal position. In June 1616 the judges were summoned to a conference with the king in which every one save Coke recanted. The case was decided against Neile in the end, but under circumstances which left James satisfied that his powers of presentation in commendam were unharmed. The issue added to the grievances which the crown bore against the chief justice. During the summer Coke found himself under increased attack, and in November he was dismissed from office.

As in Peacham's Case there was a misunderstanding between king and chief justice over the central issue. James was convinced that the conflict directly concerned him and that he had a right to be consulted. He argued that his prerogative was at stake, for the granting of livings to be held in commendam had long been a privilege of the crown. The common law bench by its refusal to delay proceedings was interfering with a rightful exercise of the prerogative. In conference with the judges, the king put the issue thus: "Whether, if at any time in a case depending before the Judges which his Majesty conceived to concern him either in power or profit, and thereupon required to consult with them and that they should stay proceedings in the mean time, they ought not to stay accordingly?"

The judges could not deny that the king was party to the action, since the dispute arose over a grant of the crown. Furthermore, Coke and his colleagues were not prepared to take the position of the plaintiffs, who questioned the right of the king to make any such presentations. Even Bacon recorded that "the Judges knew well amongst themselves that the case (as they meant to handle it) did not

22. See Holdsworth, *English Law,* 5, 439.

concern his Majesty's prerogative of grant of Commendams . . ."[23] The point of their action, maintained the judges, was that the king was a party to a dispute which involved the rights of others and this necessitated a regular trial. His Majesty should not be allowed a conference with the judges before the actual hearing, which would again be a pretrial conference whereby the judges might well have the royal position forced upon them.

It is difficult to accept James' accusation that Coke and his fellow judges were bent on destroying the prerogative of the crown. Coke even assured the king of the judges' traditional subservient relationship to the crown. The chief justice used these words in the beginning of his letter: "We are and ever will be ready with all faithful and true hearts, and think ourselves most happy to spend our lives and abilities to do your Majesty true and faithful service."

Coke, of course, interpreted "true and faithful service" as that involved in the proper administration of the king's justice. This was the task to which he and his colleagues had been appointed by the crown. To explain the meaning of judicial service, the chief justice again had recourse to the judges' oaths. One section of the oath expressly stated "that in case any letters come unto us contrary to law, that we do nothing by such letters but certify your Majesty thereof, and go forth to do the law notwithstanding the same letters." Such a letter, written by the attorney general upon command of the king, had come to the judges in the case at hand. They signified that notwithstanding they were going forth to do the law. Performance of duty in the present case required "justice and expedition" in rendering judgment on a matter which concerned "private interest and inheritance."[24] The ownership of the grant must be decided by the settled laws of the land. The king had no right to stay or delay proceedings in the courts simply because his interests were involved; in this issue the crown must be treated as a private litigant. The judges were concerned not with the destruction of the king's prerogative but with the maintenance of a fundamental point of law and justice.

Coke once more emphasized allegiance to the English legal traditions which the judiciary had been appointed to interpret and apply. James, on the other hand, believed that a principle of a higher order than ordinary law was involved in the case: the wounding of "the prerogative royal of our Crown . . . through the sides of a private

23. The quotations in this and the previous paragraphs are taken from Tanner, *Documents*, pp. 195–6.

24. *Ibid.*, p. 193, for the quotations from Coke's letter.

person." [25] The king, much exercised over the judges' action in the case of commendams, even sought to guarantee the proper reception of the crown's mandates in future issues of a similar nature. In conference with the judiciary, James demanded that forthcoming action by the courts should conform with his request for a stay in proceedings when the dispute concerned his power and profit. Face to face with the king's wrath, eleven of the judges acquiesced. Coke alone held out, maintaining that "when that case should be, he would do that should be fit for a judge to do." [26] The chief justice insisted that the function of the judges and courts was to interpret the particulars of the common law tradition in each case, present and future.

In these four cases, Coke and his colleagues occasionally took a stand which the precedents, strictly interpreted, did not support. The royalists could maintain that King James did only what the Plantagenets, Lancasters, Yorks, and Tudors had done before. Some precedents undoubtedly were for the crown, but this fact did not condone the Stuarts' extravagant dictation to the courts. James would standardize and systematize what a Henry or an Elizabeth had done occasionally. The judges stoutly resisted the universalizing of the crown's power over the administration of justice. They defended both the historic independence of the common law courts and their own judicial rights and responsibilities.

FUNDAMENTAL LAW: THE ISSUE OF SUPPLY

We turn now to a conflict which brought forth constant talk of fundamental law from the common lawyers. The issue was the king's enrichment of his treasury by direct financial levy upon his subjects, frequently called "supply" or "impositions." The complicated struggle over supply occasioned much of the common law and parliamentary opposition to the crown in the early 1600's. It was an accumulative grievance.

The 1604 and 1608 levies, the 1612 "feudal aid," the 1614 "clerical loan," the 1622 "benevolence," the 1626 "free gift," and the 1626 forced loan successively augmented the feeling against the crown. The king's right to levy on his own authority was the issue in Bate's Case in 1606, at which time the conflict between the king and the lawyers was clearly defined. The favorable decision for the crown in this leading case instigated the important debates in the 1610, 1614,

25. *Ibid.*, p. 194.
26. *Ibid.*, p. 176.

and 1626 Parliaments over the king's right to lay financial impositions on his subjects. In 1627 the king's levies brought about the contested imprisonment in Darnel's Case and produced a masterful defense of the writ of habeas corpus. Levies were the first redress demanded in the famous 1628 Petition of Right. In 1629 the king's impositions provoked an attack in Commons which was the major cause of Charles' peremptory dissolution of the last Parliament until the Short and Long Parliaments of 1640.

In addition to direct levies, the Stuarts sought to remedy their deficits by granting monopolies, patents, and charters to subjects who would pay the price. These devices were also important issues in the political and economic struggles of early seventeenth-century England, but the matter of forced impositions was the chief source of contention. Throughout the early 1600's the dire financial condition of the crown was used by the opposition as a lever to pry out important concessions. The period is a classic example of the political principle that "supply and redress of grievances go hand-in-hand." [27]

The issue should be understood as more than an instance of extravagant Stuart demands. The impositions of James and Charles were caused by genuine problems: the confused and antiquated techniques of collecting public funds, the increased expense of government in the seventeenth century, and the financing of England's growing participation in the affairs of the continent and overseas. Understandable as these problems were, the opposition insisted that their resolution be effected in accord with the legal practices of the land. The debate ranged over just what these legal practices were and whether, on special occasions, the king's command could contradict such practices. Wherever the conflict resounded—in the halls of Westminster, the chambers of the king, or the Court of the Exchequer —it was in legal terms. The 1610 debates in Commons, for example, were almost entirely in the hands of those members of Parliament who were common lawyers. Some of these were the same barristers involved in the crucial Bate's Case of four years before. In the whole matter of supply, the lawyers attempted to make their interpretation of fundamental law the criterion by which any financial program of the crown should be judged.

The lawyers were far from vague in their reference to fundamental law and its bearing on the king's impositions. They had in mind a

27. Charles H. McIlwain, *The Growth of Political Thought in the West* (New York, Macmillan, 1932), pp. 370–1.

specific procedure by which funds were to be raised for the governing of the land. Money for the maintenance of the kingdom could be gathered by the king for his treasury only after it had been approved and granted by parliamentary legislation. This method was required by both statutes and common law rules, the two chief components of the lawyers' fundamental law.

The argument of the opposition in the supply issue was perhaps first stated in 1610 when James Whitelocke upheld the "king-in-Parliament" method against James' extraparliamentary technique of levy. In the beginning of his famous speech,[28] Whitelocke rhetorically asked whether by "edict and ordinance so made by the king himselfe, by his letters patents of his own will and power absolute, without assent of parliament, he be so . . . enabled to recover these impositions by course of law." In support of a negative answer, Whitelocke first reasoned that the king's policy "is against the naturall frame and constitution of the policie of this kingdome, which is *jus publicum regni*, and so subverteth the fundamentall law of the realme, and induceth a new forme of state and government." Expounding the fundamental law basis of his argument, Whitelocke continued: "The soveraigne power is agreed to be in the king: but in the king is a two-fold power; the one in parliament, as he is assisted with consent of the whole state; the other out of parliament, as he is sole, and singular, guided merely by his own will." [29] The first is the greater, and to it belonged the crown's power of levy. The lawyers argued that the king was breaking fundamental law by doing out of Parliament what could be done only in Parliament.

The attack on the king's levies in the name of fundamental law must be described in sharper detail. James himself believed that the making of all law, including the law governing public funds, was a function of the king acting in Parliament. On several occasions the first Stuart said that he was at his highest power when he acted in Parliament. In a speech of 1610 to Lords and Commons, he declared that a certain proposal could be implemented only "by the aduise of Parliament: for the King with his Parliament here are absolute,

28. *State Trials, 2,* 477, incorrectly ascribes this speech to Sir Henry Yelverton, a lawyer whose sympathy for the crown would not have allowed him to speak thus. On Whitelocke as the speaker, see Tanner, *Documents,* p. 259, and G. W. Prothero, ed., *Select Statutes and Other Constitutional Documents Illustrative of the Reigns of Elizabeth and James I, 1559–1625* (4th ed. Oxford, Clarendon, 1913), p. 351.

29. Quotations in this paragraph are from *State Trials, 2,* 481–2.

(as I vnderstand) in making or forming of any sort of Lawes." [30]
One must probe beneath the term "king-in-Parliament" to find the real
issue between the crown and the lawyers.

BATE'S CASE

The point of the lawyers' attack on the king is grasped when the
courts are substituted for Parliament as *place de combat*. Only
when the supply issue became a case and was tried in a court of law
did the positions of the parties become clear. Bate's Case in 1606
was by far the most illuminating and important. The course of the
arguments and the final decision in this dispute were debated throughout the early seventeenth century. Bate's Case was to the impositions
issue in the early 1600's what the famous 1637 ship money case was a
generation later.

The matter had a simple beginning when a merchant named John
Bate, or Bates, refused to pay a custom levied by the crown on the
importation of Venetian currants. In Elizabethan times a certain private company had been granted a monopoly from the crown to import currants and other Venetian products. The company paid an annual £4000 to the royal treasury for its monopoly and reimbursed
itself by levying a custom of 5*s*. 6*d*. per hundredweight on all merchants engaged in the trade who were not members of the company.
Opposition increased over the crown's preferential treatment of a
particular group; at the turn of the century the company surrendered
its charter in deference to the cry against monopolies granted by
the king. The crown was then faced with an annual loss of £4000, the
yearly fee previously paid by the company. To recoup its loss, the
king threw open the trade to all merchants and levied the same 5*s*. 6*d*.
upon each merchant. For a while no opposition was encountered, but
in 1606 John Bate refused payment to the king on the ground that
the custom was illegal. The case was tried in the Court of the Exchequer, where the four barons or judges gave a verdict in favor
of the crown.[31]

The refusal of the defendant to pay the custom was held to be
nothing less than an attack on the authority of the king and, as such,
was a serious crime. Before elaborating the precise nature of the
royal authority in the case, the barons first satisfied themselves that

---

30. "A Speach to the Lords and Commons of the Parliament at White-Hall . . .
Anno 1609 [o.s.]," in McIlwain, *James' Works*, p. 311.

31. The statement of the case depends largely on the summary in Tanner, *Documents*, pp. 336–8, and Gardiner, *History*, *2*, 5–11.

the legal precedents and statutes of England would support a decision for the crown. They found overwhelming corroboration. Not only were Tudor and earlier precedents with the king, but also the common sense of the matter. The barons pointed out that the king needed the power of levy to restrict foreign competition and thus protect the economic pursuits of his own countrymen. The crown also rightly had the power of custom for the effective conduct of international diplomacy. Grave economic disadvantages could be inflicted upon a foreign prince by prohibiting the importation of his land's products. If this custom had been levied upon Bate as an ordinary subject, argued the barons, it would be an illegal imposition. Any tax levied generally upon subjects and their goods required the consent of the whole realm and this could only be given in Parliament. But the defendant was a particular kind of subject with a particular property: he was a merchant bringing foreign goods into the land. The crown was within its rights and duties as protector of the realm by taxing all such particular merchants engaged in the importation of a foreign product. Moreover, continued the barons, the currants were not Bate's actual possession anyway; the currants were still technically the goods of the Venetians. Bate's defense that his property had been confiscated when he refused to pay the tax did not stand. Finally, the judgment of the barons rested on the argument that the ports of the land were the "gates of the king." The crown could exercise over the gates such power as it deemed necessary for the governance and protection of the land. This power included the right to levy necessary customs.[32]

So flagrant was Bate's refusal to pay the 5s. 6d. custom that the barons saw fit to theorize about the king's powers. It was not uncommon for a common law court in this period to leave the roadbed of rule and statute and make a detour in the realm of political theory. Chief Baron Fleming, or Flemming, began his excursus with a description of the king's power, which he conceived as a double power. Each form had its own laws and ends. There was first the ordinary power of the king which "is for the profit of particular subjects, for the execution of civil justice, the determining of *meum;* and this is exercised by equitie and justice in ordinary courts, and by the civilians is nominated *jus privatum* and with us, common law; and these laws

---

32. These and other arguments in behalf of the crown were advanced by Chief Baron Fleming and Baron Clarke, *State Trials, 2,* 382–94. The arguments of Francis Bacon, the king's solicitor, in the 1610 Parliament embellished the barons' interpretation of the precedents; *ibid.,* pp. 395–400.

cannot be changed, without parliament . . ." The second is far greater and is called the absolute power of the king.

> The absolute power of the king is not that which is converted or executed to private use, to the benefit of any particular person, but is only that which is applied to the general benefit of the people, and is *salus populi* . . . this power is guided by the rules, which direct only at common law, and is most properly named Pollicy and Government; and as the constitution of this body varieth with the time, so varieth this absolute law, according to the wisdome of the king, for the common good . . .

Fleming insisted that the absolute power of the crown was indispensable to kingship. It gave a monarch authority to wage war, issue money, defend the kingdom, and govern the land. In the exercise of the second, higher kind of power the king was responsible solely to his own wisdom and judgment. Applying the concept to the present case, Fleming stated that "All customes, be they old or new, are . . . made by the absolute power of the king." Since Bate was challenging the king's customs which were levied in accord with the absolute power of the king, his act was against the highest authority of the land.

The chief baron continued his theorizing with an answer to an objection of Bate's counsel. If by virtue of his absolute power the king could levy at will such an impost on currants, counsel had asked, what is to prevent the future extension of levies to all private property? Here, said Fleming, the faithful subject must trust the king's judgment. "And whereas it is said, that if the king may impose, he may impose any quantitie what he pleases, true it is, that this is to be referred to the wisdome of the king, who guideth all under God by his wisdome . . ." This should not be a concern of, nor should it be disputed by, any subject. For "many things are left to his wisdome for the ordering of his power, rather than his power shall be restrained." [33]

It was clear to all participants and observers that the barons were upholding a power of the king which stood above any other authority. The judges of the Exchequer tried to ground their opinion on the safe foundation of precedent. But if any legal precedent should be opposed, they held that the absolute power of the king enabled him to levy customs which he deemed requisite.[34] Absolute and unlimited

33. The quotations in this and the two previous paragraphs can be found in *State Trials, 2,* 389, 391.

34. For a proclamation of the king couched in terms of the crown's absolute

for good reasons, the highest power of the king gave the crown the right to break ordinary law and precedent when necessary.

The common law opposition to the decision in Bate's Case developed slowly. For a while the foremost lawyers thought the case had been adjudged correctly. William Hakewill speaking before Commons in 1610 confessed his initial acquiescence in the decision:

> I was confidently perswaded, that his majesties right to impose was very cleere and not to be disputed . . . I was then present at all the arguments both at the bar and at the bench; and I do confesse that by the weighty and unanswerable reasons, as I then conceived them, of those grave and reverend Judges (Fleming, Ch. Bar. Clarke, Savil,) sitting in their seats of justice, I was much perswaded. But by those many records vouched by them I was altogether overcome . . . for syr, *ratio suadet, authoritas vincit* [reason persuades, authority conquers].

What had temporarily won over Hakewill and his colleagues was, of course, the thorough precedential support which the barons had uncovered for the king. Needless to say, the lawyers were not convinced by Chief Baron Fleming's elaboration of the king's powers.

Satisfaction with the decision was of short duration. The speeches of the parliamentarian lawyers in the 1610 and 1614 sessions indicated that further searches had been made in the records of the Exchequer in behalf of the defendant. Hakewill was one of the members assigned by the House of Commons to determine "the practice of former ages." He confided that his researches forced him to change his mind and that he would "follow the commandement of Christ to Peter, beeing converted, seeke to convert my brethren." [35] Fortified with legal authorities and fired by vigorous speeches, the lawyers gathered strength for their attack on the king's impositions.

As Coke maintained the crown's authority in his fight with James over the independence of the courts, so Hakewill and Whitelocke upheld the crown's authority in the matter of impositions. They agreed with the barons that precedents abounded for the crown's levy of custom on commodities imported to England. They further agreed that the king must have the power of levy in order to carry out his responsibilities as protector of the realm. If a custom had

---

power, see the "Commission to Levy Impositions, (1608)," in Prothero, *Documents*, pp. 353–5.

35. Hakewill's words in this and the previous paragraph are taken from *State Trials*, *2*, 408–11.

been levied against the currant merchants out of the king's efforts to defend the realm in any way, John Bate would have no case.

The lawyers were convinced, however, that the custom was not for the defense of the land. England was not at war with Venice; indeed, the two countries were on the most cordial terms. This fact eliminated from consideration the crown's right to hinder the economic prosperity of a foreign prince for reasons of state. Nor was there any domestic reason for the crown to restrict the import of currants. Such products could only be grown in the Levant and, thus, native agricultural pursuits were not endangered by foreign competition. The lawyers argued that the impost on Bate was clearly for revenue, or the enrichment of the king's treasury. The levy was an attempt of the crown to recoup the loss it sustained in the cessation of the yearly £4000 fee paid by the former monopolist company. If this were the proper interpretation of the case, then all the careful reasoning advanced by the Court of the Exchequer to confirm the action of the crown was irrelevant. The court had never discussed the matter of revenue. It simply assumed the king had acted as protector in Bate's Case and therefore was within his right.

With this interpretation as a foundation, the lawyers tore asunder the argument of the barons. The ports were the gates of the king, agreed the barristers, but only for purposes of protection, not revenue. James had a right to commandeer these gates to combat an enemy—not to enrich his depleted coffers. It was a thin argument that set Bate apart as a special subject to be dealt with in a particular way because he was a merchant. Similarly fictitious was the barons' claim that the levy was on currants and not on Bate and his fellow merchants. Clearly the tax was on Bate and his fellows, who alone were affected by the demanded impost. There was no need to defend the land against currants, only to lay demands on merchants. It was obvious, finally, that the king had taxed Bate's property and not that of the Venetians, over whose property the king had no control anyway. The defendant's servant was actually hauling away his master's currants from the waterfront when apprehended by the king's officers. Hakewill capsuled the common law interpretation of the case by stating that the king, on his sole initiative, may levy for defense and protection but not, on just his own authority, impose for reasons of taxation or revenue.

For my part, I think the King cannot restrain the passage of merchants, but for some speciall cause. . . . let me inform you, that there is not one of these presidents [sic] vouched by them to prove the king's power to restraine, but they are upon speciall reasons ; as by reason of enmity with such a nation . . . or because such a commodity may not be spared within the kingdome. . . . But is the consequence good, that because the king restraine, therefore he may impose upon such as passe? [36]

The political significance of the lawyers' argument was the claim that the impost in Bate's Case could be established only by parliamentary grant. Hakewill, Whitelocke, and the others found precedents to prove that the historic procedure for supplying the crown its financial needs had been by act of king-in-Parliament. The barons acknowledged the existence of such precedents, but they were ruled irrelevant since Bate's Case did not fall within the category of revenue or supply. Hakewill assured his hearers that "all the kings of this realm since Hen. 3. have sought and obtained an increase of Custome, more or lesse, by the name of Subsidie, or the gift of their subjects in parliament."

Kings went to Parliament not because this was the easy way to obtain funds for the government of the land, but because such a procedure was required by law. "Is it likely, that if any or all these kings had thought they had had in them any lawfull power by just prerogative to have laid impositions at their pleasure, they would not have rather have made use of that, than have taken this course by act of parliament, so full of delay, so prejudiciall to their right . . ." [37] Former kings could not do otherwise, however, because an act of Parliament was fundamental law for the collection of revenue.

Hakewill made a complete listing of the possible sources of financial supply for the king's governance of the land. Each item of income was seen to originate in statute or common law. Should the amount granted by these two sources be insufficient, the king was to ask Parliament for an additional supply. If the king followed any other course, Whitelocke added in his subsequent speech, "He must either take his subjects goods from them, without assent of the party, which is against the law ; or else he must give his own letters pattents the force of a law, to alter the property of his subjects goods, which is also against the law."

Whitelocke, Hakewill, and their associates were, like Coke, perhaps

---

36. *State Trials, 2,* 471–2.
37. *Ibid.,* p. 421, for the quotations in this and the previous paragraphs.

guilty of legal exaggeration and artifice. Before 1606 few cases on impositions had actually been adjudged. The barristers were thus hard pressed to find decisions in the records of the Exchequer which could be used as on-the-point precedents. They had to depend on the sometimes ambiguous, badly recorded financial practices of the Tudor age and on extrajudicial opinions. Furthermore, there was probably more agreement among all concerned on the difference between the crown's ordinary and absolute power than the lawyers were willing to admit.[38] The lawyers were arguing, however, for the spirit of the fundamental law rather than its letter. The implication of Fleming's theory was that the king's absolute power gave him the authority to break law. This was precisely the issue—the lawyers saw it more clearly than the crown and the barons of the Exchequer. "It hath been alleadged," declared Whitelocke, "that those, which in this cause have enforced their reasons from this maxime of ours, 'That the king cannot alter the law,' have diverted from the question.—I say under favor they have not; for that in effect is the very question now in hand; for if he alone out of parliament may impose, he altereth the law of England . . ."[39]

DARNEL'S CASE

A further instance of the lawyers' use of fundamental law against the Stuart crown occurred early in Charles' reign. The conflict can again be described pointedly in terms of a leading case brought before the common law courts. We refer to Darnel's Case of November 1627, popularly called the "Case of the Five Knights."

Once again litigation resulted from the depleted condition of the royal treasury. In order to alleviate serious financial needs in 1626–27, Charles tried various ways of gathering funds. The most ambitious, and most resisted, device was a forced loan that was to be gathered from certain wealthy subjects of the realm. Charles, angered over the continuing and increasing opposition to the crown's imposi-

38. Consult G. D. G. Hall, "Impositions and the Courts, 1554–1606," *Law Quarterly Review, 69,* No. 274 (April 1953). See also Mr. Hall's article "Bate's Case and 'Lane's Reports': The Authenticity of a Seventeenth-Century Legal Text," *Bulletin of the John Rylands Library, Manchester, 35,* No. 2 (March 1953), which deals with the inadequacies of "Lane's Reports," the source of most of the selections in *State Trials.*

39. Whitelocke's words in this and the previous paragraphs are taken from *State Trials, 2,* 483.

tions, peremptorily imprisoned five leaders of a group who refused subscription to the loan. The five were incarcerated *per speciale mandatum domini regis* [by special order of the lord and king]. Charles did not dare give the real reason for imprisonment, which was, of course, the knights' refusal to comply with the royal demand for money.

The prisoners applied for a writ of habeas corpus, which would have required the king to set forth the cause of their imprisonment. An issue would thus have been stated which could go before a jury in regular trial. The granting of the writ would also have allowed the prisoners to be released on bail. Without habeas corpus, the prisoners had to remain in the Fleet until and if the king granted them liberty. Everything depended on the whim of the crown. The uproar over the imprisonment was so tumultuous that the case was finally heard in the Court of the King's Bench. After ingenious argument on both sides, judgment was given for the crown. Habeas corpus was denied, and the five knights were sent back to prison. The royalist judges held that the only way for the prisoners to effect their delivery was by petition to the king, throwing themselves completely on his mercy. The prisoners did resort to petition and at the end of January 1628 the king ordered them to be released. Several of the knights were promptly elected to the 1628 Parliament where in the company of Coke they carried on the debate over the crown's power of arbitrary imprisonment.[40]

In his arguments before the court, Attorney General Heath amassed an array of precedents in support of the king's right to imprison without showing cause. Like Chief Baron Fleming, Heath then proceeded to speculate on the king's authority. That the crown should have such power resulted from the king's *absoluta potestas*. The power derived from the king's position as head of the commonwealth: "All justice is derived from him, and what he doth, he doth . . . as the head of the commonwealth, as *justiciarius regni* [the justice of the kingdom], yea, the very essence of justice under God upon earth is him." [41] In questions of state, the king's absolute power could not be contravened by any other authority. The judges found the precedents cited by Heath to be overwhelming, although they apparently did not endorse the attorney general's speculations on the king's absolute power. In fact, the common law bench—even after the removal of Coke—was

40. Consult Gardiner, *Documents*, pp. xviii–xix; *idem, History, 6,* 212–17; *State Trials, 3,* 1–3, 59–60.
41. Gardiner, *Documents*, p. 60.

reluctant to grant the crown an arbitrary and extensive right to imprison as a function of royal prerogative. In the present case, however, the precedents clearly favored the king's action.

Serjeant John Bramston and the influential John Selden were leading counsel for the prisoners. They agreed that precedents did exist for imprisonment on special order of the king without the showing of any other cause. Such imprisonments, argued counsel, had resulted from the requisite incarceration of traitors or criminals, or from some other necessarily swift administration of the king's justice. The lawyers thus admitted that the crown had exceptional emergency powers which could throw a man into prison upon mere command of the king.[42] But there was no emergency in the present issue. It was clear to counsel, as it was to all who knew the origin of the case, that the king's special order was a disguise of his true reason for imprisonment. The reason was that the five prisoners had refused subscription to the forced loan.

The crux of John Selden's argument was his insistence that, in the matter of imprisonment, the king must proceed within the "constant and settled laws of this kingdom, without which we have nothing . . ." Selden referred to Magna Carta, chapter 29, as the foundation of this procedure: "Nullus liber homo capiatur vel imprisonetur nisi per legem terrae [No free man is seized or imprisoned unless by law of the land]."[43] "Per legem terrae" needed refinement in the light of previous practice before its relevance for the case at hand could be determined. Selden pointed out to the court that the crucial phrase had come to mean that a man could be imprisoned only by presentment or indictment. Neither had been done in the present case; the five prisoners were held in the Fleet simply *per speciale mandatum domini regis*. Selden argued that the law of the land had been broken. Imprisonment by special order of the crown contradicted the fundamental law, which allowed imprisonment only when cause was shown, assured freedom upon payment of bail, and guaranteed trial without delay.

The royal viewpoint was irrevocably opposed to that of Bramston and Selden. Attorney General Heath admitted that the king's right to imprison without showing cause might at times result in hardships and

42. Neither Bramston, Selden, nor any other of the counsel disputed a decision of *34 Elizabeth* (1591), wherein it was held that if a man were committed by the crown under certain circumstances he was not bailable. This case was a key precedent cited by Attorney General Heath in his argument and by Chief Justice Hyde in judgment for the king. See Gardiner, *Documents*, pp. 62, 64.

43. See *ibid.*, p. 59, for the quotations from Selden's argument.

even inequities. But such rare occurrences were to be endured so that the king's absoluta potestas would be untrammeled. As Chief Baron Fleming had said before him, the subject must, in the end, trust his sovereign's judgment and sagacity. To hold that the king was limited by any other authority was an affront to his absolute power. "But shall any say, The king cannot do this? No: we may only say, He will not do this." [44] Whatever the law of the land, the king's absolute power was of a higher order, and if need be the king could break the law. There was such a need in Darnel's Case and the king had acted within his right.

In Bate's Case and Darnel's Case, the fundamental issue was the nature of the king's absolute power. How broad was it, and what was its relation to the lawyers' fundamental law? These questions were asked in nearly all the conflicts between the common lawyers and the crown in the early 1600's. The four grievances of the 1628 Petition of Right in Parliament laid open the same questions. Throughout their struggle with the king in law court or Parliament, the lawyers took a narrow view of the king's absoluta potestas. Such power did exist in the crown, but only for use in particular circumstances, such as the direct levy of a tax to defend the realm or the right to imprison a dangerous criminal without showing cause. These particular uses of the king's power were stipulated in common law rules and statutes. The power of the king was derived from rather than stood above the components of the fundamental law.

The judges and barristers thought of the king more in terms of prerogative than absolute power. It can even be said that the lawyers conceived of prerogatives, rather than *the* prerogative.[45] Royal power was a distillation from the fundamental law, issuing in the form of particular rights and privileges for the crown. Coke recorded the matter boldly: "the King hath no prerogative, but that which the law of the land allows him." [46] The fundamental law of common law rules and statutes was always superior to the power of a king. In the case of conflict, the lower must yield to the higher.

44. *Ibid.,* p. 63.

45. See S. B. Chrimes, *English Constitutional Ideas in the Fifteenth Century* (Cambridge, The University Press, 1936), pp. 42–3. In this section the author looks beyond his period to the 17th-century dispute over the powers of the king.

46. *The Reports of Sir Edward Coke, Knight. In Thirteen Parts,* J. H. Thomas and J. F. Fraser, eds. (London, Butterworth, 1826), Pt. 12, *6,* 76.

6 PURITANS AND LAWYERS ON POLITICAL AUTHORITY

AUTHORITY AND OBEDIENCE

IN A PREFATORY ESSAY to the political works of James I, Charles H. Mc-Ilwain states that the chief political issue of the sixteenth and seventeenth centuries was obedience.[1] The issue could be put in the form of a question: What authority was to be obeyed above all others? The matter usually had a religious dimension, for it was asked which entity in society God had placed supreme. Mr. McIlwain believes that William Tyndale set the stage for the dispute in England with his book *The Obedience of a Christian Man* (1528).[2] Tyndale, translator of the Bible and staunch supporter of the Tudor Reformation, declared that final and complete obedience was due the king by divine decree. He spoke against Roman Catholics who held that God had created the pope supreme and that full obedience should therefore be rendered the Roman pontiff. In his insistence on complete and unquestioned allegiance to the king, Tyndale also chastised those who would divide their loyalty. Protestants and Catholics who allotted their homage between king and ruler of the church, whether the latter was pope, synod, or convocation, were anathema. Obedience was monolithic in structure, the sole foundation being the crown.

Henry VIII, James I, Charles I, and James II were sixteenth- and seventeenth-century English monarchs who took their Tyndale seriously. The Henrician writer was succeeded by many political theorists who supplied additional justification for rulers who sought absolute power. Thomas Hobbes is the leader of those who followed in the direction set by Tyndale. In *De Cive* of 1642 and the *Leviathan* of 1651

---

1. McIlwain, *James' Works*, pp. xx ff.
2. See also Harold J. Laski, *The Foundations of Sovereignty, and Other Essays* (New York, Harcourt, Brace, 1921), p. 294.

Hobbes argued for complete, undivided obedience to a single authority—this time notably without religious sanction.

Those who stressed full obedience to a particular authority had a difficult time with their countrymen in the sixteenth and seventeenth centuries. In fact, both the theoreticians and the implementers of the idea were a minority party. Most Englishmen were unsympathetic toward the Tyndales, Jameses, and Hobbeses; they were unwilling to say what earthly authority should be obeyed in any final sense; they were particularly suspicious of the claim of a monarch to be the only object of obedience. Queen Elizabeth recognized the suspicion and, with more inherent shrewdness than was possessed by Henry VIII or James I, declined to represent herself as the sole base upon which all political and ecclesiastical loyalty should be constructed.

The early seventeenth-century Puritans and lawyers were prime examples of Englishmen unwilling to give complete obedience to the crown. Indeed, all forms of earthly power were subjected to their criticism—king, council, Parliament, pope, and synod. The divines and barristers never confessed to "where sovereignty lay" among the present, competing powers nor stated which power was to be obeyed above all others. They represented the dominant political mood of their fellow citizens in the sixteenth and seventeenth centuries.

This does not mean that the Puritans and the lawyers were against organized government. The early seventeenth-century divines affirmed the role of the state, unlike certain branches of the Reformation's left wing. The organized political body was not a source of contamination for the pure believer, or a punishment for human sin, or a necessary evil whose *raison d'être* was to restrain wayward men. It was a positive force for the proper management of society. The Puritans inherited the Old Testament emphasis on the "life of the nation" and, like the prophets, maintained that one condition of a nation living under God was effective political organization.

The lawyers similarly insisted on the necessity of the state. Consider, for instance, the 1608 case of the *post-nati*, or Calvin's Case, in which Chief Justice Coke made it clear that strong political authority was the only alternative to chaos. The crux of the case was the determination of the national status of persons born in Scotland after the death of Queen Elizabeth I. Those born in Scotland before Elizabeth's death (the *ante-nati*) were held as aliens and were disallowed, at first, the full privileges of English citizenship. But were the post-nati subjects or aliens? Coke saw only confusion, let alone injustice, if the post-nati Scots were declared aliens: "If there were not a soveraign to prescribe laws, and people of allegiance to obey them, there could be no laws made nor executed." [3] If James was not the rightful king of the post-nati, endowing his Scottish subjects with English citizenship, government in Scotland would be impossible.

For both Puritans and lawyers, government was a necessary good. It was quite another matter, however, to hold that king, or Parliament, or any other conceivable form of government deserved absolute obedience.

The issue of obedience is a helpful key to the political history of the time, but its promise fades when the word is applied solely to concrete authorities. For the Puritans and the lawyers, final loyalty was rendered to objects which no contemporary formulation of political power fully represented. Unqualified obedience could only be given to God and law. Puritans swore allegiance to divine sovereignty and lawyers to fundamental law. When the judges refused to obey the king's commands, they did so partly on the basis of their oath to administer the law of the land. The order of the king to stay proceedings in the Case of Commendams in 1616 was held contrary to the judges' commission which bound them "upon their oaths, and according to their best knowledge and learning . . . to deliver the true understanding [of law] faithfully and uprightly." [4] Likewise the Puritans were bound to obey God. There was no formal oath as in the case of the judges, but there was explicit opposition to any other sworn loyalty. Many Puritans were against all manner of oath taking. As with other groups in the history of the church, these men were determined to obey God even at the expense of disobeying men of high authority. One Puritan minister closed a sermon preached before the judges in Norwich at summer assizes in 1620 with this prayer: "Blesse *the people*, and teach them to obey *for conscience sake;* and withall wisely to know where, and how *it is better to obey thee, then* [sic] *man.*" [5] God and law alone provoked ultimate loyalty. They alone could be obeyed unquestioningly.

The Puritans and lawyers were confident that God and law merited absolute obedience. For the Puritans, divine sovereignty was a matter to be reckoned with immediately in any question of loyalty. It was, as we have seen, the cornerstone of Puritan faith and morals. The rule of God was no temporary expediency created on the moment to deal

3. *State Trials, 2,* 570.
4. Tanner, *Documents,* p. 193.
5. "The Proiector. Teaching a Direct . . . Way to Restore the Decayes of the Church and State," in Scot, *Workes,* p. 39.

with a particular situation. It had come into the world from without
and had existed from eternity. The divine origin, comprehensiveness,
and perpetuity of God's rule made it incomparably superior to other
forms of authority.

In a similar way the lawyers construed fundamental law. As "pure
reason," or the perfection of reason, the logic and harmony of common law rules and statutes made them natural first sources of obedience. But there was more to commend the fundamental law than just
reasonableness. The source of the ancient common law was somewhere
in the dim beginnings of Anglo-Saxon history. Coke and others
cleverly spun the tale of a law originating in the bliss of pre-Norman
times when all things existed in an uncontaminated state prior to the
coming of William the Conqueror. Coke appropriated the Christian
myth of creation and fall, even the motif of the Garden of Eden, in
order to validate the superiority of the fundamental law. The ancient
law of the land had a mystical aura, even a blessedness, which rightly
called forth man's highest loyalty.[6] The more extreme apologists
among the common lawyers were not averse to pushing the matter all
the way: The fundamental law was "grounded upon the Law of

6. See Coke, *Reports*, Pt. 8, *4*, iv, in "To the Reader": "the grounds of our common laws at this day were beyond the memory or register of any beginning, and
the same which the Norman conqueror then found within this realm of England.
The laws that William the Conqueror swore to observe, were *bonae et approbatae
antiquae regni leges,* that is, the laws of this kingdom were in the beginning of the
Conqueror's reign good, approved, and ancient." In both the *Reports* and the *Institutes* Coke rejoices when he finds that a certain law or usage has come down from
Saxon times and thereby antedates the coming of the Conqueror. Such a law has
great authority. An offense against the ancient, pre-Norman common law is *malum
in se* (evil in itself), not merely *malum prohibitum.* See the comments of the chief
justice in the proclamations dispute (Tanner, *Documents,* p. 188).

In his search for older and older precedents, Coke followed the lead of a late
13th-century legal work *The Mirror of Justices,* generally thought to have been
written by one Andrew Horn. In the 2d Pt. of the *Institutes,* Coke refers constantly to "the Mirrour" in order to substantiate his claim that the origin of the
"good, approved, and ancient" laws of the land is to be found in the age before
1066. Frederic W. Maitland spoke the truth when he wrote about Horn: "The
right to lie he exercises unblushingly," in William J. Wittaker, ed., *The Mirror
of Justices,* Publications of the Selden Society (London, Quaritch, 1895), intro.,
p. xxvi. The anachronistic and artificial reasoning of Coke based on the unreliable
Mirror of Justices does produce grave problems. The point for our study, however, is that Coke's attempt to "pre-Normanize" the law was simply the way he
would prove what he already believed, namely, that the ancient law of the land
is worthy of veneration. Consult William Haller and Godfrey Davies, eds., *The
Leveller Tracts, 1647–1653* (New York, Columbia University Press, 1944), pp.
46–7, for the later significance of the method followed by Horn and Coke.

God." [7] Occasionally the lawyers' law of God was equated with the Bible; the ancient common law rules were then seen to have their base in scripture. More often the law of God was cited as a vague foundation superior to other equally ill-defined bases, such as the law of nature or the law of nations. Particular laws constructed on this law of God were of greater worth than those built on lesser foundations. The absence of clarity and logic does not prevent the generalization that the lawyers honored and revered their fundamental law. It was at least a "vital principle" [8] to which early seventeenth-century judges and barristers were as attached as Puritan divines and teachers were to divine sovereignty.

For both Puritans and lawyers, the ultimate authorities had a direct relationship to the world of practical affairs. The relationship is indicated by the emphasis on "sovereignty" for God and "fundamental" for law. The omnipresence of fundamental law was a commonplace and demonstrable proposition for the lawyers. Common law rules and statutes were simply unavoidable when any practical questions or issues were raised.

The worldly relevance of divine sovereignty was less apparent. One might ask of the Puritans, Was not the way of God forever beyond the knowing of men, was not the infinite rule forever a mystery to man's finite mind? The answer is yes, in part; but the Puritans lived in the conviction that God's rule was manifested in the here and now and that the marks of his sway were known by men in their day-to-day affairs.[9] The eternal was always breaking through into the temporal. The divines were fond of saying that fair England under God possessed more signs of divine rule than did ancient Israel:

> this then is the matter of praise, that we are in such a Kingdome whereof not man, but *God* is King. *Israel* the type of us, they had Kings indeed, but all were flesh, served their times, and dyed: But our King is *God*, whose Throne is for ever; this the men of *God* fore-saw and rejoyced in, *Thy God reigneth, O Sion,* &c. And in

7. See Dugdale, *Origines,* p. 3, quoting the early 17th-century chancellor Lord Ellesmere. In the 2d Pt. of the *Institutes,* Coke himself leads the reader to believe that the ancient laws come from God. For the use to which this idea was put in the early 1640's, when the 2d Pt. of the *Institutes* was published, see William Haller, *Liberty and Reformation in the Puritan Revolution* (New York, Columbia University Press, 1955), p. 71.

8. *Ibid.,* p. 70.

9. The above description of divine sovereignty depends in part on the analysis found in Niebuhr, *Kingdom,* pp. 56 ff.

truth this is altogether it which doth so credit this kingdome of ours, this is all the glory of our Israel.[10]

The immediateness of God's rule was seen most clearly in the matter of the church, where Christ "a head of pure gold indeed," as described by one Puritan, ruled directly without the aid of "vice-ministeriall heads." "As if Kings cannot governe all their Countreyes, though their Persons be at their Court onely : How much more our King who is with us in Spirit, where two or three are gathered in His name?" [11] Richard Holdsworth spoke for his colleagues when he once used the figure of a silver and a golden stream to describe the felicity of the land. He was preaching on Psalm 144:15: "Blessed are the people, that be so, yea blessed are the people, whose God is the Lord." The silver stream was civil order and harmony, created and directed by the left hand of God. God's right hand controlled the golden stream in which was found the religious happiness of the nation. The works of each hand were perceptible to all and were evidence of God's universal rule.[12]

Divine sovereignty and fundamental law applied everywhere and were to be reckoned with in all matters of early seventeenth-century life.

THE ROLE OF LAWS

How did divine sovereignty and fundamental law wield their ultimate authority in society? In the practical world the sway of God and fundamental law, believed the Puritans and the lawyers, was shown forth through individual laws.

This conviction made our subjects legalists par excellence. Among both divines and barristers there was a marked disinclination to generalize about political authority. Rather there was a scurrying to respective law books to discover what was commanded by a particular legal norm, be it a common law rule, a biblical pronouncement, or a statute. No sweeping constitutional documents were produced by the Puritan–common law opposition in the prewar period. The heralded 1628 Petition of Right, for example, simply "placed on record the King's acceptance of the statement that according to these laws certain definite grievances were illegal. . . . [it was] the recognition of a claim that every subject of the Crown had been wronged

10. Bayne, *Colossians*, p. 74.
11. *Ibid.*, p. 97.
12. Richard Holdsworth, *A Sermon Preached in St. Maries in Cambridge* (Cambridge, 1642), pp. 1–2.

in certain specific matters, and that, in the future, in those matters, the laws would be observed." [13] The petition asked for no prohibition of the crown's financial impositions, save under the particular circumstances of the 1626 forced loan. In the ship money case of 1637 the whole issue of supply had to be fought through again, and a thorough examination of precedents was made once more by both sides.

The panegyric of a parliamentarian lawyer in the 1628 Parliament displayed the spirit of the age:

> Our Lawes, which are the rules of this Justice, they are the *ne plus ultra* to both the King and the Subject: and as they are *Hercules* Pillar, so they are the pillar to every *Hercules*, to every *Prince*, which he must not passe. Give me leave to resemble her to *Nebuchadnezzar's* tree: for she is so great, that she doth shade not onely the Pallace of the King, and the house of the Nobles, but doth also shelter the Cottage of the poorest beggar.[14]

As one scholar has written of the period before the Civil War, "Of legalism there is much; of political science, none." [15]

Arrogance often tinged the legalism of the Puritans and the lawyers. The divines wrestled with the laws of scripture and immodestly proclaimed their superiority in the interpretation of God's word. The lawyers argued that they alone possessed the knowledge needed for the understanding and application of the laws of the land. Unless one had studied the common law diligently, Coke told James in the prohibitions issue, the requisite "artificial reason" could not be acquired. The divines and barristers frequently represented themselves as unfailing experts in the multifarious laws of the time.

For the Puritans, as we have seen, the Bible was the primary law book. It was scripture that displayed in best form the specifics of divine sovereignty. Biblical norms did not relate just to matters of salvation, the good life, or the organization of the church. The laws of the Bible were more extensive and applied generally to the vaster realms of political and social life. The precise coverage of scriptural pronouncement was a matter of debate among the international Cal-

13. E. R. Adair, "The Petition of Right," *History, 5,* No. 18 (July 1920), 102–3. Also consult Frances H. Relf, *The Petition of Right,* Minneapolis [University of Minnesota Press], 1917.

14. Fuller, *Prerogative,* p. 22, part of a speech given by the parliamentarian-lawyer Creswell in the first session of the 1628 Parliament.

15. William A. Dunning, *A History of Political Theories from Luther to Montesquieu* (New York, Macmillan, 1905), p. 194; see also McIlwain, *High Court,* p. 97.

vinist brotherhood. The English Puritans, as already indicated, did not find in the Bible a complete form of ecclesiastical organization as did the Genevan and Scotch Presbyterians. The divines also had reservations over making scripture the sole criterion in issues relating to the body politic. But the Puritans always began with God's word when searching for authoritative answers to their problems.

The particular laws which the Bible did not or could not provide must be found elsewhere. When scripture would carry the early seventeenth-century divines no further into the practical world, they seized upon another readily available corpus of law. The Puritans turned to the common law tradition of England and affirmed with the common lawyers the authority of the fundamental law. Time and again, the divines looked for help to common law rules and statutes when aroused by Stuart demands and interferences. Thomas Scott spoke of certain "high-waies" on which the king must travel in all his journeys. The highways were none other than the components of the lawyers' fundamental law.[16] Scott agreed with James that a king was to govern his domain by virtue of powers which had been specially accorded the crown. These powers, however, were hardly the absolute points of kingship which the Stuarts claimed under the divine right of kings. Rulers were set aside by a "special spirit" which God had given them to rule properly. The special spirit, continued Scott in the *High-Waies*, was that given the crown by the law of the land. Scott did not use the word "spirit" in a vague sense. The special spirit given to kings was precise and knowable in the form of the particular laws of the common law tradition.

The law of the land did not have the sanction of scriptural law, for biblical commandments were fundamentally different from other laws inasmuch as they comprised the very word of God. But the common law rules and statutes had an authority which allowed them a station close to that held by scriptural law. One anonymous Puritan writer began his description of the laws of England with these words: "The Lawes of England wch now wee enjoy, were not first framed and fashioned after the Lawes of the Romans & other Heathens wch were in many things Corrupt & prophane; but after ye pure & undefiled

16. "The High-Waies of God and the King: Wherein All Men Ought to Walke in Holinesse Here to Happiness Hereafter," in Scot, *Workes*. Consult Judson, *Crisis*, pp. 328 ff., for an evaluation of this divine's political importance. Miss Judson points out that Scott's special spirit of kingly rule was based on the "public voice of the people," known explicitly in Parliament, as well as on the law of the land.

Lawes of God; & are at this day more agreeable to ye Law of God than ye Civill or Cannon Lawes, or any other Lawes in ye World." [17] As evidence of the agreeableness of England's laws with the law of God, the writer cited the origin of the former. The first English laws resulted from the promulgation of King Lucius acting on the advice of Eleutherius, a Christian bishop, who had urged that England's law be fashioned after God's law in the Bible.[18] King Lucius heeded the advice of God's representative. Throughout English legal history, continued the author, the close accord of the common law with God's law was apparent. The writer never maintained that God had decreed the particulars of England's law of the land, but he did imply that the Almighty could not have done better if He had tried.

In order to establish similarity between the two kinds of law, the author used the common Puritan analogy of England as the new Israel. The meaning of the figure was not only that England and Israel were chosen lands, but that the laws by which the biblical and the British nation were governed were alike in origin and content. God had decreed laws for Israel throughout its life as a nation. These laws had a history, a development; they were an unfolding of God's will for His children, His ways of dealing with His Israel. Similarly God had treated England. As He had smiled on Israel through the laws of the Old Testament, so now He smiled on England through its common law rules and statutes. The laws of England comprised the story of God's dealing with His present chosen nation.

In such a wholehearted approbation of secular law, the Puritans once again demonstrated their Calvinist inheritance. John Calvin had found in Geneva, as later Calvinists did elsewhere, that the clarity and force of law were useful in the political structure. The laws of a land provided order and efficiency; they were protection against a would-be tyrant; and they could even implement the principle of mu-

17. Anon., "The Lawes of England" ([London] n.d.), p. 1. The original MS of this work is in the Ellesmere Collection of the Huntington Library, San Marino, Calif. In a note prefixed to the microfilm copy, George L. Mosse sets the probable date of composition between 1624 and 1629. I would say that it can be ascribed to a Puritan, possibly a divine, because of the extensive biblical exegesis, the near-sermonic outline, the attempts to square common law with biblical law, the elaborate comparison of England with Israel, and the belief in divine sovereignty. Miss Judson corroborates assignment of authorship to a Puritan; see *Crisis,* p. 335. The political significance of the MS, writes Miss Judson, accords the unknown author a place of honor beside Coke, Gataker, Scott, and other Puritan and common law opponents of Stuart absolutism (p. 339).

18. Anon., "Lawes," pp. 35 ff.

tual love. Civil laws could thus be framed and used with God's blessing.

The early seventeenth-century Puritans also stood in the tradition of John Wyclif, the English proto-reformer of the late fourteenth century. Wyclif insisted on "positive law" as the only means of properly governing church and state. Wyclif's use of positive law, meaning any law whatever made by man, was one of the earliest uses of the term.[19] In *De Officio Regis*, the dissenter urged the supremacy of the ancient laws of the land over those found in civil and canon law.[20] The support of the common law tradition was part of his attack on the bishops, who were urging the introduction of civil law study in the universities. But there was more than the usual Wyclifite attack on the papists. Wyclif acknowledged the peculiar authority of those legal particulars which were natively English and which had become established precedent. Such laws were of greater authority than those found in the elaborate system of Roman law or in the contrivances of canon law. Wyclif neither asserted that the positive law was a limitation on the king nor that it possessed a near divine status, but he did consider the law of the land to be a requisite authority in the function of society.

The Puritans went beyond both Wyclif and Calvin. Common law rules and statutes were not only necessary for political harmony. They had an even higher value inasmuch as they, like the laws of the Bible, were manifestations of God's rule. Puritans examined the fundamental law and saw there the guiding hand of the one God who ruled everywhere.

The legalism of the lawyers was rooted in statutes and common law rules. Their professional lives were bound up with a never ending study and exegesis of the particulars of England's legal tradition. But the legalism of the early seventeenth-century judges and barristers did not rest solely on acts of Parliament and ancient legal customs. The lawyers turned to Puritan norms, much as the divines had turned to the standards of the legal profession. Whenever a biblical saying could be found that corroborated the meaning of a common law rule or statute, it was eagerly seized upon.

Consider the statements of Nicholas Fuller as he took up the Puritan cause in the ex officio oath cases during the first decade of the century. In his arguments against the extensive malpractices of the

19. See Chrimes, *Constitutional Ideas*, p. 197, n. 3. Wyclif's "positive law" is similar to Thomas Aquinas' "human law."

20. Consult Frederic W. Maitland, "Wyclif on English and Roman Law," *Law Quarterly Review, 12* No. 45 (Jan. 1896), 76–8.

Court of High Commission, Fuller found both the Old and the New Testaments useful.

> To force a man in a criminall cause to accuse himselfe, was . . . directly against the rule of the law of God. For it is said in *Deut. cap.* 19. 15 that one witnesse shall not arise against a man for any trespas, or for any sin, or for any fault that he offendeth in; but at the mouth of two witnesses, or 3 witnesses shall the matter be established. Which rule is confirmed under the Gospell, as appeareth *Math.* 18. 16. 2 *Cor.* 13. 1 where it is said, In the mouth of two or three witnesses shall every word stand; and Christ said to the woman accused of adultery, *where be thine accusers?* . . .[21]

In the 1628 Parliament, Sir Edward Coke spoke out against false imprisonment and summed up his argument thus: "I will conclude with the highest authority, that is, 25. chap. of the *Acts* of the Apostles, the last verse, where Saint *Paul* saith, *It is against reason to send a man to prison without shewing a Cause.*" [22] The great jurist could stay with the best of the divines on the authority of the Bible: "To those lawes which [the] holy church hath out of scripture, we ought to yield credit; for that . . . is the common law, upon which all lawes are founded." [23]

Coke and his colleagues were hardly innovators, for repeated use of the Bible had been the practice of nearly every medieval commentator on the common law. Fortescue, the famed sage of the law in the fifteenth century, employed fifty-two biblical quotations in his short treatise *De Laudibus Legum Angliae*.[24] The Bible supported, in the mind of the lawyers, the authority of ancient common law rules and parliamentary enactments and thus helped to effect the ultimate authority of fundamental law.

The legalism of the Puritans and the lawyers demonstrated once more an ideological parallelism. The Puritans held that divine sover-

21. *The Argument of Nicholas Fuller . . . in the Case of Tho. Lad, and Rich. Mansell His Clients: Wherein It Is Plainly Proved, that the Ecclesiasticall Commissioners Have No Power . . . to Put Them to the Oath "Ex Officio"* (London, 1641), p. 11. Fuller made use of certain biblical passages which Coke had employed before in Slade's Case.

22. Fuller, *Prerogative,* p. 40.

23. *Institutes,* 2d Pt., *2,* sec. viii, p. 625, quoting Sir John Prisot, a 15th-century chief justice of the Common Pleas.

24. Gerald Hurst, *A Short History of Lincoln's Inn* (London, Constable, 1946), p. 9.

eignty manifested its authority through particular laws. This is also what the lawyers believed about fundamental law. Actual reciprocity existed among the divines and the barristers, for they coopted each other's particular laws. The Puritans found the whole common law tradition to be a part of God's extensive rule of the world, while the lawyers discovered that the Bible undergirded the authority of common law rules and statutes and thereby augmented the supremacy of fundamental law. Indeed, it might be said that the two groups possessed a mutual set of legal standards, consisting of the word of God in scripture and the word of fundamental law in ancient customs and parliamentary enactments.

Dissimilarity is found, of course, amidst the parallelism. In the end, the mutual common law of the Puritans and the lawyers pointed to differently conceived final authorities. Divine sovereignty was more substantive for the divines than fundamental law was for the lawyers. The Puritan principle was a source of loyalty for men because it portrayed the one absolute which was God; in divine sovereignty the Puritans beheld how God ruled, ordered, and willed. Back of divine sovereignty was always found God. For the lawyers, fundamental law *was* the absolute; there was nothing behind it.[25] Divine sovereignty and

25. A few judges and barristers held that God somehow was behind the fundamental law. Most of them, however, were pointedly nontheological. The refusal to be theological was not incompatible with the ascription of divine attributes to fundamental law. Fundamental law was a "vital principle," a lawmaker, and, as we shall see, an entity which could be said to have revealed itself to the world. The lawyers' final authority was believed to rule, order, and will, implying that fundamental law was in some sense an actor. Herein lie some problems. It is difficult to accept the proposition that fundamental law wills and acts unless more is said about the qualities of this absolute authority. The divines predicated that the very nature of God was to relate himself to the world by his action. Thus God gave the law, both the biblical and the common, and was involved in the larger dramas of creation and redemption. Willing and acting as functions of the ultimate authority naturally followed from the Puritan doctrine of God. That fundamental law wills and acts does not follow from the undeveloped thought of the lawyers. The judges and barristers either have to be content with an ambiguous conception of their final authority, or equate fundamental law with God. Many of them choose the second alternative. (To this the author would reply: Nothing can be God except God, not even fundamental law.)

But suppose fundamental law in its own right could be thought of as an actor. We must then ask whether an authority which acts only in the realm of customs, rules, and statutes is a universal authority. I feel that it is not. Or could it be said that fundamental law *does* act in some broader way, analogous to the Puritan doctrine of creation and even redemption? A few lawyers spoke of fundamental law as if it did so act. Magna Carta in 1215 was thought of as the redemption of the fallen state incurred by the events of 1066. Still, granted that the broader

fundamental law were not, therefore, fully correlative terms. Nevertheless, this discrepancy did not stand in the way of an alliance between the divines and barristers. In matters to be decided by specific laws they could speak the same language for they had joint referents.

Furthermore, neither group proclaimed a blind, dead-end legalism, for laws themselves were not the supreme authorities which called men to absolute obedience. Particular norms always pointed beyond to a lawmaker—fundamental law or God known in divine sovereignty. The justification for obeying laws was that they led one to be obedient to the lawmaker.

Natural Law

The relationship of particular laws to absolute authorities in the thought of the Puritans and the lawyers can be further explained by comparing our subjects with those who held natural law concepts. Such a comparison will also help to locate the divines and the barristers in the general stream of political thought.

These men lived in an age when the incoming tide of natural law was running swiftly. The result was flood tide which engulfed many folk in the seventeenth and eighteenth centuries. Those carried along by the surge of natural law were principally continental thinkers, ranging from Grotius in the early 1600's to Kant and Fichte at the beginning of the 1800's. Within the two-century span lived the other formulators of modern natural law: Hobbes, Pufendorf, Spinoza, Locke, Montesquieu, Burlamaqui, and Rousseau. The application of natural law to political thought was not something newly attempted in the seventeenth and eighteenth centuries. The attempt had been made, of course, in classical antiquity by the Stoics and the Roman jurists. The Middle Ages also had proved receptive to natural law— Thomas Aquinas aptly showed the uses to which natural law could be put in political and social theory. Even in England before the seventeenth century the term was freqently employed. Consider the writ-

---

interpretation were possible, could an authority that willed and brought about only an English way of life be ultimate and final? Again, an affirmative answer is difficult.

The action and willing of God was not, for the Puritans, totally restricted to laws. God's action in religious experience, for example, could not be explained by laws, not even those of the Bible. Nor, on the other hand, did God's action relate only to England. On many counts, the author finds the thought of the Puritans about the nature of absolute authority more cogent and meaningful than that of the common lawyers.

ings of the Henrician judge Christopher St. German, in the early part of the 1500's, and those of Richard Hooker at the end of the century.

Nor did natural law die with the passage of its golden age in the late seventeenth and eighteenth centuries, for it continued to be a recognizable motif in the political thought of the nineteenth century. In our own time, an earnest resurgence of natural law interpretation is at hand.[26] More than a few contemporary writers see natural law as a major ingredient in the present constitutional law of the United States.[27] Nothing has arisen in the last 150 years, however, to match the high-water mark of natural law in the seventeenth and eighteenth centuries. In that period natural law shook itself loose from the classical and medieval past; proclaimed its emancipation by taking on secular rather than Christian or Stoic form; became individualistic; and adopted pure *ratio* for its base rather than the *ratio scripta* of the Roman law.[28] Natural law found strength in its new freedom and pervaded all crannies of political, social, and legal inquiry until the early 1800's. The beginning of the modern natural law school coincided with activity of the Puritans and lawyers, and the relationship of the school to Puritan–common law thought cannot be overlooked.

Who is the wise man who can define natural law? The words "natural" and "law" are themselves capable of varying meanings, but when the two are joined together in a single term the problems of definition are more than doubled. Here is something more evasive than even fundamental law. No consistent use of the term "natural law" appeared in the ages that lie between classical antiquity and our own; the Greco-Roman period differed from the medieval which in turn differed from the modern. And, of course, there have been varying definitions within the divisions of Greco-Roman, medieval, and modern. The author does not suppose that he is wise enough to say what natural law meant in the seventeenth and eighteenth centuries. But,

26. *Natural Law Forum,* beginning annual publication in July 1956, is indicative of a new interest. The journal is published under the auspices of the Natural Law Institute of the University of Notre Dame Law School.

27. Consult Charles G. Haines, *The Revival of Natural Law Concepts,* (Cambridge, Harvard University Press, 1930). Also John Wild, *Plato's Modern Enemies and the Theory of Natural Law,* Chicago, University of Chicago Press, 1953; and John Wild, ed., *The Return to Reason. Essays in Realistic Philosophy,* Chicago, Regnery, 1953, particularly William A. Banner's essay, "Natural Law and Social Order."

28. Ernest Barker's introduction in Otto F. von Gierke, *Natural Law and the Theory of Society, 1500–1800* (Cambridge, The University Press, 1934), pp. xli–l.

with the help of competent authorities and at the risk of saying nothing by saying too little, a working description can be offered for our comparative purposes.

In the school of the seventeenth and eighteenth centuries, natural law had perhaps four important meanings.[29] First, the term was equated with the basic pattern of man's life in a supposed "state of nature." This form of natural law spoke to the questions, How did man qua man behave in his natural state before the advent of organized government, and what qualities did he manifest in relation to his fellows? The alleged behavior and qualities of individual, primitive man comprised the natural law. Sometimes the descriptive norms were held to relate not primarily to man himself but to some group, such as the nation or the family, within which man was held to be naturally incorporated. Grotius represented this divergency; he began with "social natural law" and thereon constructed his theory of international law. The chief concern of the school, however, was with the individual existing in a simple, unorganized state of nature.

There were conflicting opinions over the fundamental behavior and qualities of the individual. Hobbes believed that man was warlike; Locke held him to be peaceable and cooperative; and Montesquieu saw him as timid, trembling at the motion of a leaf. Hobbes was able to reduce the natural law essentially to the rule of self-preservation and its corollaries. From such a conception of natural law, he then developed the necessity and goodness of a totalitarian regime. Locke viewed the first meaning of natural law in a more extensive fashion. Man had certain rights as well as basic qualities in the state of nature—for example, the rights of property protection and inviolability of contracts. Private possession and dependable agreements were intrinsically part of man's life among his primordial fellows and were, thus, natural law. Moving from these and other premises of natural law it is small wonder that Locke's theory of government differed radically from Hobbes'. Montesquieu was something of a radical reductionist like Hobbes but, unlike Hobbes and Locke, natural law was for him a form of interesting speculation rather than a foundation for subsequent political construction.

The second meaning of natural law dealt with the very matter of political construction, or with the actual state which was thought to

29. The author depends on the work of many experts in natural law. He has found Benjamin F. Wright, *American Interpretations of Natural Law. A Study in the History of Political Thought* (Cambridge, Harvard University Press, 1931), especially the introduction, to be helpful.

be an outgrowth of the indeterminate state of nature. Frequently the transition from nature to politics was accomplished by the device of a contract, as with Hobbes and Locke, although Montesquieu, Burlamaqui, and Rousseau in the eighteenth century found the idea of a contract to be of little use. They might disagree over the means by which the state was created, but all concurred that the natural law of the state of nature implicitly contained certain principles of government which must be established if the good state were to exist. Hobbes emphasized prudent absolutism; Locke stressed the sovereignty of the people; and Rousseau held for a state where equality and freedom were conjoined. These principles of good government were an extension of the state of nature into the realm of the state, and were themselves natural law.

On the other hand, the desiderata of the good state were deductions from a principle which itself was a third kind of natural law. Nearly all members of the school spoke of a higher law which was not to be equated with either the state of nature or the principles of good government which were to fructify in the actual state. The higher law was known by many names: God, the natural order, conscience, the moral ideal, or reason. Burlamaqui was perhaps the chief higher law thinker of the natural law school, believing that everything from a general theory of sovereignty to the particular rights of ambassadors could be deduced from the higher natural law of "divine order." [30] The third type of natural law could exist in many forms: it could be a higher law within man, such as conscience and the moral ideal, or a higher law outside man such as God, the natural order, and Burlamaqui's divine order. Or it could be both within and without, such as reason.[31] Whatever its location, the higher law acted with the natural law of the state of nature to effect the necessary principles of good government. These principles of the state, or the second kind of natural law, were thus a joint product, the result of induction from the state of nature and abstraction from the higher law.

A practical corollary followed hard upon these three meanings of natural law. Particular civil laws requisite for the implementation of the good state were also natural law. Locke's writings are the best example of what may be called the fourth meaning of natural law.

30. See Jean J. Burlamaqui, *The Principles of Natural and Political Law,* trans. Thomas Nugent, 5th ed. Cambridge, The University Press, 1807.

31. Consult Roland H. Bainton, "The Appeal to Reason and the American Constitution," in *The Constitution Reconsidered,* ed. Conyers Read, New York, Columbia University Press, 1938.

He held that certain personal rights and liberties not yet framed in the laws of a nation necessarily followed from the state of nature, the principles of government, and the higher natural law. The positive law which would enact and implement these rights and liberties was likewise natural law. At this point the school displayed a visionary as well as a practical character, for the implementing statutes were not yet in existence. Natural law referred in its fourth significance to the concrete civil laws that "ought to be."

These conceptions of natural law had important ramifications for seventeenth- and eighteenth-century political theory. They led first of all to a scientific examination of man as a political animal. The inquiry was made in the conviction that man's true political role and the real nature of the civilized state could be discovered by an analysis of the natural laws governing man's conduct in the state of nature. It was held that such an analysis would lead inevitably to a logically coherent, systematic understanding of man and the state. All the natural law thinkers were "scientific" to this extent; Hobbes, Spinoza, Pufendorf, Locke, and Rousseau stand out especially. The school also became deeply involved in assertions of the political world as it must become. Natural law offered the promise and the guarantee of a better political world.

Now the Puritans and the lawyers had little connection with this kind of political thought. They never believed in—or perhaps never thought of—a scientific analysis of man in the state of nature. Even if such an examination could have been made, they would probably have questioned what it all meant. Both groups shared the reticence of their contemporary Hugo Grotius over viewing geometry and political life as analogous—the basic natural laws of man's life in society defied simple enumeration and facile description.[32] Nor did the Puritans and the lawyers ever speculate on the ought-to-be, or on the concept of the "ideal state." As we shall see, the divines and the lawyers in their conservatism rebelled at the idea of promulgating new laws whereby the good state would be erected.

When a member of either group did refer to natural law, the reference scarcely had political potential. Puritans and lawyers used natural law primarily to denote laws relating to man's physical existence. The divines and barristers would have agreed with the work of revisionists in the school such as Montesquieu, the mid-eighteenth-century admirer of the English constitution, who did not conceive

32. See the discussion of Grotius in George H. Sabine, *A History of Political Theory* (rev. ed. New York, Holt, 1950), pp. 420 ff.

natural law to be a set of universal principles and norms for political society. Like the writer of *L'Esprit des lois*, the early seventeenth-century opponents of the king employed natural law to describe the utterly commonplace drives of man: the seeking of nourishment, existence in peace, and life in association.[33] There were, of course, some exceptions among the Puritans. The prewar Independent William Ames found natural law to be a cosmic principle of great usefulness in his arguments for the adoption of Independency by the established church; he also used natural law in his discussion of conscience. But Ames, as mentioned before,[34] was more connected with American Puritanism in the 1630's than with English Puritanism in the earlier decades of the century.

Most Puritans and common lawyers eschewed natural law when it meant anything more than physical or mechanical law. Coke's decision in the 1608 case of the Scottish post-nati who were claiming English citizenship is relevant at this point. The jurist spoke against Edwin Sandys and others who declared that the ancient *jus gentium* and "natural reason" necessitated an alien status for those born in Scotland after the accession of James to the English throne. The decision must not be made, said Coke, on such foreign and specious grounds. English common law rules and statutes provided the only grounds for justice in the case and they were clearly in favor of admitting the post-nati to citizenship.[35] The Puritans and lawyers were critical of natural law thought and saw it to be of small account in the determination of the vast issues in English ecclesiastical and political life.

The general English suspicion of natural law in the early 1600's was typified by these men. In the days of the Tudors, writers such as Christopher St. German, John Major, John Ponet, and Richard Hooker had gainfully employed the idea of natural law as a political principle. Shortly after the period of our study in the 1640's natural law again returned to vogue in the appeals of Henry Parker, John Goodwin, John Lilburne, and other liberals. The early seventeenth century, however, was dead water in the flow of natural law political thought in England.

There are even grounds for asserting that the early seventeenth-century attitude represented the dominant English view of natural

33. Baron de Montesquieu, *The Spirit of the Laws,* trans. Thomas Nugent, rev. J. V. Prichard (New York, Appleton, 1900), *1,* 4–5.
34. See Ch. 1, p. 14, n. 6.
35. *State Trials, 2,* 593–4, 607 ff.

law in medieval and modern times. Certainly England was less receptive toward the concept than were continental countries. Even in the
case of the aforementioned Englishmen who are so often classified as
natural law thinkers, there was an insistence on the prior authority
of the concrete laws of the English past. St. German, for example,
conducting a pamphlet war with Thomas More over the ex officio
oath, attacked the oath because it was against the ancient law of the
land. The latter law, he held, was always superior to canon law in the
case of conflict.[36] Tudor canon law, like the Roman Catholic canons
which it superseded, openly espoused natural law doctrine. Despite
the evidence of some natural law thought, the judgment of Mr.
McIlwain appears sound: "The law of nature, or whatever that
speculative basis may be called . . . comes largely as an attempt
[in England] . . . to account for a body of customary law which
has long been in existence, and whose binding charter is unquestioned,
though its beginnings are lost in antiquity." [37] Whatever one's position on the relationship of English political thought and natural law,
there can be no debate over the Puritans and the lawyers in the early
1600's. They had little use for the idea.[38]

And yet the divines and the barristers had some connection with
natural law thought. They did believe in a concept of higher law, as
did the leaders of the natural law school. The appeal to higher law
was typical not only of seventeenth- and eighteenth-century natural
law thought, but has been found in all kinds of natural law, whether
Stoic, Christian, secular, second- or thirteenth-century. The appeal
to reason as the higher law dominated the modern school of natural
law, at least as the eighteenth-century leaders carried on the work of
the seventeenth-century formulators. But the age of Montesquieu
had no monopoly of the law of reason. Appeals to the higher law of
reason were made in England before the period of our study. St.
German and Hooker serve again as prominent early and late six-

36. Consult Mary Hume Maguire, "Attack of the Common Lawyers on the
Oath *ex officio* as Administered in the Ecclesiastical Courts in England," in
Essays in History and Political Theory. In Honor of Charles Howard McIlwain
(Cambridge, Harvard University Press, 1936), pp. 209 ff.

37. *High Court,* p. 97. See also John W. Gough, *John Locke's Political Philosophy, Eight Studies* (Oxford, Clarendon Press, 1950), p. 111, n. 2, and Frederic W. Maitland, *English Law and the Renaissance,* Cambridge, The University
Press, 1901.

38. A rejection of natural law places the Puritans and the lawyers partly within
the movement analyzed by Hiram Haydn, *The Counter-Renaissance,* New York,
Scribner's, 1950.

teenth-century English examples of this kind of natural law thought. In the period of the Civil War, references to reason reappeared.

The early 1600's, however, were a significant hiatus in the English use of reason as a higher law. The Puritans and the lawyers stand out once more in the anti-natural law persuasion of the period. Divines and barristers talked about reason, to be sure, but it was never a first principle of the universe. It was rather a unique faculty of man which enabled him to make inquiry and to come to decisions—to interpret the Bible and the common law tradition. It was a means of comprehension. In fact, it was the wisdom or "artificial reason" given to those who on the one hand had wrestled with the commandments of scripture and on the other had steeped themselves in the ancient law of the land. The Puritans and the lawyers had their higher law, but it was not reason. It was divine sovereignty and fundamental law.

The conception of a higher law found among the divines and the barristers was fundamentally different from that of the natural law thinkers. The Puritans and the lawyers believed in an English *civitas* governed by God and law; their higher law was an other-worldly, commanding rule. The natural law thinkers, on the other hand, envisioned their higher law as a rational model or a cognizable pattern to which actual existence conformed and on which the good society of the present and the future must be constructed. Natural order, divine force, reason, or whatever the higher law was called became in the thought of the school a kind of Platonic form.[39] It had a sublime quality, but it was clearly part of this world. Indeed, all things had emanated from the higher law and were connected to it. Man's reason was associated with the cosmic reason; the organic functions of the body were part of a wider, all-inclusive organism; and the smallest unity of existence was but a microcosm of the universal order of all things. Moreover, finite beings could know the full import of the higher law. The qualities of the law of reason, or the law of natural order, could be predicated and its application to political structure could be lucidly explained.

The divines and barristers were less facile in their understanding of divine sovereignty and fundamental law. Both groups stood in awe of the absolute rule of their respective higher law. Divine sovereignty for the Puritans was shrouded in the mystery of God's creation and governance and no man could fully conceive its specifications. In the same manner, fundamental law for the lawyers was a mystical standard of justice dating from the golden age of pre-

39. Sabine, *Political Theory,* p. 428.

Norman antiquity. Barristers and judges spoke not about some clearly detailed *law* of reason to describe the common law tradition, but about "pure reason." Like divine sovereignty, pure reason could not be fully understood by men.

Furthermore, both the Puritans and the lawyers saw the need for intermediaries between men and the absolute authorities. The need was met by the particular laws of the biblical and the common law tradition. For the natural law thinkers, the higher law was clearly present among and comprehended by all men. For the divines and the barristers, the higher law was not of this world and required mediation to those who lived in the world.

The subjects of our book demonstrated a further variance with the natural law school in their understanding of the significance of particular laws. The Puritans and the lawyers viewed the positive, concrete norms of the Bible and the common law tradition as means by which God and fundamental law related themselves to the world. It may not be too much to say that the lawyers as well as the Puritans were religious men inasmuch as both groups believed that particular laws were the revelations of an ultimate authority which transcended the world. The divines and the barristers did not search out the observable rules of the so-called natural order of things with an eye to constructing a political system. They did not attempt to deduce the specifics of political and social life from the all-determining natural law, as did a Hobbes or a Pufendorf. Rather they accepted the particular laws which they believed had been bestowed upon the land. The laws of the Bible and the common law tradition did not set forth a people's experience in the practical world, or a kind of English *jus gentium*. Their final significance was that they recorded the way in which God and fundamental law had dealt with the nation.

The meaning of the ultimate authorities for practical life was found in the laws, but it was also hidden in the laws. The Puritans and the lawyers had to struggle with the commandments, rules, and statutes in order to discover the contemporary meaning of divine sovereignty and fundamental law. Hence the insistence was made that divines wrestle with scripture and that barristers employ "artificial reason." Both groups were of necessity casuists when it came to the laws of the Bible and the common law tradition.[40] The never ending array of laws had to be studied, interpreted, and com-

40. On political casuistry among English Puritans, see the following by George L. Mosse: "Puritanism and Reason of State in Old and New England," *William and Mary Quarterly*, 3d series, *9*, No. 1 (Jan. 1952); "The Assimilation of Machia-

pared. Out of the process came assertions about the nature of the state, the exercise of authority, and other matters of political concern. But these statements were not the great principles of the natural law tradition. The Puritans and the lawyers did not spin a theory of the equality of men, the meaning of justice, or the inalienable rights of man. Something more particular, less dramatic, came out of the laws which they examined. Their assertions had not the ring of a trumpet but more the dry rustle of a sheaf of legal parchment.[41]

Consider the famous Dr. Bonham's Case of 1610, a case often held to be a crucial step in the development of Anglo-American constitutionalism. The president and censors of the Royal College of Physicians in London imposed a fine on one Thomas Bonham, a graduate of Cambridge, for practicing medicine in London without the certificate of the college.[42] Bonham was also forbidden to practice, but he continued in his profession on the grounds that the censors had no legal jurisdiction in his case. The doctor was summoned again by the president and censors and fined an additional amount. He defaulted in payment of the second fine and eventually was incarcerated in the Counter of Fleet Street by order of the Royal College. Bonham then brought an action of false imprisonment against the chief members of the college; the case was heard before the Court of Common Pleas with Chief Justice Coke presiding. The censors claimed their authority had been established by letters patent dating from the time of Henry VIII and had been definitively substantiated by enactments of Parliament. Despite the weight of these precedents, the bench gave judgment for Bonham the plaintiff.

As a graduate of Cambridge, Dr. Bonham was automatically exempt from the college's surveillance, but the court saw fit to bypass this technicality and render judgment on deeper issues. It is frequently thought that one of the arguments which Coke used to set aside the statute upon which the Royal College based its action dis-

---

velli in English Thought: The Casuistry of William Perkins and William Ames," *Huntington Library Quarterly*, *17*, No. 4 (Aug. 1954); and *The Holy Pretence. A Study in Christianity and Reason of State From William Perkins to John Winthrop*, Oxford, Blackwell, 1957.

41. I am indebted for this figure to John C. Murray, "The Problem of Pluralism in America," *Thought*, *29*, No. 113 (summer 1954), 207, who used it in a discussion of the *Federalist* papers.

42. The interpretation of the case which follows depends on Samuel E. Thorne, "Dr. Bonham's Case," *Law Quarterly Review*, *54*, No. 216 (Oct. 1938); the same essay can be found in Read, *Constitution*, entitled "The Constitution and the Courts: A Reëxamination of the Famous Case of Dr. Bonham."

played an appeal to some high principle of justice. The principle is believed to have significance for the modern democratic state. Coke stated, "it appears in our books, that in many cases, the common law will controul acts of parliament, and sometimes adjudge them to be utterly void: for *when an act of parliament is against common right or reason,* or repugnant, or impossible to be performed, the common law will controul it and adjudge such act to be void . . ."[43]

Some commentators argue that Coke was appealing to the higher law of reason. The jurist was at the same time proclaiming, it is held, a momentous natural law principle of judicial review, a principle which was to become part of American constitutionalism. An examination of the precedents cited by the chief justice shows that the judgment for Bonham was based on less spectacular reasoning. Coke pointed out that the statute under which the Royal College had acted allowed the president and censors to receive one-half the fines which they imposed. The college was therefore not only a judge but a party in any case that came to its attention. The president and censors would benefit materially from any punishment of unlicensed physicians, even those who were rightfully qualified because of training at Oxford and Cambridge. Any statute which allowed a person to be both judge and party, Coke maintained, was repugnant or contradictory and could not stand. Out of a difficult, complicated review of precedents came the simple assertion that no man can be judge in his own case. It was this point, not the right of a high court to void legislation by an appeal to reason or natural law, which resulted in judgment for Bonham.

In the ex officio oath cases before the High Commission, involving both divines and barristers, the point that emerged from the review of biblical, common, and statute law was that no man can be forced to witness against himself. In Bate's Case and the impositions debate in Commons, it was no supply without an act of Parliament; in Darnel's Case, no imprisonment without showing cause. Only in their conception of the authority of institutions did the Puritans and the lawyers approach the ring of the trumpet.

In the next section we deal with this most important aspect of Puritan–common law thought, namely, that authority had been "distributed" among the present institutions of society. Here the move was made from narrow proscription to positive declaration. The rustle of legal parchment, however, was still clearly heard. Authority had been apportioned among institutions not out of con-

43. Coke, *Reports,* Pt. 8, *4,* 375, my italics.

formity with some discernible natural principle but because of the
requirements of particular laws which revealed the practical meaning
of divine sovereignty and fundamental law for institutional life.

These pithy axioms of the laws—no man judge in his own case,
no self-incrimination, no supply without act of Parliament, no imprisonment without showing cause, even the distribution of institutional authority—all these differed from natural law pronouncements
in formulation as well as in extent. The natural law thinkers worked
with an immanental higher law and then fashioned a theory of
justice, freedom, equality, or natural right. The Puritans and the
lawyers lived under the rule of God and fundamental law. They did
not trust their own creating powers; they did not believe they could
or were required to fashion anything. Rather they were called to look
into the laws which had been given them and there to find the relevance of divine sovereignty and fundamental law for the issues of the
day.

The axioms which emerged from biblical pronouncement, common
law rule, and parliamentary enactment were, in the first instance,
summaries or restatements of the laws. But their raison d'être went
beyond mere summation. They were distillations which made sense out
of the scattered, sometimes contradictory laws. When a Puritan or a
lawyer was called to interpret the multifarious marks of God's or
law's supremacy, he found he was guided by a set of rules which had
grown out of the laws. The axioms effected clarity where previously
there had often been confusion; in their consistency was dissolved the
disharmony of commandment, custom, and statute. The meaning of a
particular law was determined by comparing it with the distillations,
a process which was part of Puritan wrestling and common law artificial reason.

The problem of legal interpretation entered precisely at this point.
A law, statute, or biblical commandment could not contradict an
axiom. Such was Coke's position in Dr. Bonham's Case: An act of
Parliament which allowed a person to be judge in his own case could
not stand. When a particular norm was seemingly opposed to an established maxim, every attempt at reconciliation must be made, but
if the individual law could not be interpreted so as to accord with the
axiom, the particular law must give way. As Mr. Gough has indicated,
that which was unalterable was not a collection of laws, but something
that had grown out of the laws and now stood over them.[44]

44. J. W. Gough, "Fundamental Law in the Seventeenth Century," *Political
Studies, 1,* No. 2 (June 1953), 168. "What was thought of as fundamental in the

For all their archaic and narrow legalism, it must be said that the Puritans and lawyers displayed a certain flexibility in their understanding and use of particular laws. Paul Baynes in his commentary on Ephesians urged his readers to be mindful of the laws which do not change, of those whose meaning constantly changes, and of those whose usefulness is spent.[45] Richard Sibbes, John Cotton, and John Davenport joined Baynes in the process of interpreting the disjointed pronouncements of scripture by comparing them with the biblical axioms that abide forever. Mr. Foster rightly speaks of a "fearless spirit of re-examination of premises . . . that appears in the English-speaking of a certain type, the Puritans."[46] It is known that Coke reversed his own previous interpretation of specific laws and admitted that he had been wrong in several early seventeenth-century issues, for example, royal impositions and imprisonment by the king's command.[47] For both Puritans and lawyers, the point of the Lancastrian judge Fortescue that individual laws are supreme but not immutable seems highly applicable.[48]

A further difference from the natural law thinkers should be noted at this point. The particular laws governing man's societal life as asserted by a Hobbes or a Locke were incapable of varying interpretation. There was nothing to compare these laws with, for they were a projection of the overriding natural law into the world, and hence were absolute. The inflexibility of the natural law school made possible the detailed political systems which the school was forever erecting in different forms. The Puritans and the lawyers, on the other hand, believed that their laws constantly needed interpretation and even adjustment. Mr. Holdsworth makes the following observation about

---

seventeenth century was not a body of unalterable common law but, in the first place, the traditional legal constitution, in virtue of which the monarchy was a limited monarchy, and subjects enjoyed their rights and liberties."

45. *An Entire Commentary upon the Whole Epistle of St. Paul to the Ephesians* (Edinburgh, Nichol, 1866), pp. 161 ff.

46. "Liberal Calvinism. The Remonstrants at the Synod of Dort in 1618," in *Collected Papers of Herbert D. Foster* ([New York] priv. print., 1929), p. 118. On the same page Mr. Foster refers to the flexibility of Calvin, citing the reformer's "Farewell to Genevan Magistrates" address: " 'We must walk forward, and grow, so that our hearts may be capable of things we cannot now understand. If our last day finds us going forward, we shall learn beyond this world what we could not learn here.' " Liberalism in the interpretation of laws, however, seldom broke through Calvin's strict, normative pattern of thought.

47. Holdsworth, *English Law, 5,* 427–8, 449–51.

48. Chrimes, *Constitutional Ideas,* pp. 202–3.

the barristers: "the common lawyers, helped by their system of case law, have always kept sufficiently in touch with changing needs and circumstances, and with the main currents of public opinion, to adapt the machinery of the law and its rules to suit new needs and circumstances." [49] Certainly the Puritans of the early 1600's shared the capacity of the lawyers for adaptability. A thesis on the legal flexibility of the two groups can be distorted to the point of untruth, but the point remains that the divines and the barristers were less rigid in their legalism than were many of those who drew out immutable particular laws from natural law.

The citation of axioms that stood above the particular laws suggests once again the work of Montesquieu. The eighteenth-century Frenchman called attention to the "spirit of the laws" which transcended custom, enactment, and commandment. The spirit of the laws created and defined for Montesquieu the characteristics and *esprit* of a nation. F. D. Maurice caught the sense of the matter, although no one, not even Montesquieu, could describe the spirit of the laws satisfactorily. "There was something Montesquieu perceived in every country besides the laws, written on tables or parchments; something besides its different institutions, Monarchical, Aristocratical, Republican. There was a mind which corresponded to these; it was fostered by them; in turn it sustained them; if it was lost they must perish." [50] Fair England—the Puritans' new Israel and the lawyers' land of fundamental law—found its spirit of the laws in the axioms which had emerged from the norms of the Bible and the common law tradition.

Montesquieu did make it clear that the function of the spirit of the laws was relation. The spirit was the medium through which the particular laws of a nation were related to each other and, more significantly, to the physical and sociological factors which ultimately determined the polity of each nation. The spirit of the laws revealed the interrelationship of laws as it partly existed in fact and as it must become.

> They [the laws] should be adapted in such a manner to the people for whom they are framed that it should be a great chance if those of one nation suit another.

49. William S. Holdsworth, *Some Lessons from Our Legal History* (New York, Macmillan, 1928), p. 94.

50. F. D. Maurice, *Social Morality. Twenty-One Lectures* (London, Macmillan, 1869), p. 5.

They should be in relation to the nature and principle of each goverment; whether they form it, as may be said of politic laws; or whether they support it, as in the case of civil institutions.

They should be in relation to the climate of each country, to the quality of its soil, to its situation and extent . . . to the religion of the inhabitants . . . In fine, they have relations to each other, as also to their origin, to the intent of the legislator, and to the order of things on which they are established; in all of which different lights they ought to be considered. . . . These relations I shall examine, since all these together constitute what I call the "Spirit of the Laws." [51]

The Puritans and the lawyers shared with Montesquieu the insistence on the relational function of the spirit of the laws, but the object of relation was not other laws, nor the whole complex of physical and sociological factors that constituted the national character of a nation. The spirit of the laws found in the Puritan–common law axioms had divine sovereignty and fundamental law as the objects of relation. The spirit of the laws became a "working revelation" of the transcendental authorities, a medium through which the authority of God and fundamental law was always revealed, no matter what the inadequacies and failures of the particular laws in the sight of men. At the risk of being too theological in the case of the lawyers (the Puritans would not have objected), one can point to the soteriological nature of the relation. The spirit or the axioms had been given by God and fundamental law to save the laws, to bring order out of confusion and contradiction, to restore proper interrelation. The spirit of the laws made possible the right function of the biblical commandments and the common law tradition.

As this section reaches its conclusion Paul Tillich's concept of "belief-ful realism" would appear useful. Tillich describes belief-ful realism as "a basic attitude in every realm of life, expressing itself in the shaping of every realm." Belief-ful or self-transcending realism "tries to point to the spiritual meaning of the real by using its given forms." The Puritans and the lawyers looked at more than simply laws in questions of authority. Laws *were* inescapable; they were the real things to be encountered when any ecclesiastical, legal, or political issue was at stake. However, the true interest was not in these "natural forms of things for their own sake, but for their power of expressing

51. Montesquieu, *Spirit*, pp. 7–8.

the profounder levels and the universal significance of things." [52] The divines and the barristers employed belief-ful realism inasmuch as they were involved in "a turning toward reality, a questioning of reality . . . a driving to the level where reality points beyond itself to its ground and ultimate meaning." [53] Beyond the laws, known through the spirit of the laws, lay the transcendental rule of God and law. The divines and the barristers believed that the laws of the Bible and the common law tradition were not ultimate reality or final authority. They were grounded in something else; indeed, they had come from something else to which men owed their supreme allegiance.

The foregoing discussion shows little similarity between the early seventeenth-century Puritans and lawyers and the natural law thinkers. Affinity there may have been at some points, particularly in the Puritan-common law appeal to a higher law. But the affinity is broken when one examines the meaning of higher law for the Puritans and lawyers. The higher law of our subjects stood above the world. To be sure, it was known in the world—not, however, because it functioned in an emanative way like some Platonic form, but because it had revealed itself through particular laws and the spirit of the laws. The distinction was maintained between that which had been revealed and the revealer. The laws were not final and absolute in themselves but must be continually examined and compared with the spirit of the laws. Only then could the meaning of divine sovereignty and fundamental law be discovered.

DISTRIBUTIVE AUTHORITY

The conviction that there were ultimate authorities ruling through laws determined the function and relationship of all institutions for the Puritans and lawyers. Both groups held a view of institutional authority which distinguished them from those who would centralize power and control. The divines and the barristers especially stood apart from and opposed the position of the early Stuarts. James I and Charles I pictured English society as a rigid hierarchy wherein the king derived his power from God and other institutions derived their powers from the king. The crown had given a place in the hier-

52. Paul Tillich, *The Protestant Era*, trans. James L. Adams (Chicago, University of Chicago Press, 1948), p. 67, for all the quotations used so far in the paragraph.

53. As quoted by James L. Adams, "Tillich's Concept of the Protestant Era," in Tillich, *Protestant Era*, p. 296.

archy to each institution; the assigned stations determined the relationship of one entity to another. The Court of Star Chamber, for
instance, was in the judgment of the Stuarts rightly superior to the
common law courts because the king had bestowed more authority
upon this prerogative court than upon the courts of Common Pleas,
the Exchequer, and King's Bench. The concept of the king as an
earthly giver of power pervaded the Stuart "free monarchy."

Among the Puritans and the lawyers the issue was not how much
power had been given by the crown to various institutions. God and
fundamental law were the bestowers, and they had given specific, distinct authority to church, court, university, inn of court, king,
Parliament, and council. One institution could not usurp the function
and responsibility of one or more of the others, as the Stuart crown
sought to do. A concept of authority distributed among all institutions by ultimate authorities was explicit in the thought and activity
of our early seventeenth-century subjects.

Even in the case of the church and the courts, the Puritans and the
lawyers clung to a belief and a practice of distributive authority. Although mightily concerned with the church and the courts, the two
groups did not clamor for the supremacy of these two institutions over
all others. The body of Christ and the seat of justice were institutions
which more than any others represented the direct authority of God
and law in the world. But this unique qualification did not enable them
to impose their authority on other entities, not even on the Stuart
kings who opposed them. The charge leveled against Coke—that he
was bent on making the judiciary a ruling aristocracy—is extremely
difficult to substantiate. The great jurist was forever insisting on the
authority of the king and Parliament as coordinate with that of the
courts. No Puritan leaders of the time, as we have seen, proposed a
theocracy in which the church should become the governmental organ
of society. The common law courts and the church were, like all other
institutions, independent of the king, but just because they were the
fountainhead of justice and the holy community they had no license
to extend their authority over that rightly located in other realms.

The Puritans and the lawyers also insisted on what they considered
to be a necessary counterpart to institutional freedom. They stressed
the *inter*dependence of king, council, Parliament, church, court,
university, and inn of court. The institutions of English life were free
from one another, yet they were also bound together. Each needed the
others for the proper function of its own tasks. At this point both the
divines and the barristers displayed a resemblance to Richard Hooker,

a similarity which we have considered before in the case of the Puritans. Hooker dealt with the two institutions of church and state in his *Laws* and argued that the Church of England and the crown were bound together in one commonwealth. The king needed the Anglican church and likewise the church needed the king. The happy joining of the body of Christ and the body politic had in large measure produced the English community, the benefits of which were all too obvious to Hooker. The Puritans and lawyers extended the thought of the Anglican apologist to include the many institutions of English life, not just church and state. All needed and depended on each other and out of their union came the felicity that was England.

But the Puritans and the lawyers never forgot about the independence and nonsubordination amidst the connectedness and interdependence. They might agree with Richard Hooker that the institutions of the early 1600's were auspiciously joined with one another and that the cohesion effected the English commonwealth. This is especially true in the case of the Puritans who, as we have seen, held for the union of church and state so long as there was conformity to their interpretation of the Tudor establishment. Both Hooker and our subjects might be said to have an organismic understanding of national community. But the political organism which the Puritans and the lawyers envisioned had visible parts, sections, and joints. Hooker's *Laws* pictured the commonwealth centering in the crown wherein the body politic and the church were naturally fused. Both the monarchy and the Church of England were constructed in accord with the law of nature or the law of reason; the civil laws of the one and the canon laws of the other faithfully reflected the common higher norm. The union of church and state also accorded with scripture and history. This line of reasoning smacked of too much union and togetherness for the divines and barristers.

The Puritans and the lawyers entered a demurrer on two counts. First, Hooker's analysis permitted an easy concentration of power and authority in the king, a matter not to be taken lightly by those struggling for the independence of the church, the universities, the courts, and the inns of court. Secondly, there was no clear distinction between the laws of the state and the laws of the church. In the formulation of major ecclesiastical legislation the monarch was the prime mover, promulgator, and executor. The law of the state became the law of the church. This was not a matter of alarm for Hooker because natural law and reason had decreed that unity in the crown should prevail over a meaningless and, as he felt, unchristian diversity. The

higher law would always act as a check on any monarchial excesses.
For the Puritans and the lawyers, the rule of God and the rule of law,
on the other hand, had given clearly different laws to the many institutions of early seventeenth-century England. There were tenure rules
in the universities, procedural laws for the courts, ordination statutes
in the church, hearing rules in the king's council, committee regulations in Parliament, succession laws for the crown, and governing
rules for the benchers in the inns of court. These sets of laws were all
distinct from one another; indeed, they were so variant that they frequently conflicted with one another. Hooker half accepted the existence of the parts, but he saw a beneficent, easily achieved harmony
which the Puritans and the lawyers denied.

Here is demonstrated once more the gap between natural law thinkers and the subjects of our book. The law of nature or the law of
reason pervaded everywhere and joined things together in a readily
comprehensible scheme. Divine sovereignty and fundamental law were,
once again, authorities which revealed themselves through the Bible,
the common law tradition, the spirit of the laws, and the particular laws of institutions. If there be harmony, it existed only within
the other-worldly rule of God and fundamental law. The ultimate authorities had revealed laws for the here and the now and these laws
proclaimed and sanctioned real difference among the institutions of
the land. Church, courts, universities, and the rest were bound together, but each was unique so that it could better discharge its functions and fulfill its purpose. Togetherness *and* separateness were
needed. Both motifs showed forth the glory of God and the pure reason
of the law and gave meaning to the English community.

The themes of responsibility to higher authority, independence, and
interdependence dominate the conception of institutional authority as
held by the Puritans and the lawyers. Our subjects can be likened to
others beside Hooker, whose *modus operandi* was drawn from the
Middle Ages. There is a relation between Puritan–common law
thought and the medieval theory of dominium which postulated an
ultimate realm above all earthly powers.[54] The higher realm had both
legal and religious formulations. The two groups made a special use
of dominium thought, however, in their application of distributive
authority to the early seventeenth-century struggle for political
power. This matter will engage us for the remainder of the present
chapter and in the one ahead.

The Puritans and the lawyers proclaimed first of all that govern-

54. Consult Chrimes, *Constitutional Ideas,* pp. 307–28.

mental power was limited. The Stuart insistence on an unrestrained divine right of kings and on free monarchy cast a sinister shadow in the light of distributive authority. Kings, like all other forms of human power, were subject to the higher rule of God and of law. No better spokesman appeared for the Puritans than Thomas Gataker when he preached at Serjeants Inn in Fleet Street on the text: "I have sayd, Ye are gods, and ye all of you are children of the most High. But ye shall die as a man, and ye princes shall fall like others. O God, arise, *therefore* judge thou the earth: for thou shalt inherit all nations" (Ps. 82: 6–8). In his sermon, which was dedicated to Sir Henry Hobart, Chief Justice of the Court of Common Pleas, and delivered to a congregation of lawyers, Gataker spoke thus about the limitation of kings:

> For 1. hee [God] is absolute and independent. Other Kings and Princes are not absolute. They hold all from him; they depend all upon him; they doe service all to him. As *the sheilds* [sic] *of the world,* so *the Crownes,* and *the kingdomes of the world are all his:* and he disposeth them at his pleasure. For *he dispenseth the kingdomes of the world* . . .[55]

If fundamental law were substituted for the references to God, the above quotation could well have been a legal opinion delivered by a common law judge rather than a sermon preached by a divine. Gataker's congregation of lawyers and judges doubtless agreed with the preacher's further reminder that kings were also limited because they were only frail, human officeholders.

> Princes therefore . . . though they be *Gods by name,* yet are they *not* so *by nature.* It is not *Iah* or *Iehovah* a name of *Essence,* but *Eloah* or *Elohim* a name of *Office* that is given them. . . . Though they sit above others, yet must they die as others. Though they may live *like Gods,* yet must they die *like men,* even *as other ordinary men* are wont to doe.[56]

Contemporary forms of political power were restricted not only in a general way because of the derivation of authority from God and law, but specifically. Particular laws prescribed bounds for the function of king, Parliament, and council. The limitations of the Bible and the common law tradition were not always apparent, as we have seen, and

55. Thomas Gataker, *Gods Parley with Princes. With an Appeale from Them to Him* (London, 1620), pp. 54–5.

56. *Ibid.,* pp. 32–3.

had to be determined in a trial, a hearing, a debate, or perhaps a pamphlet war. When a concrete issue did arise, the two groups sought to pin down the specific authority allowed the various forms of political power. The Puritans contested with the crown over its claim to legislate at will for the church and found that both the Bible and the common law tradition proscribed the king's unrestrained lawmaking for the church. In the 1610 parliamentary debate over Bate's Case, William Hakewill argued against the crown's position, which was based on deliberate indefiniteness and left all to the discretion of the king's absolute power. Hakewill's words portrayed the Puritan–common law belief that specific limitations could be found in particular laws: "I lay this as a ground which will not be denied me by any man, that the Common Law of England, as also all other wise laws in the world, delight in certainty and abandon uncertainty, as the mother of all debate and confusion . . ." [57]

The divines and the barristers searched their laws to discover the specific roles which political litigants were allowed to play. Roscoe Pound reminds us that the common law's primary concern has always been with the *role* of the parties in a transaction—the role of principal and agent, for example, in the law of agency—not with the will of the parties. Roman and later civil law systems, on the other hand, have singled out the act of the parties, or the manifestation of their will, as the essential matter in a legal dispute. As a result the common law, more than the civil, has insisted on a strict formulation of the duties, rights, and liabilities incumbent upon parties engaged in certain relations. [58] A concern with the proper relation of parties was part of the Puritan–common law ideology and found its way into the political scene, where the roles of king, Parliament, and council were held to be carefully specified by law.

The Puritans and the lawyers were united in refusing allegiance to any form of political authority which claimed power on a basis other than that prescribed by distributive authority. Mr. Holdsworth calls attention to the affinity between Puritan leaders and the political opponents of the crown, chiefly lawyers, at the point of common refusal to respect persons. [59] Position, prestige, royalty, de facto authority, and emergency powers did not by themselves command obedience and loyalty.

Not even the principle of consent justified the authority of a king

57. Tanner, *Documents*, p. 249.
58. Roscoe Pound, *The Spirit of the Common Law* (Francestown, N.H., Marshall Jones, 1921), pp. 21 ff.
59. *English Law*, 6, 128.

or a Parliament. The few cries in the early 1600's that political power should represent the "voice of the people" were scattered.[60] It can rightly be said the idea of an English *Volksstaat* did not emerge until the 1640's, when Parliament claimed unlimited sovereignty as representative of the whole realm. When such a claim was made during the Civil War, first by Parliament and later by the army, it was ill received by those of our Puritans and lawyers who were still alive.

Nor did the artifice of contract between ruler and people provide vindication for political power. When obedient to present powers the divines and barristers had more pressing reasons. A king, a Parliament, a council, or an army was said to govern correctly and to merit allegiance when and if it used the powers bestowed by God and fundamental law as found in the Bible, the common law tradition, and the spirit of the laws. Good government also demanded respect for the laws of other institutions. The concept of a *Rechtsstaat* was continually to the fore in the early part of the century.[61]

Finally, there remains the Puritan–common law insistence that the greater the power bestowed upon a political institution, the greater its responsibility to use its authority correctly. Gataker, in the sermon referred to above, made the point in this fashion: "the higher their places are, the lesse liberty is leaft them: Not in regard of God onely: because *where he hath conferred much: there he expecteth the more:* And, as he said sometime of Christians, so may wee well say of great Ones . . . A city, saith our Sauiour, *set on a hill cannot be hid.*" [62] The congregation of lawyers was in probable accord with the preacher's stress on responsibility.

The foregoing conception of political authority is hardly a detailed theory of the state as found in the thought of the Stuart kings, the radical parliamentarians, the leaders of the New Model Army, the Thomas Hobbeses, or the natural law thinkers. Sovereign powers of government were not assigned to any person, group, or institution; there was no declaration of rights; checks and balances were not devised. Numerous historians have called attention to the ambiguity and nondirection of political thought in the early seventeenth century.[63] Without question the Puritan–common law concept of distributive

60. For a discussion of political arguments among the Puritans based on consent and the voice of the people, see Judson, *Crisis*, pp. 311–48.

61. Francis D. Wormuth, *The Royal Prerogative, 1603–1649. A Study in English Political and Constitutional Ideas* (Ithaca, N. Y., Cornell University Press, 1939), p. 29.

62. Gataker, *God's Parley*, p. 15.

63. See Allen, *English Political Thought, 1,* 35–9, for a negative estimate of Coke's political contribution.

authority was incomplete and produced not a few practical dilemmas. However, the insistence that authority was derived from prior authorities and exercised by various institutions according to laws proved to be an important political idea in early seventeenth-century England. Far from being an antiquated inheritance, the conception was incorporated in the most crucial political development of the time, namely, the growth of Parliament.

In the pre-1630 era Puritans and lawyers indoctrinated the House of Commons with the same concept of authority which they had invoked against the Stuart kings. To be sure, Parliament was soon to abandon the Puritan–common law interpretation of its governing powers. Made headstrong by initial successes, urged on by new leadership, and compelled by the exigencies of war, the Long Parliament of the 1640's claimed a power which was the near equal of the free monarchy of the Stuarts. But the concept of distributive authority based on laws did not perish with the bellicose demands of John Pym or the charges of Cromwellian horse. The idea returned to become part of the very marrow of English political life.

7 PURITAN–COMMON LAW INFLUENCE
ON PARLIAMENT

THE EARLY SEVENTEENTH CENTURY

THE GROWTH of Parliament from a medieval council and court to a supreme governmental body is an engrossing political story. The narrative contains some chapters that move with dramatic swiftness and significance and others that are dull and apparently meaningless. Authorities have often called attention to the exciting chapters, such as the beginning of committee initiative in the late medieval House of Commons and the periods of great legislative activity in the reigns of Edward I and Henry VIII. Chapters dealing with the Long Parliament, the Civil War, the Restoration, and the Revolution have been written many times. The reader of the story can find excellent accounts of the eighteenth century when Parliament's power was fully and unmistakably asserted. Today his attention is caught by a foreboding chapter whose theme is that of Commons' demise, as some claim, in the suffocating clutches of administrative law.[1] Parliament's story rightly consists of all these parts, each one of which has contributed something unique to the development of the institution.

It is understandable but unfortunate that the less dramatic periods have been neglected. A faithful political narrative demands the account of both the fast and the slow, the quick and the dead—the long years of tyranny in the *ancien régime* need to be related before one can understand the cataclysmic events of the French Revolution. We would call attention to a relatively drab period of parliamentary development in the early seventeenth century, the period before the telling events of the 1640's, of 1660 and 1688. No declaration of human rights, no triennial act, no express statement of parliamentary sovereignty occurred within its span. Nevertheless, the chapter writ-

1. Consult George W. Keeton, *The Passing of Parliament,* London, Benn, 1952.

ten in the early 1600's made possible that which was to come and, more important, made a significant contribution to the growth of the chief political institution in the life of England.

Mr. Holdsworth speaks thus of the early seventeenth-century opposition in Commons:

> It is clear . . . that the Parliamentary opposition down to 1629 was essentially a legal opposition. It did not aim at change. It aimed only at securing the observance of the law, interpreted as its leaders interpreted it, and the punishment of those who had broken it. It recognized that both the king (who was always spoken of with the greatest respect), and Parliament, had important functions in the state; and it aimed at delimiting their respective spheres of action, and securing for them liberty of action within these spheres.[2]

The pre-1630 Parliaments were dominated by the Puritans and common lawyers. These antagonists of the king, as we have seen, brought their particular grievances to the House of Commons for redress. Of greater significance was the fact that they came to the lower house with a conception of authority. During the early 1600's, the Puritan–common law idea of distributive authority was at work in every conflict between the crown and Commons. The opposition in the lower house was legalistic; it sought to limit political power; it recognized the authority of other institutions in society; it attempted to establish proper bounds for the functions of these institutions; and it proposed no radical seizure of power for itself.

IMPEACHMENTS

A refusal to respect persons simply because they possessed de facto power was a hallmark of parliamentary activity in the early seventeenth century. Examples abound of the attempt in the House of Commons to apply existing laws to the king and thus define his proper bounds. The parliamentary opposition also sought to limit the power of the crown's ministers and representatives. We have already noted the attacks of the Puritans and the lawyers outside Parliament on those representatives of the king who interfered with the church and the courts. Likewise in the House of Commons, the two groups and their representatives acted to curb the powers of certain persons of state.

2. *English Law, 6,* 103.

In 1621 the long-dormant proceedings of impeachment were revived by the lower house. There had been no impeachment and trial
at the suit of Commons since the proceedings against Lord Stanley
in the mid-fifteenth century. Sir Giles Mompesson, a monopolist en-
joying the benefits of three royal patents, was the first victim of the
revival.[3] Coke, now a member of Commons, was prominent in the
action. The case against Mompesson was politically unimportant,
save that James considered the suit of the lower house a vicious attack on his power to grant monopolies.[4] Other impeachment proceedings followed, however, which were of crucial political significance
because important public officials were removed from office.

In the same year of Mompesson's impeachment and conviction,
1621, Francis Bacon was called to task by the House of Commons.
Now Viscount St. Alban and lord chancellor of the realm, Bacon
had long associated himself with the absolutism of James. He was
impeached for bribery, to which he made a humble confession and
implored the mercy of Parliament. His conviction signified more than
the bringing of a corrupt minister to justice. The lawyers in Parliament had not forgotten that it was Bacon who, in Peacham's
Case of 1615, had argued with Chief Justice Coke that judges must
render their opinions separately upon demand of the crown. The
Puritans recalled that the lord chancellor had acquiesced in and
encouraged the proceedings of the crown against nonconformists in
the courts of High Commission and Star Chamber. Bacon was thus
known to be a persistent interferer in the special interests of the
Puritans and the lawyers.

The continual meddling of the lord chancellor helps to account for
his harsh sentence. Bacon was fined £40,000, imprisoned in the
Tower, prevented from holding any future position in state or commonwealth, debarred from sitting in Parliament, and outlawed within
an area twelve miles about the royal court. One antagonist proposed
that he also be stripped of his titles, but the house refused to add
this further disgrace.[5] In the eyes of the Commoners, Bacon was
rightfully dismissed from this office and severely punished because,
like the king he served so faithfully, he had frequently exceeded the
authority of his offices.

In 1624 another high official of the crown, Lionel Cranfield, Earl

3. The proceedings in Parliament against Mompesson can be found in *State
Trials, 2,* 1119–36.
4. See Tanner, *Documents,* p. 322.
5. Gardiner, *History, 4,* 102–3.

of Middlesex and lord treasurer, was impeached and discharged from office. The charges against Middlesex were "Bribery, Extortions, Oppressions, and other grievous Misdemeanors committed by his lordship . . ." [6] Middlesex was not charged with as many unwarranted extensions of official power as Bacon, nor was Middlesex treated as severely. The significance of the lord treasurer's impeachment lies in the fact that Commons was able, for the first time, to carry through an action against a minister of state on its own initiative and authority. In the proceedings against Mompesson and Bacon, the lower house had turned evidence over to Lords for investigation and, as it turned out, conviction. Edward Coke, in a conference in Whitehall between representatives of the two houses on the Middlesex impeachment, stated: "My Lords do enjoy your Places by Blood and Descent . . . but the Members of the House of Commons by free Election. They appear for Multitudes and bind Multitudes; and therefore they have no Proxies. They are the Representative Body of the Realm . . . and therefore, by the Wisdom of the State, and by Parliament Orders, the Commons are appointed the Inquisitors General of the Grievances of the Kingdom . . ." [7] The lower house gave notice in the Middlesex affair that, by the exercise of its own power, it would seek out and present charges against those officials of the state who abused their offices.

Impeachment proceedings created a great stir in the celebrated case of the Duke of Buckingham, favorite of Charles I and holder of many governmental posts. The articles drawn up against Buckingham by Commons in 1626 were legion. He was accused of bribery, misuse of military funds and equipment, bad judgment, neglect of duty, and a long list of other crimes and failings.[8] Like Bacon, Buckingham had long been attacked by Puritans, common lawyers, and other opponents of the crown. Although he had made numerous enemies for personal reasons, there is little question that Parliament's attack resulted chiefly from arrogant misuse of the authority that had been entrusted to him.

These impeachments, convictions, and sentences of persons of state who exceeded the prescribed limits of their offices only presaged the wrath which was to come. In the early 1640's, Thomas Wentworth,

---

6. *State Trials, 2,* 1250.

7. *Journals of the House of Lords* (n.p., n.d.), *3,* 307. See also Godfrey Davies, *The Early Stuarts, 1603–1660* (Oxford, Clarendon, 1937), p. 28.

8. Consult Gardiner, *Documents,* pp. 8–22, for the 13 charges of the lower house against Buckingham.

Earl of Strafford and late supporter of Charles I, was impeached by Commons and, following the use of a bill of attainder, decapitated before some 200,000 people. In the middle of the decade, Archbishop Laud likewise went to the scaffold after the employment of attainder by the now all-powerful Long Parliament. Such violent treatment of enemies did not occur in the prewar years. The early seventeenth-century parliamentarians did uphold, however, the conception of distributive authority against ministers of state who transgressed the bounds of their official responsibilities.

INSTITUTIONAL INDEPENDENCE

The most significant application of distributive authority occurred in the realm of institutional life. All forms of earthly dominion—ecclesiastical, legal, political—were seen by Parliament to stand directly under God or fundamental law. The king had definite powers and duties, as did Commons and Lords, the church, the courts, and the king's council. One institution could not assume the powers of another, for each was independent of the other, depending on divine sovereignty or fundamental law for its justification and proper function. The political motif of institutional autonomy was constantly to the fore in the early seventeenth-century chapter of Parliament's story.

In the 1604 Apology and Satisfaction, the first presentation of grievances to the crown by a Jacobean Parliament, the lower house protested the crown's interference with the church. "For matter of religion," declared the members of Parliament, "it will appear by examination of truth and right that your Majesty should be misinformed if any man should deliver that Kings of England have any absolute power in themselves either to alter Religion (which God defend should be in the power of any mortal man whatsoever), or to make any laws concerning the same otherwise than as in temporal causes . . ." [9] The 1604 Apology, which has been called a lecture to a foreign king on the constitutional customs of the realm (James was fresh from Scotland), also protested the crown's interference with the privileges of Parliament.

The crown's dictation to the church continued to be a familiar complaint in the early Stuart Parliaments. It was taken up again in the petition of 1610, which supported the cause of the recently deprived ministers. Soon, however, the whole range of Stuart absolutism

9. Tanner, *Documents*, p. 226.

was challenged by the Commoners. The interference of the king as it affected judicial procedures, the legislative powers of the lower house, and the rights of citizens was decried in the impositions debates, the protestation of 1621, the 1628 Petition of Right, the 1628 remonstrance against tonnage and poundage, and the protestation of 1629.

Parliament not only criticized the crown for usurpation of power, but it forbade emulation of the Stuarts by any other authorities. Most important was the assertion in the House of Commons that Parliament itself was a limited governing body. Just as the king should allow Parliament its independence, so should Parliament grant and even safeguard the independence and sway of other institutions. Respect for the king and his rightful powers was genuinely displayed in the beginning of each grievance presented to the crown by Commons. No parliamentarian of this period proposed an Erastian control of the church by the lower house, although Prynne and others were not to balk at the idea in the 1640's. Even the most radical parliamentarians made no suggestion that Commons take over the function of the courts. Parliament, too, had definite bounds over which it could not step to invade the province of other institutions.

How does this interpretation fit the strong words with which many of our subjects described the House of Commons? Coke depicted Parliament in the *Institutes* as "so transcendent and absolute, as it cannot be confined either for causes or persons within any bounds." [10] It does not appear, however, that this and similar assertions were used by Coke or any other leading figure of the time to proclaim Parliament's unlimited legislative or governmental authority. Such words were rather employed to describe its historic function as the highest court in the land. The conception of Parliament as a high court prevailed in the Middle Ages and was much in evidence in the early 1600's. Indeed, traces of the idea are to be found in British political life today. Coke spoke of "transcendent" Parliament much as present-day Americans speak of the Supreme Court, an institution which is supreme because it is the highest of courts, not because it has unrestrained powers of government. [11]

10. 4th Pt., sec. i, p. 36.

11. For Coke's understanding of Parliament's supremacy, as well as the above analogy to the U.S. Supreme Court, see McIlwain, *High Court,* pp. 139 ff. Mr. McIlwain believes that Coke stands in line of descent from certain 16th-century political writers (e.g., Sir Thomas Smith, Elizabethan author of the *Discourse on the Commonwealth of England*), who likewise conceived of Parliament as a high court (pp. 121 ff.). McIlwain thus opposes the older view of Bryce, Dicey, Maitland,

The Commoners were so watchful of the house's power that they harkened to those outside who asserted that Parliament was, if not overbearing, at least meddlesome. Shortly before the outbreak of war, Richard Holdsworth spoke against the interference of the lower house in the affairs of Cambridge University and Emmanuel College. Parliament attempted in 1640 to enforce a frequently ignored technicality which stipulated that fellowships should end within one year of an incumbent's receipt of his doctorate. Several months later, in an incident connected with the dispute over the tenure problem, Commons annulled the election of a certain fellow to Emmanuel College.[12] The vice-chancellor and many of his colleagues felt that both matters were unwarranted interference with the life of the university and the college, and they made protest to Parliament.[13] The two issues were undoubtedly in Holdsworth's mind when he lamented the decline of learning in his moving commencement address of 1641. In July of the same year Parliament "Ordered, That the Information given concerning an Oration made in the University of *Cambridge*, touching the Decay of Learning, *&c* by Dr. *Holdsworth* the *Vice-chancellor;* wherein it was alleged were Reflections on Parliaments proceedings, be referred to a Committee." [14] Not much was done to alleviate the grievances to which Holdsworth had called attention—more crucial affairs now occupied the House of Commons —but at least notice was taken. Throughout the early part of the century, the parliamentary leaders not only refused to claim absolute power but often proved receptive to the criticism of those who asserted that Commons interfered with the life of other institutions.

A MODERN MEDIEVALISM

What contribution did the early seventeenth-century House of Commons make to parliamentary development? Conformity with the principle of distributive authority is apparent in the House of Commons, but does this mark a departure from the medieval, or traditional, concept of Parliament's powers? Are not the themes of independence and restricted authority simply continuations of well-

and Pollock who see parliamentary sovereignty emerging in the thought of 16th- and early 17th-century figures. The author of *High Court* is supported by Messrs. Figgis, Gough, Thorne, Mosse, and other authorities.

12. For these actions of the House of Commons, see Charles H. Cooper, ed., *Annals of Cambridge* (Cambridge, Warwick, 1845), *3*, 306–7, 307, n. 1.

13. *DNB, 27,* 125.

14. Rushworth, *Collections,* Pt. 3, *1,* 355.

established ideas? Doubtless they are. Mr. Chrimes rightly points to the limitation of an institution's sphere of action as a familiar political theme of the Middle Ages.[15] Similarly, the conviction that one institution should not be under the authoritarian control of another was widely held in the centuries just preceding our study. Mr. Mosse, another student of English political development, considers the thought of Edward Coke so medieval in character that he compares the jurist with Sir John Fortescue, the Lancastrian chief justice and political writer. Coke's understanding of political power reminds Mosse of Fortescue's *dominium politicum et regale*, in which no political entity was supreme and each kept within its own bounds and customs.[16]

A case can be made for the medieval character of distributive authority, but the concept existed now against the backdrop of unfeigned allegiance to Parliament. By the time of the Puritans and lawyers, the House of Commons had without question become a major factor in the government of England.[17] The divines and lawyers were not suspicious of this development; they rather encouraged it. With church, courts, council, and Lords under the king's thumb, where else could opposition be effectively offered? The lower house became the final hope of those who opposed the Stuart kings, and aroused enthusiasm and support more passionately than it ever had in Tudor, Yorkist, and Lancastrian times. Distributive authority was active in a new setting, in the center of which was Parliament.

The growth of Commons' power and popularity has led many authorities to ascribe the inception of parliamentary sovereignty to the late Elizabethan or early Jacobean period. Many scholars find in one or more of the events discussed in Chapters 4 and 5 the beginning of such an idea. Mr. Holdsworth believes with others that the first proclamation of parliamentary sovereignty occurred in Whitelocke's celebrated "king-in-Parliament" speech of 1610.[18] Still others argue that later crises produced the birth of the concept.[19] The present writer finds it difficult to ascribe parliamentary sovereignty

15. *Constitutional Ideas*, pp. 59–62.

16. "Here we seem to be back with Fortescue." George L. Mosse, *The Struggle for Sovereignty in England. From the Reign of Queen Elizabeth to the Petition of Right* (East Lansing, Mich., Michigan State College Press, 1950), p. 163.

17. Consult John E. Neale, *The Elizabethan House of Commons*, London, Cape, 1949, and *Elizabeth I and Her Parliaments, 1559–1581*, London, Cape, 1953; and Wallace Notestein's still indispensable essay, "The Winning of the Initiative by the House of Commons," London, Oxford University Press, 1924.

18. Holdsworth, *Lessons*, pp. 124–5. See Ch. 5, pp. 103 ff.

19. See McIlwain, *High Court*, pp. 103–5, for note entitled, "The Beginning

to the 1603–30 period. Such a doctrine does not seem to appear in the words of Sir James Whitelocke, who was speaking to the particular point of whether the king could levy impositions for revenue without act of Parliament. The Puritan–common law opposition always phrased its contest with the king in terms of pinpointed legal issues. The Puritans and the lawyers were not disposed to propound a theory of sovereignty, for according to their understanding of political authority no institution was sovereign over another.

John Pym, the Long Parliament leader who later was to claim unlimited powers for the lower house, declared in 1628 that he did not know the meaning of the word "sovereign." In the debate over the Petition of Right, the upper house asked Commons to affirm the king's rule, or to leave his sovereign power undiminished. Pym spoke against this request on the basis that Parliament could not leave or give what it had never possessed.[20] In the same debate, Coke also denied any acquaintance with "sovereign," whether applied to king or Parliament. The great jurist proclaimed, "*Magna Charta* is such a Fellow, that he will have no Sovereign." [21] Before the Civil War there was neither an attempt to promulgate, nor an interest in, a comprehensive theory of Parliament's power.

The chronology of parliamentary sovereignty is a thorny issue. It is probably impossible to say exactly when the concept became the accepted mode of government in England. The House of Commons asserted its powers over the direction of various parts of the body politic at different times. Henry VIII called a Parliament to confirm his break with Rome and thereafter Commons insisted on a dominant role in legislation for the church. In Elizabeth's time, members of the lower house took upon their shoulders governmental responsibility through seizure of power for parliamentary committees. We have observed the claim of the House of Commons to decide matters of

of Practical Legislative Sovereignty by Parliament." While commending the theories of others, the author asserts, "We must not overlook the importance of the activity of the Long Parliament and the Parliaments of the Protectorate . . ." Mr. Allen calls attention to the parliamentary events of early 1642 in *English Political Thought, 1,* 373. Consult Gough, *Fundamental Law,* for a review of parliamentary sovereignty from Elizabethan times through the 18th century.

20. Parliamentary MSS differ slightly in the recording of Pym's speech; see Gardiner, *History, 6,* 280, n. 3. Mr. Gardiner believes that "Pym may have meant, 'We can only leave what we have control over. This is beyond our control.' " Rushworth, *Collections,* Pt. 1, p. 562, records his words as follows: "And we cannot leave to him a Sovereign Power: Also we never were possessed of it."

21. Rushworth, *Collections,* Pt. 1, p. 562.

revenue in the early 1600's. But many aspects of parliamentary sovereignty did not occur until the Whig administration of the early eighteenth century. And if we would speak of Parliament's sovereign power over the courts, we must wait for the Common Law Procedure Acts in the last half of the nineteenth. Parliamentary sovereignty has accumulated over the centuries. It is now, of course, undeniably operative in British government,[22] but it is impossible to allege that it suddenly emerged at such and such a time. At least its full-blown appearance was not seen in the early seventeenth century. Sovereignty was not the contribution made by the Puritans, the lawyers, and their allies to the growth of the House of Commons.

The contribution of the early seventeenth-century Commoners was the adaptation of a traditional concept to a new political situation. They took the familiar medieval idea of the limitation of power and applied it as a checkrein to their beloved, high-spirited House of Commons. In especial, the parliamentary Puritans and lawyers embedded in the headstrong house a theory of and a procedure for lawmaking. The Puritan–common law conception of legislative authority was to become a permanent feature of Parliament's supremacy in the years ahead.

The lawyers and the Puritans chose to side with the House of Commons against the king, but they insisted that the lower house act in accord with traditional authority. Commons' time-honored responsibility and power had been to enact statutes, or new laws, jointly with the House of Lords and the king, thus playing only one role in the traditional "threefold assent" required for the promulgation of new laws. Coke put the matter thus in the *Institutes:* "There is no act of parliament but must have the consent of the lords, the commons, and the royall assent of the king, and as it appeareth by records and our books whatsoever passeth in parliament by this threefold consent, hath the force of an act of parliament." [23]

In the pre-1630 period no parliamentarian proposed that the lower house make new laws without the cooperation of Lords and the king. The scrupulous maintenance of the authority of these two latter institutions was the primary reason why no strikingly new legislation was passed in the early part of the century. Not until the king's lawmaking role was denied could Parliament push ahead with its dras-

22. For the contemporary significance of the principle, consult Geoffrey Marshall, "What Is Parliament? The Changing Concept of Parliamentary Sovereignty," *Political Studies, 2,* No. 3 (Oct. 1954).

23. 4th Pt., sec. i, p. 24. See also Chrimes, *Constitutional Ideas,* pp. 218 ff.

tic legislative program, but the leaders of the early seventeenth-century Parliaments consistently refused to make the denial.

Moreover, the parliamentarians insisted that old laws should provide the basis for legislative activities. The authority of ancient norms, found in both the Bible and the common law tradition, was religiously maintained in the early seventeenth-century House of Commons. Whenever new laws were under consideration for the church, the bewildering precedents of the Tudor period had to be consulted. Specific biblical commandments were frequently cited on the floor of the lower house as an additional directive for ecclesiastical legislation. In the 1610 dispute over impositions, Hakewill and others were dispatched by the house "to make search in the Exchequer for records which by the practice of former ages might guide our judgments in this weighty point . . ." [24] Sir Edward Coke captured the spirit of the prewar Parliaments when he wrote, "The very lock and key to set open the windows of the statute, whereby it might be known whether the act were introductory of new law or affirmative of the old, was to know what the common law was before the making of any statute." [25]

In the early seventeenth century there was an open suspicion of all attempts to make new law in Parliament. Coke's advice in the *Institutes* was taken literally: "A good caveat to parliaments [is] to leave all causes to be measured by the golden and streight met wand of the law, and not to the incertain and crooked cord of discretion." [26] The purpose of legislation according to the prevailing theory was, as Mr. McIlwain points out, *jus dicere*, not *jus dare*—to proclaim, not to give the law.[27] Parliamentary lawmaking did not have as its goal the creation of new law, but the clarification and adaptation of laws already in existence. Statutes were regarded principally as declarations of ancient laws and customs. This was, of course, a widely held concept in the Middle Ages; it continued to be professed in England long after it had fallen into disaffection in other Western countries.[28] The jus dicere idea of legislation was firmly fixed in the minds of lawyers, Puritans, and even a few monarchs in the late sixteenth and seventeenth centuries.

The prevalence of the jus dicere theory of legislation in the early

24. Tanner, *Documents*, p. 248.
25. As quoted by Chrimes, *Constitutional Ideas*, p. 249.
26. 4th Pt., sec. i, pp. 40–1.
27. *High Court*, p. 94.
28. Chrimes, *Constitutional Ideas*, pp. 193–4.

1600's has probably been exaggerated. Some scholars claim that the shift to jus dare, often held to have occurred during the sway of the Long Parliament, had actually transpired long before. There is evidence that Parliament did not regard itself just as a high court but as a true legislative body—and this not only in the early 1600's but in the Middle Ages. Mr. Theodore Plucknett has demonstrated in *Statutes and Their Interpretation* [29] and elsewhere that certain acts of medieval Parliament were commonly held to have made new law. Perhaps our subjects were preaching one thing about their powers in Commons, but practicing something else. The point of whether the right hand knew what the left was doing will be discussed *ad infinitum*. More important than settling the debate is to see that the Puritans and the lawyers *believed* in the process of jus dicere and that this conviction had important ramifications for the theory and practice of English government as it centered in the House of Commons during the following centuries.

Later in its history, the lower house became an independent lawmaker. Commons was no longer required to cooperate with the king and Lords in the making of statutes. In the subsequent exercise of its legislative powers, however, the lower house seldom forgot that it was in a real sense a cooperator with, not a dictator to, other institutions and groups. In the future Commons was also to make law that had little connection with the old laws of the Bible and of the realm. Still, the authority of the ancient laws was not neglected. The Puritan–common law opposition was instrumental in adapting the traditional notion of the limitation of power to a modern political institution which was later to admit no peers.

LATER PARLIAMENTARY HISTORY

Our account cannot include a detailed rendering of parliamentary development beyond the first few decades of the seventeenth century. Brief allusions will be made, however, to certain periods which illustrate the course of distributive authority. Looking ahead, one's first impression might be that the concept fared badly. Yet the principle of distributive authority, despite apparent absences, continued to be at work in the House of Commons and is a powerful influence today.

The Long Parliament entered the first dissent to the concept of

29. Cambridge, The University Press, 1922. Consult the discussion of the high court theory of Parliament in John W. Gough, "Fundamental Law in the Seventeenth Century," *Political Studies, 1,* No. 2 (June 1953), 163–7.

legislative power held by the prewar House of Commons. The leaders of Commons in the 1640's were innovators. Pym and his colleagues made a pretense of searching for precedents to their acts, even when they were in the novel process of doing away with the High Commission and other aspects of kingly rule. But in reality, the members of the Long Parliament passed legislation which was neither based on the old laws nor promulgated according to the customary procedure of king-in-Parliament. As the Civil War advanced, the more radical parliamentarians joined other groups, military and religious, with the purpose of destroying even the crown itself. Only vestiges of distributive authority remained in the drive for unrestrained political power in the 1640's. The Restoration of 1660 saw the return of the king and, it might be said, of certain aspects of distributive authority. Parliament was now clearly the major partner in the government of the land, but no longer in a mood to exercise its powers as violently as it had in the Puritan Revolution. Still the lower house dominated the government of the land. When James II refused to acknowledge the shift of authority from crown to Commons, it was a relatively simple matter in 1688 to impress parliamentary supremacy upon that grandson of the first Stuart.

The principle of distributive authority was ignored throughout most of the eighteenth century, by which time the preeminence of the House of Commons was firmly established. The Whigs, who maintained supremacy in the government from 1688 until their downfall in 1790, frequently sought to exercise unlimited power in Commons. The third quarter of the century witnessed a display of parliamentary powers similar to that of the 1640's and 1650's. One commentator even compares the Whigs in Parliament with the would-be absolutist government of James II:

> It seems no exaggeration to say that the Whig theory of the state after 1760 is hardly to be distinguished from the principles of James II which had brought on the Revolution of 1688. In one, as in the other, the government assumed authority to impose laws *arbitrarily*. The only difference lay in the fact that in the one case this arbitrary government was under control of an unreformed parliament and that in the other it was dominated by the will of a despotic king.[30]

30. Charles H. McIlwain, *Constitutionalism Ancient and Modern* (Ithaca, N.Y., Cornell University Press, 1947), p. 7. See the author's note pp. 149–52 for instances of the Whig use of Parliament's lawmaking power earlier in the century: (1) imprisonment of the Kentish petitioners, 1701; (2) the case of Ashby vs.

At the end of the eighteenth century, the utilitarianism of Jeremy Bentham and his disciple John Stuart Mill led to a reform program whose implementation demanded lawmaking powers heretofore unpossessed by Parliament. One political historian writes that "distrust of custom and its complete subordination to legislation were among the principal characteristics of Bentham's jurisprudence. With them was connected an indifference to, or rather contempt for, history . . ." [31] Bentham's whole political orientation, as well as his specific proposals, would have been foreign to the early seventeenth-century parliamentarians.

Distributive authority was also disregarded in certain periods of the nineteenth century. John Austin, the great jurisprudential writer of the first half of the 1800's, declared that the only true laws were those promulgated by the sovereign body of the state, which was Parliament. Unfettered lawmaking power was the mark of sovereignty.[32] Breaches in distributive authority continued to appear after Austin's time, abetted by his forceful analysis of law, the state, and sovereignty.

To recognize is not to condemn the later absence of the early seventeenth-century conception of Parliament's authority. Certainly by the eighteenth century, the day had passed when the balanced, medieval-like, Puritan–common law theory of the body politic was practicable for the government of England. The lapses of distributive authority must be judged against constantly changing political and social conditions. The excesses of the Whigs in the eighteenth century may be interpreted as a new form of tyranny, or as consolidation of the parliamentary gains made in the Revolution of 1688. The former view is fair enough, but it should not be forgotten that on occasions the House of Hanover showed a penchant for Stuart ways and it was well that consolidation had taken place.

The reform of Jeremy Bentham and his school may be judged inimical if not harmful to the British system of law and politics, especially Bentham's proposed codification of English law. But here again,

---

White, 1704–05; and (3) the Septennial Act, 1716. The Septennial Act, which postponed a scheduled parliamentary election, was defended as an extraordinary use of Parliament's power in view of the Jacobite uprising of 1715. The arguments in support of the act resembled the doctrine of the crown's emergency powers advanced in the conflicts of the early 17th century.

31. Sabine, *Political Theory*, p. 680.

32. John Austin, *Lectures on Jurisprudence. Or the Philosophy of Positive Law* (5th ed. London, Murray, 1885), especially lects. 1, 5, and 6 in Vol. *1*.

he who judges must not forget that the old laws failed to provide remedies for the legal and governmental defects noted by the Benthamites. The common law had hindered rather than helped the development of equity, the establishment of commercial and maritime law, the growth of family law, and the reorganization of the courts.[33] Every major reform in English law during the nineteenth century can be traced in part to the influence of the Benthamites.[34] New laws were required to cut through the narrow constructionism and inadequacies of an earlier era.

Reforms were possible only after Parliament had made some new laws pertaining to its own structure. The idea of an institution making law for itself would have been ill received by the seventeenth-century Puritans and lawyers. And yet once more political good was accomplished, as seen in the great reform bills of 1832 and 1867 by which Commons widened the franchise. The abolition of the corn laws in 1846 serves as another example of the needed use of Parliament's lawmaking power. Even the potentially dangerous, monistic theory of John Austin played a helpful role in the development of Parliament. An unlimited, sovereign lawmaking body could quickly make the statutes which were necessary for the efficient and equitable administration of the state.

The rapid growth of the House of Commons has occasioned injustice and political discomfort in the English nation, but the institution's exercise of its power has been largely beneficent. Today, fully grown, Parliament can make and unmake whatever laws it desires; no written constitution prescribes the limits of legislative activity. And yet, as the genius of British government attests, Parliament has not done and does not do whatever it pleases. Or it does what it pleases, perhaps, but its pleasure accords with certain principles rooted in the political life of the nation.

A. V. Dicey, in his classic *Introduction to the Study of the Law of the Constitution*,[35] cites three standards of the English constitution: (1) the sovereignty of Parliament, or the legislative supremacy of the House of Commons; (2) the rule of law, or the guarantee of individual rights; (3) the authority of constitutional conventions, or the influence of certain customs and practices upon the formal ad-

---

33. See Holdsworth, *English Law, 5,* 424.

34. Sabine, *Political Theory,* pp. 683–6. Bentham began his criticism in the *Fragment on Government* (1776) with an attack on the *Commentaries* of Blackstone, who was in many ways the 18th-century successor to Coke.

35. 9th ed. London, Macmillan, 1950, ed. and intro. E. C. S. Wade (1st ed. 1885).

ministration of government.[36] The sovereignty of Parliament is, according to Dicey, the keystone of British politics. The other two are pillars which support and rigidly hold the central stone in its appointed place. Dicey's rule of law, or what can be called the primary of the two pillars, has a connection with early seventeenth-century history. Its emphasis upon a "rule" and on "law" suggest the Puritan–common law understanding of how all power, including that of Parliament, must be limited.

Mr. Dicey interprets the rule of law to mean chiefly the preservation of individual rights and liberties, upon which Parliament may never trespass. The term did not originate, of course, with the *Introduction of the Study of the Constitution,* which was written in the last quarter of the nineteenth century. "Rule of law" had a medieval provenance and, at that time, enjoyed a wider meaning than Dicey chose to give it later. In the Middle Ages, as well as in the time of our study, the term referred primarily to the authority of ancient laws, regardless of whether such laws applied to personal rights and liberties. The guarantees to the individual which Dicey saw fit to emphasize were chiefly a modern addition. Although the two uses of the principle are different in scope, they have much in common: both point to norms which qualify Parliament's lawmaking powers. We shall use the rule of law in its older, broader meaning as we describe the abiding influence of the early seventeenth century in the House of Commons.

The continuation of the earlier idea of the rule of law is seen today, first, in the authority which the ancient laws of the land still possess in an age of parliamentary supremacy. The customary, particular laws and statutes of the ancient common law tradition are considered the foundation of modern legislation, possessing an intrinsic authority with which the House of Commons may not tamper. Whatever the insufficiency of the common law tradition, the suggestion that Parliament codify the law of the land is not taken seriously. Codification would deny the particular authority that each ancient law has in its own right without an act of Parliament. Also it would presume that Parliament at the moment of codification possessed the correct interpretation of the vast number of rules, customs, and statutes which comprise the English legal tradition. Statutes are needed to correct the old laws and even to make new. But, as Coke said over three centuries ago, good statute making depends on a

36. To Dicey's three guiding principles of the constitution, Mr. Wade adds a fourth: "The crown can do no wrong," pp. cxlvi–cli.

knowledge of and a respect for the ancient law of the land. Coke's words have been heeded by the generations of lawyers who succeeded in Parliament.

Secondly, Parliament's lawmaking powers have always respected the authority and the laws of other institutions. Today other groups in the national community do not depend on the sovereign body for their existence and their laws. England has never fully accepted the so-called "fiction" or "concession" theory of incorporation developed by the civil lawyers and canonists. This theory, dominant in continental law, is founded on the twofold assumption that legal existence is possible only upon conferral by the state and that such status is bestowed upon "persons." Besides natural, individual human beings, the only other entities to which the state grants legal existence are fictitious persons, or corporations. The crux of the theory is that the sovereign alone can create fictitious persons or corporations. A rigid subscription to this school of thought requires that all groups —political, religious, or purely social—must be incorporated on terms prescribed by the sovereign. The state gives or concedes existence to them. "The corporation is, and must be, the creature of the State. Into its nostrils the State must breathe the breath of a fictitious life, for otherwise it would be no animated body but individualistic dust." [37]

The concession theory has been adopted in part by English law. Many oracles of the common law, including Blackstone, have boasted of England's adherence to the idea. Doubtless the theory has a purpose in the function of the modern state, for without some laws of incorporation, promulgated by sovereign authority, anarchy and the usurpation of individual liberty by powerful, uncontrolled groups could result.[38] England has put the theory to use, but has added beneficial modifications. "So wide," as Mr. Maitland puts it, "was that blessed back stair" of the common law that the idea of concession could enter into the nation's legal and political life and yet, in the process, be uniquely Anglicized.[39]

The English accommodation of the concession theory has shown itself in at least three ways.[40] First, Parliament's incorporation statutes have enabled groups of men associated for lawful purposes

---

37. Otto Gierke, *Political Theories of the Middle Age* [sic], trans. and intro. Frederic W. Maitland (Cambridge, The University Press, 1900), p. xxx in Mr. Maitland's introduction.

38. Holdsworth, *Lessons*, pp. 149–51.

39. Gierke, *Middle Age*, p. xxxi in Maitland's introduction.

40. Consult Holdsworth, *Lessons*, pp. 142 ff.

to obtain corporate form easily. There are no elaborate incorporation laws which might enable Parliament to implement the conviction
held elsewhere that corporate life is the gift of the state. Parliament
thus does not exercise a severe regulative control over the life of
other institutions. Secondly, most of the unique institutions of British
society—the established church, counties, justices of the peace, inns
of court, universities, common law courts, boroughs, and parishes—
continue to depend for their legal existence on the law of the land
and their own promulgations. Parliament honors these norms; it
does not seek to control or manipulate them. The House of Commons
does not say to these institutions, as James I once wrote to Cambridge University officials, that the orders of the sovereign body
must be observed "without immutation upon any pretense of local
statutes . . ." [41] The Commons sides rather with Coke's words to
Cambridge: "it is not possible for any one generall Lawe to fitt every
particular Colledge especially when your private Statutes and Or-
dynaunces be not knowne . . ." [42] Thirdly, the trust principle which
enables property to be held by trustees for various purposes is not
subject to incorporation laws. The trust has preserved the medieval
theory of semiautonomous groups in legal and political terms suit-
able for the modern age. Under its aegis, unincorporate groups are
able to maintain a legal existence alongside of incorporate, fictitious
persons. Here is something especially English. "If we are to visit a
land where Roman law has been 'received,' we must leave this great
loose 'trust concept' at the Custom House . . ." [43]

So far our analogy to Mr. Dicey's principle has been at the level
of law. "Rule" also connotes the presence of the Puritan–common law
conception of authority which has continued to qualify the supremacy
of the House of Commons. In addition to the restriction of other
laws upon its statute-making power, Parliament's rule or supremacy
has been subjected to a conscious articulation of the principle of
self-limitation. Even the eighteenth-century Whigs, Jeremy Bentham,
and John Austin did not consider Parliament to be a monolithic
leviathan, identified by an insatiable and uncontrollable thirst for
power. For Austin, the lower house as maker of positive law was necessarily the only all-powerful sovereign in the state, although theo-

41. Corrie, *Interference*, p. 51.
42. "Sir Edward Coke's Letter to the University of Cambridge [March 12,
1603]," as printed in Millicent B. Rex, *University Representation in England,
1604–1690* (New York, Barnes & Noble, 1954), app. 1, p. 351.
43. Gierke, *Middle Age*, pp. xxix–xxx in Maitland's introduction.

retically Commons shared sovereignty with the king and Lords.[44] But even an omnipotent sovereign operated within the confines of general jurisprudence, which is concerned with "principles, notions, and distinctions which are common to systems of law [for example] . . . 1. The notions of Duty, Right, Liberty, Injury, Punishment, Redress; with their various relations to one another . . . 2. The distinction between written or promulged, and unwritten or unpromulged law . . ."[45] Parliament's power grew to be unquestioned, but the rule of the House of Commons was surveyed, limited, and criticized by elements from within.

No chapter in the parliamentary story illustrates the concept of self-limitation better than the one dealing with the rise of an organized opposition party. The word "opposition" has the generic political meaning of resistance or contrariety.[46] Although often used in a nonspecific way, the term refers in modern English parliamentary history to that particular group of parliamentarians opposed to the current ministry. The first concrete application of the idea of opposition occurred in the opening years of the eighteenth century. Certainly by the third decade of the next century, a recognized group of Commoners opposed to fellow members, who were at the moment in power, became an established feature of British political government.

Lord Bolingbroke, leader of the Tory party during Queen Anne's reign, exile in France, and repatriated critic of Walpole's administration, was among the first to urge the formation of an organized opposition. Bolingbroke believed in a "balanced constitution," which he felt Walpole was laying waste in the late 1730's by corrupt appointments and connivings with the king. The Tory leader pleaded for an alliance of the people and "patriot king" George III to upset the oligarchy of Orange Whigs in Parliament and public office. Opposition was a duty, he claimed, and the avoidance of it was a sin. Bolingbroke said he believed his balanced constitution to be in accord with the divine plan.

Edmund Burke, leader of the Rockingham Whigs midway in the

44. Austin, *Jurisprudence, 1,* 245.

45. *Ibid., 2,* 1073.

46. Archibald S. Foord, "The Development of the Parliamentary Opposition. Chapters in the History of 'His Majesty's Loyal Opposition,'" (unpub. diss., Yale, 1942), p. 112. Mr. Foord's study is the basis for the following section on the opposition; he traces the rise of the opposition in the unreformed Parliaments from 1714 to 1830. Mr. Foord's forthcoming book on this crucial development will add much to our perspective and knowledge of English political institutions.

last half of the eighteenth century and founder of modern conservatism, further embedded the concept of opposition in English political life. Burke rallied the "old corps" of Whigs, who had been unsympathetic to any former opposition until they were put out of office in 1762. The parliamentarians led by Burke at first attacked the king's theory of cabinet appointments. The House of Commons, they argued, must refuse to support the government when the crown's ministers were unacceptable to the people whom Parliament represented. Burke helped to destroy the theory that ministers should be supported because of appointment by the king. His efforts proved of long-range significance in British political life.

Edmund Burke also deplored the undue exercise of the authority of Parliament as well as that of the crown. Although he lamented revolutions, in particular the events across the Channel, he joined with those who defended the American colonists against parliamentary encroachments. He continued the attack of Lord Camden and others on the position of Northington and Mansfield in the 1760's that "every *government* can *arbitrarily* impose laws on all its subjects." In 1791 he stated that the rebellious Americans stood "in the same relation to England, as England did to King James the second, in 1688." [47] Parliament's rule had exceeded its rightful limits, Burke claimed, in dealing with the colonists. The opposition must call the sovereign body to account.

More so than Bolingbroke, Burke founded his criticism and opposition upon religious as well as political conviction. He viewed the nation state as an historical entity within an over-all spiritual community. The state stood under the same divine moral order wherewith God governed the wider community.[48] Whenever the political balance and integrity of the British nation were upset, it was the task of the opposition to restore these qualities so that the political would accord with the higher, divine realm.

It should be remembered, nevertheless, that Bolingbroke and Burke developed their justification of opposition within the framework of political realism. Opposition based upon lofty principles of political philosophy was a practical means to a practical end. They wanted

47. McIlwain, *Constitutionalism*, p. 5, for both quotations.

48. See Sabine, *Political Theory*, p. 616. Consult this citation also for Burke's attack on the East India Company and Warren Hastings because of their interference with indigenous Indian ways. Burke was convinced that the Asiatic Indians must be governed "upon their own principles and not upon ours." As with Englishmen engaged in far-flung enterprises, so with parliamentarians in domestic politics: there are some things not within their province to determine and control.

power. Bolingbroke, though his writings are full of transcendental moralizing, was not concerned to follow his own high precepts either in personal life or in the political arena. Furthermore, there is no evidence to show that Bolingbroke viewed the opposition as an indispensable feature of British politics,—necessary even if *he* were in office. Burke is perhaps more convinced that opposition is a *sine qua non* of English political life. Still, it is not until the middle of the next century that opposition is held to be an elemental and distinctive principle of British constitutionalism.[49]

Despite these qualifications, it must be said that both Bolingbroke and Burke did appeal to something above mere political expediency to justify their concept of opposition. Their views set them apart from the conventional eighteenth-century place-hunters, to whom politics was only a game that offered rich rewards to the winner. The thinking of these two leaders continues the Puritan–common law stress on a supreme authority. The Puritans were convinced of God's rule in the universe; all men owed final obedience and loyalty to this rule. So it was with the lawyers in regard to fundamental law. In the eighteenth century, Bolingbroke and Burke acknowledged an ultimate authority or rule in the universe, standing above Parliament's supremacy. This higher rule, understood primarily by Burke in terms strikingly similar to those of the early seventeenth-century Puritans, was a rule prior in time and authority to Parliament. It was a rule which determined the exercise of sovereign power by the House of Commons. The function of the opposition was to see that Parliament responded to God's rule in the world and abided by the restrictions which this ultimate authority placed on all persons and groups in power.

Neither Bolingbroke nor Burke developed actual tactics for an opposition group in the political life of the time.[50] They did stimulate, however, the development of political parties. Bolingbroke organized and directed what might be called the first party organ, the *Craftsman* (1726–36). He began a newspaper to mold public opinion and "went to the country" to win adherents to his opposition.[51]

49. For the first systematic exposition of the modern theory, see 'Art. I—Hansard's Parliamentary Debates. Parliamentary Opposition," *Edinburgh Review. Or Critical Journal, 101,* No. 205 (Jan. 1855), 1–22. The author is indebted to Mr. Foord for both this reference and the gist of the above paragraph.

50. Consult Foord, "Opposition," pp. 125–32, for the inadequacy of Bolingbroke's thought for practical politics.

51. See Crane Brinton's article on Bolingbroke in the *Encyclopaedia of the Social Sciences, 2,* 622.

Burke's attempts to infuse new vigor into the old Whig party led him to assert the necessity of party organization. His *Thoughts on the Cause of the Present Discontents* (1770) defined a party and sounded the note of personal involvement: "Party is a body of men united for promoting by their joint endeavors the national interest upon some particular principle in which they are all agreed. For my part, I find it impossible to conceive, that any one believes in his own politics, or thinks them to be of any weight, who refuses to adopt the means of having them reduced into practice." [52] In the minds of these eighteenth-century figures, the idea of opposition was being slowly welded to the structure of a political party. A fully organized opposition party was to become a regular feature of nineteenth- and twentieth-century English politics.

The inchoate program of the eighteenth-century opposition has developed today into the party known as "his majesty's opposition," or the "loyal opposition." [53] In the British government this party has a dual role: it supports *and* criticizes. The opposition affirms the form and constitution of the English government, yet it opposes those in power. Its opposition is founded on differences with his majesty's government over specific issues, yet also on the conviction that some group in Parliament must oppose those who exercise the power of the House of Commons. The opposition is traditionally loyal to the constitution and the crown, but perhaps its loyalty and support have another meaning. The opposition is loyal to the rule of some higher authority, whether it be God, law, the democratic principle, or the balanced constitution. It is the party's loyalty to the higher authority which necessitates its opposition to the party in power. The loyal opposition party is the nation's critic and conscience. It insists that the rule of supreme Parliament be exercised in accord with the limitations which a transcendental rule has imposed. Self-limitation under the higher rule has taken concrete form in the modern parliamentary system.

Like Dicey's principle, these seventeenth-century elements of law and rule temper the sovereignty of the House of Commons. Not all of Parliament's story, of course, was told in the early seventeenth century; chapters perhaps more significant were written centuries

52. *The Works of the Right Honorable Edmund Burke* (rev. ed. Boston, Little, Brown, 1865), *1, 530.*

53. Mr. Foord believes that the Rockinghamites and their Whig successors laid the foundation for the 19th- and 20th-century development ("Opposition," pp. 161–2).

before and others equally important have been written since. But certainly one dominant theme in the age-long story was proclaimed effectively for the first time by the Puritans and common lawyers of the early 1600's. In their struggle with James and Charles, these groups took their grievances to parliament where they asserted the Commons' supremacy while at the same time they set forth its limitations. The assertion of parliamentary supremacy later took forms which the early seventeenth-century parliamentarians would have deplored. But the inordinate use of Parliament's power never destroyed the seventeenth-century heritage. The theme of limitation persisted through the times of excess.

With a few exceptions, notably the Civil War period immediately following the span of our study, Parliament has exercised its statute-making power in accord with certain principles. The authority of the ancient statutes and customary laws of the land has been preserved. The independence, laws of operation, functions, and rights of other institutions and groups have also been respected by the supreme body. Rather than making fictitious corporations through intricate incorporation proceedings, the House of Commons simply acknowledges the existence of real ones. Parliament does not presume to lay down detailed laws under which other groups live, move, and have their being. Even the crown, that institution most restricted by Parliament from the seventeenth century on, remains a separate entity in British society with a province unclaimed by the sovereign Commons. The church, the courts, the universities, the inns of courts, and other institutions have continued to exert their own particular authority with only rare interference from the legislature.

Lastly, Parliament has given evidence that it considers the exercise of its powers to be responsive to the rule of some higher authority. This ultimate rule, however conceived, is not fully represented by Parliament or by any other institution in society. Its presence requires that the House of Commons as a sovereign body exercise proper self-limitation. These aspects of Parliament's authority in an age of its supremacy witness the persistence of a political heritage to which the Puritans and lawyers were major contributors.

8 SOVEREIGNTY AND THE STUFF OF POLITICAL HISTORY

A BEQUEST FOR SOVEREIGNTY

THE PURITANS and the lawyers contributed to the development of political theory as well as to the growth of the institution Parliament. At least one segment of current political philosophy stands indebted to the early seventeenth-century opponents of James and Charles. The divines and the barristers bequeathed a way of thinking about the power of state which was conducive to a later theory of sovereignty. That school of thought which advocates societal pluralism and cites the necessity of legal limitations upon the ruling power is in line of succession from our subjects.

Elements of affirmation and denial are present in the Puritan–common law contribution to future thinking about sovereignty. The climate of opinion produced by our subjects, while favoring the growth of one theory of the state, has proved inimical toward others. Certainly it may be said that the divines and the barristers were not responsible for the political philosophy which gave birth to the monist theory of sovereignty, propounded by such men as Hobbes, Spinoza, Bentham, Hegel, and Austin. The monist conception of sovereignty, often called the "classical" or "analytical" theory of the state, holds that sovereign power, wherever it resides in the government, is unlimited in its action.[1] The Puritans and the lawyers

---

1. The author's discussion is indebted to many classificatory studies of sovereignty and jurisprudence, particularly Stanley I. Benn, "The Uses of 'Sovereignty,'" *Political Studies, 3,* No. 2 (June 1955); Huntington Cairns, *Law and the Social Sciences,* New York, Harcourt, Brace, 1935; Edwin W. Patterson, "Historical and Evolutionary Theories of Law," *Columbia Law Review, 51,* No. 6 (June 1951), and *Jurisprudence. Men and Ideas of the Law,* Brooklyn, Foundation Press, 1953.

spent their lives fighting James I and Charles I, two monists of the
first order. The contribution of the former to political thought can
hardly be claimed as propitious for later theories of monism.

The divines and the barristers waged a peculiar battle with the
Stuarts. They opposed the absolutist crown with a determined assertion of the authority of ancient laws. Such strategy seemingly had
little to do with the matter of sovereignty. But the Puritans and the
lawyers did proclaim a dominant role for Parliament in the political
life of England. By an ascription of governing power to Parliament,
they helped to solve the medieval constitutional dilemma of the inability of ancient laws to stand firm against the exercise of the king's
power. Royal *gubernaculum*, or government, to borrow the thought
and phraseology of Bracton the mid-thirteenth-century jurist, had
usually prevailed over *jurisdictio*.[2] The Puritans and the lawyers in
the early seventeenth century fought the crown not only with the
authority of the ancient laws, or jurisdictio, but with another gubernaculum, that of Parliament.

As we have seen, the divines and the barristers did not proclaim a
theory of parliamentary sovereignty. The idea of sovereignty was
foreign to their medieval inheritance. Nor, in the realm of tactics,
were they able to break completely the grip in which the early Stuarts
held Parliament. Yet, by asserting Parliament's authority to make
statutes which, they believed, declared and clarified the old law, our
subjects were ready to give Parliament the governmental power
necessary to redress their grievances. This Puritan–common law
claim of definite, though restricted, authority for Parliament produced a political atmosphere unfavorable to a second type of modern
sovereignty thinking, namely, extreme pluralism. The divines and the
barristers were convinced that someone must rule and they held that
it should be Parliament functioning in a certain way.

There is a stark contrast between the Puritans and the lawyers and
such a modern figure as Harold J. Laski, the pluralist of pluralists.
The late British socialist conceived the state as a federation in which
a frictionless and equitable relationship between all members of society could be maintained without assertions of political authority
by any group or person. "We have, therefore, to find the true meaning of sovereignty not in the coercive power possessed by its instru-
ment, but in the fused good-will for which it stands." "We begin to
see the State as akin to that medieval empire which was above all a

2. See the consideration of Bracton's terms and of medieval constitutionalism
in McIlwain, *Constitutionalism*, pp. 67 ff.

community of communities." [3] Laski viewed the political sovereign as simply one among other entities in society with no particular governing powers. Such unrestrained, almost anarchic pluralism had no foundation in the political thought of the early seventeenth-century divines and barristers.

The Puritans and the lawyers, however, did espouse the general idea of pluralism. Their legalism displayed the prevalence of the concept. All authority, especially political, was affirmed or condemned on the basis of its agreement with or variance from numerous unsystematized laws. All institutions had access to the laws and governed their existence by what was found therein. The standards of judgment found in the laws and in the spirit of the laws were many; they were not gathered together in one place; they were incapable of being manipulated in a facile way by any power-seeking group or person. Moreover, no individual or institution could fashion the spirit of the laws or create the particular laws of the Bible and the common law tradition. Their provenance was divine sovereignty and fundamental law. The conviction of the Puritans and the lawyers about the nature and function of laws and the relation of legal norms to ultimate authorities formed a prototype for modern pluralist thought.

The concept of distributive authority is an even more patent illustration of the affinity of our subjects for pluralism. The Puritan–common law conception of authority can, without anachronism, be called a pluralist theory of society. Many contemporary political thinkers have reaped where these men of the seventeenth century sowed, and have maintained, like the divines and the barristers, that the authority of each institution is independent of the power of the sovereign. Sometimes a modern pluralist position is taken for functional reasons: the organized parts of society are held to have reached a point of development where they cannot be forced into logically controlled categories. A leviathan state is a physical impossibility because of the proliferation and essential differences of groups and institutions.[4] Occasionally political theorists advance arguments identical to those of the Puritans and lawyers. Mr. Figgis,

3. Harold J. Laski, *Studies in the Problem of Sovereignty* (New Haven, Yale University Press, 1917), pp. 12, 274. Laski apparently saw no compromise or middle ground between himself and the leaders of the monist school.

4. George H. Sabine, "Pluralism: A Point of View," *American Political Science Review, 17*, No. 1 (Feb. 1923). Mr. Sabine is himself a quasi-pluralist; he reserves "the right to be a monist when I can and a pluralist when I must" (p. 50).

for example, upholds the independence of the church in the face of advancing statism; in the last analysis, the church can never depend on the state, only on God.[5] Lastly, one might call attention to the common ground between our subjects and Messrs. Gierke and Maitland, who propound an "associations theory" of society. This theory, close in some ways to Laski's out-and-out pluralism, upholds the "group personality" of institutions and associations. Distinct social personalities together comprise society. The state has neither created nor can it arbitrarily control the "group persons." [6]

All these nonextremist pluralist schools of thought emphasize a decentralized, distributive, nonmonistic concept of sovereignty. With the possible exception of Gierke's scheme, which draws heavily on German Romanticism, they are indebted to a climate of opinion for which the Puritans and lawyers are in part responsible.

The thought of the nonextremist pluralists falls roughly between the monism of John Austin and the thoroughgoing pluralism of Harold Laski. The chief formulator of this position is Charles H. McIlwain. The median theory clearly insists on the necessity of a ruling body in the state. Man's disorder and inevitable conflict with his fellows requires political authority in order to structure the nation and to prevent the disintegration of the national community. The leaders of this school prefer to call the governing body the "legal sovereign," however, rather than the political sovereign. Wherever sovereignty may be rooted in the state, it has no proper application beyond the domain of law; the sovereign power can use only those governmental procedures which the law of the land prescribes. Political power is based on right, and right is concretely defined in legal norms. All members of the school agree that sovereignty is essentially a "juristic" term.[7]

5. John N. Figgis, *Churches in the Modern State* (2d ed. London, Longmans, 1914), especially lect. 1, "A Free Church in a Free State." Mr. Figgis argues against the "lawyers" (typified for him by Hobbes, Austin, and Bismarck), who hold that the church is simply a part of the state.

6. Consult Gierke, *Natural Law,* which is a translation by Ernest Barker of five subsections in the 4th vol. of *Das deutsche Genossenschaftsrecht;* Maitland's introduction to Gierke, *Middle Age; The Collected Papers of Frederic William Maitland* (3 vols. Cambridge, The University Press, 1911), especially "A Historical Sketch of Liberty and Equality" and "Mr. Herbert Spencer's Theory of Society"; and Ernst Troeltsch, "The Ideas of Natural Law and Humanity in World Politics," in Gierke, *Natural Law, 1,* 201–22.

7. See Charles H. McIlwain, "Sovereignty Again," *Economica, 6,* No. 18 (Nov. 1926), and John Dickinson, "A Working Theory of Sovereignty," *Political Science Quarterly, 42,* No. 4 (Dec. 1927).

The median theory, which prescribes actual sovereignty yet limits it by law, is the modernized form of a concept of the state which goes back to the late sixteenth and early seventeenth centuries. Jean Bodin, whose *Republic* of 1576 had probably the first careful discussion of political sovereignty or *majestas*, stands near the beginning of the source. A curious figure of both medieval and modern times—similar to the Puritans and the lawyers—Bodin was among the first to understand the need for *potestas* in the proper functioning of the national state. Potestas always meant, however, *auctoritas*. Whatever power the sovereign possessed came from the authority which law conferred. Bodin is often remembered for the application of the term *legibus solutus* to the sovereign power. *Legibus tentus* was also part of his system. The supreme political body or person was restricted by natural law, divine law, the law of nations, customary law, and constitutional laws.[8] Freedom from the laws, legibus solutus, must always be balanced with an equally important aspect of sovereignty, namely, the acceptance of legal limitations, or subscription to legibus tentus.[9] Bodin held for de jure power, not merely de facto. His sovereign possessed lawful authority, not sheer might.[10]

A similar limitation of the sovereign prevailed among certain religious leaders of the late sixteenth century. Calvinist political thought did not possess the *Republic's* clear articulation of the concept of sovereignty, but at least the Huguenots and the Scottish reformers asserted the necessity of some form of political power. As with Bodin, all princes were again limited by law. John Knox and the author of *Vindiciae contra Tyrannos* held that God conferred all political authority and that his laws in the Bible, as well as civil laws, governed the exercise of this authority. The scriptural laws were especially binding on the sovereign. If a prince disregarded biblical norms, the radical step of revolution could be taken.

8. Bodin's use of natural law, among other things, made him suspect in the eyes of the Puritans and the lawyers. Consult George L. Mosse, "The Influence of Jean Bodin's *Republique* on English Political Thought," *Medievalia et Humanistica, 5* (July 1948). One Puritan, William Loe, decried in 1621 those who "study Bodin's *Commentaries*, Lipsius' *Politics*, and such quodlibets more than the Holy Scriptures," as quoted by Mosse, p. 77. Nonetheless, a translation of the *Republic* was made by Richard Knolles in 1606 and the work became widely known in England.

9. This is the judgment of Max A. Shepard, "Sovereignty at the Crossroads: A Study of Bodin," *Political Science Quarterly, 45*, No. 4 (Dec. 1930).

10. See McIlwain, "Sovereignty," pp. 253 ff.

The idea of sovereignty bound by laws found its most telling formulation for practical politics among the early seventeenth-century Puritans and common lawyers. They ascribed supremacy to Parliament, but they insisted that the authority of the House of Commons stand under divine sovereignty and fundamental law. The particular laws and the spirit of the laws given by the ultimate sources of men's obedience and loyalty determined the power of Parliament. The early seventeenth-century Puritans and lawyers helped significantly to create the climate of opinion which fostered the modern juristic concept of sovereignty.[11]

THE STUFF OF POLITICAL HISTORY

The political activity of the divines and the barristers has not been easy to uncover. Sermons, reports, tracts, pamphlets, speeches, and occasional treatises tell the unsystematic story of the conflicts between them and the first two Stuarts. The whole political history of the prewar period is found in a series of seemingly minor clashes between the crown and its opponents. If this period tells us anything about man's life in organized society it is that political history exists in the form of these frequently unconnected, sometimes inexplicable crises. It is not to be discovered in the majestic unfolding of political ideals, nor in the logical development of "the State" masquerading as an Hegelian march of God in the world. The specific interplay of

11. One possible conveyor of Puritan–common law thought to modern times is John Locke. The great justifier of the Revolution of 1688 is traditionally described as a propagator of a theory of rights, not of sovereignty. However, his discussion of the extent of legislative power in the second of the *Two Treatises on Civil Government* (London, Routledge, 1887), ch. 11, secs. 134–48, pp. 260 ff., displays some interest in the problem of sovereignty. The legislative body as *governmental* sovereign is supreme in the state; but it is a fiduciary body responsible to the people, which is the *political* sovereign. This is not a forerunner of a Montesquieu-like theory of checks and balances. It is an actual ascription of governmental power to one unit in the body politic, i.e., the legislature. But such power is limited: the legislature "is not arbitrary by being absolute" (*ibid.*, 2d treatise, sec. 139, p. 265). See also McIlwain, *High Court*, p. 130. The limitations on the governmental sovereign are certain fundamental principles of the British constitution which, in Locke's view, are best preserved and enforced by the people.

Any discussion of sovereignty in Locke, however, runs into the debate among scholars over whether Locke actually concerned himself with the problem. See a listing of positions in Wilfrid Harrison, "Texts in Political Theory," *Political Studies, 3,* No. 1 (Feb. 1955), 38, n. 1.

power and countervailing power at given times has determined the course of the body politic.[12]

Conflict is the key to the content of political history as well as to its form. Out of specific conflicts between the Puritans and lawyers and the Stuart kings came ideas on the nature of authority, the use of laws, the power of Parliament, and the role of institutions. These concepts evolved not because the divines and the lawyers were a priori political, but because their germane concerns became targets for Stuart absolutism. When the two groups were forced to define the role of the king, ascribe governmental supremacy to the House of Commons, and speak their mind on political authority, they used the only ideas they had. These were the guiding principles of their ecclesiastical and legal pursuits. Divine sovereignty, fundamental law, institutional independence, the meaning of laws, and the spirit of the laws were applied to the whole political struggle with the Stuart crown.

The ultimate significance of the Puritan–common law struggle with the king is that ideas developed in a context quite other than the political were brought to bear on politics. This is frequently the case in the life of the body politic. The meaning of political authority stands as a good example. The effort to define the power of the state has not been conducted in a vacuum; many groups in various conflicts throughout time have converged upon the problem and have added emphases drawn from their own activities and convictions. Gierke's concept of the "personality" of the state carries out this line of thought. Other "group persons" which are part of loosely organized society have contributed to the growth of the sovereign power and have left upon it the impress of their personality. Gierke even asks whether the ruling body has any personality other than that contributed by the outside group persons.[13]

Might it not be that the roots of political ideas are the intrinsic concerns and beliefs of particular groups who have been cast into

12. See Earl Latham, "The Group Basis of Politics: Notes for a Theory," *American Political Science Review, 46,* No. 2 (June 1952).

13. Consult Francis W. Coker, *Organismic Theories of the State. Nineteenth-Century Interpretations of the State as Organism or as Person,* New York, Longmans, 1910; John D. Lewis, *The Genossenschaft-Theory of Otto von Gierke,* Madison, Wis. [University of Wisconsin Press], 1935; and Sobei Mogi, *Otto von Gierke. His Political Teaching and Jurisprudence,* London, King, 1932. In his concept of the state as orgänism, Gierke wrestles with the problem of the one and the many: the state has its own real being, yet its life is seen only in the purposes and functions of its organs, or the individuals and associations of society.

the political arena? If so, a study of these groups and their conflicts is perhaps more important for the student of politics than the study of the great political philosophers who often are outside the arena. Thucydides' history of the Peloponnesian Wars is at least as important for the understanding of Greek political history as Plato's *Republic* and *Laws*. So it is with the seventeenth century in England, where an understanding of political development must be sought in the activities of the Puritans, the lawyers, and their fellow strugglers as much as in the formal thought of Hobbes, Filmer, Halifax, and Locke. The stuff of political history comes in the main from the ideas of essentially nonpolitical groups who contend with the powers that be.

A final word must be said about the struggle of the Puritans and common lawyers with the crown. Our subjects held a firm conviction about the nature of political life. They conceived divine sovereignty and fundamental law to be the ultimate authorities under which all human activity was conducted. But they were more than idealistic preachers and lofty jurists. They warred against the king on the basis of particulars—the specific laws of the Bible and the common law tradition, which were the instruments and the manifestations of the ultimate rule of God and fundamental law. The relationship of the universal to the particular in their political thought is of crucial significance. The divines and the barristers never considered individual laws to be the absolute authorities. Only God and fundamental law belonged in this category. Despite the biblicism of the Puritans and the intense legalism of the lawyers, both groups insisted, as we have seen, on the flexibility of particular laws. The scattered, individual norms constantly needed interpretation and clarification in order to produce the good ordering of society. The use of the old laws and the refashioning of them to meet new situations was always done in response to divine sovereignty and fundamental law. The particular authority was forever relative to the universal.

Many others have insisted on a similar relationship of the particular to the universal in political life. Thomas Paine once described a constitution as "antecedent." Although the apologist for the American Revolution used the term "antecedent" primarily in a chronological sense, meaning that a constitution must be drawn up before a government could be formed, the word has a wider application of which Paine himself was aware. There were principles of the first order in political life which later elaborations only maintained and made explicit. Paine saw the American constitution as a response to such antecedent principles as the limitation of governmental authority and the preservation of individual rights.[14] Many contemporary British authorities speak of English political activity as conformity to, if not response to, the "constitutional principles" of the land. Several American writers cite the balance between unity and diversity as the universal to which the particulars of political life must respond.

The Puritans and the lawyers were acutely responsive. Their legalism, their understanding of institutional life, and all other aspects of their political activity were conceived in the form of a response to divine sovereignty and fundamental law. Personally as well as politically they were aware of the profound relationship of the particular to the universal, the relative to the absolute. Their joint struggle against the crown was an attempt to structure society in accord with the ultimate principles which demanded the supreme loyalty and obedience of all men.

There were differences between the early seventeenth-century divines and barristers, inasmuch as their professions and basic convictions were distinct. Both groups, however, had much the same grasp on the essentials of political life. They discerned similar ongoing rules in the affairs of this world. All activity was to be conducted under divine sovereignty and fundamental law and by them it was to be judged. The Puritans and the lawyers bequeathed a conception of authority which helped to shape the course of modern political history.

14. McIlwain, *Constitutionalism*, pp. 8 ff.

KEY TO BIBLIOGRAPHY

BIBLIOGRAPHY

I. Bibliographical Aids.

British Tracts, Chronology File, [1481]–1800, New Haven,
Sterling Library, Yale University. The materials are classified
by author or title under date of publication.

*Calendar of State Papers and Manuscripts, Relating to English
Affairs, Existing in the Archives and Collections of Venice, and
in Other Libraries of Northern Italy.* 38 vols. (1202–1675),
London, Longmans and His Majesty's Stationery Office, 1864–
1947. Although the listings here and in the following work are
unobtainable in this country (save on occasional microfilm),
the complete descriptions and summaries of the papers are
useful.

*Calendar of State Papers, Domestic Series . . . Preserved in
. . . Her Majesty's Public Record Office.* 15 vols. (1547–
1640). London, Longmans, 1856–80.

Godfrey Davies, *Bibliography of British History, Stuart Period,
1603–1714.* Oxford, Clarendon, 1928. An authority on all aspects of the Stuart age.

Charles R. Gillett, ed., *Catalogue of the McAlpin Collection of
British History and Theology.* 5 vols. (1501–1700), New
York, Plimpton, 1927–30. A useful guide to a leading collec-
tion in this country, located at Union Theological Seminary,
New York City.

M. S. Giuseppi, *A Guide to the Manuscripts Preserved in the
Public Record Office.* 2 vols. London, His Majesty's Stationery Office, 1923–24. Helpful description, commentary, and
listings.

Hubert Hall, ed., *List and Index of the Publications of the Royal
Historical Society 1871–1924 and of the Camden Society
1840–1897.* London, Offices of the Society, 1925. An excellent

reference, containing extensive indices. In 1897 the Camden Society was amalgamated with the Royal Historical Society and the Camden series of publications transferred to the new organization.

The Harleian Miscellany, a Collection of Scarce, Curious, and Entertaining Pamphlets and Tracts, as well in Manuscript as in Print Selected from the Library of Edward Harley, Second Earl of Oxford [1689–1741]. 10 vols. Annotations by William Oldys and Thomas Park. London, White, Murray, and Harding, 1808–13. At the end of Vol. *10*, pp. 357 ff., are located helpful catalogues and an index (author, title, and subject).

William Haller, *The Rise of Puritanism. Or, the Way to the New Jerusalem as Set Forth in Pulpit and Press from Thomas Cartwright to John Lilburne and John Milton, 1570–1643.* New York, Columbia University Press, 1938. The Bibliographical Notes, pp. 405–40, are extensive.

Marshall M. Knappen, *Tudor Puritanism. A Chapter in the History of Idealism.* Chicago, University of Chicago Press, 1939. "The Historiography of Puritanism," App. III, pp. 494–518, is a helpful survey of works which tell the story of Puritanism. Also contains a Select Bibliography, pp. 521–31.

John G. Nichols, *A Descriptive Catalogue of the First Series of the Works of the Camden Society.* 2d ed. Westminster, Nichols, 1872. The careful descriptions in this book and in the following provide a good survey of the society's work, some of which is important for the early 17th century.

———, *A Descriptive Catalogue of the Works of the Camden Society.* Westminster, Nichols, 1862.

Wallace Notestein and Frances H. Relf, eds., *Commons Debates for 1629 Critically Edited, and an Introduction Dealing with Parliamentary Sources for the Early Stuarts.* Minneapolis, University of Minnesota, 1921. The excellent introduction helps to guide an inquirer through both the sources and the problems of parliamentary research in the early 17th century.

Wallace Notestein, *The English People on the Eve of Colonization, 1603–1630.* New York, Harper, 1954. Contains a first-rate bibliographical essay, pp. 267–79.

Alfred W. Pollard and G. R. Redgrave, et al., *A Short-Title Catalogue of Books Printed in England, Scotland, and Ireland and of English Books Printed Abroad, 1475–1640.* London, The Bibliographical Society, 1926. An invaluable check-list.

[Somers Tracts], *A Collection of Scarce and Valuable Tracts, on the Most Interesting and Entertaining Subjects. But Chiefly such as Relate to the History and Constitution of These Kingdoms. Selected from an Infinite Number . . . Particularly that of the Late Lord Somers* [1651–1716], ed. Walter Scott. 13 vols. 2d ed. London, Cadell, 1809–15. The volumes are arranged chronologically according to the reigns of English monarchs. The tracts of each reign are placed under four classifications; an index concludes each volume.

Eleanor S. Upton and George P. Winship, Jr., *Guide to Sources of English History from 1603 to 1660 in Reports of the Royal Commission on Historical Manuscripts.* Washington, D.C., Scarecrow, 1952. Contains excellent indices and descriptions. The commission was appointed in 1869 to examine and catalogue private collections of MSS; its reports have been appearing since 1870.

Eleanor S. Upton, "A Guide to Sources of Seventeenth-Century English History in Selected Reports of the Royal Commission on Historical Manuscripts," *Abstracts of Theses. Humanistic Series* (University of Chicago), *8*, 1929–30.

Donald G. Wing, *Short-Title Catalogues of Books Printed in England, Scotland, Ireland, Wales, and British America and of English Books Printed in Other Countries, 1641–1700.* New York, The Index Society, 1945. Indispensable.

II. Early 17th-Century Materials.

A. manuscripts.

Anon., "The Lawes of England." [London, 1624–29.] In the Ellesmere Manuscript Collection, Huntington Library, San Marino, Calif. This work illustrates better than any other the favorable Puritan attitude toward the common law of England.

Anon., "Policies in Parliament." [London, early 1600's.] In the Stowe MSS at the British Museum. The fragments contain a discussion of parliamentary rules and procedures, probably composed during Jacobean times.

Francis Tate, "A Discourse Importing the Assembly of a Parliament . . ." [London], Elizabeth's reign. A common lawyer of the Middle Temple discusses the need for a parliament.

B. RELIGIOUS WORKS.

1. *Puritan.*

a. Anon.

Certaine Considerations Drawne from the Canons of the Last Sinod. And Other the King's Ecclesiasticall and Statute Law . . . for not Subscription, for the not Exact Use of the Order and Forme of the Booke of Common Prayer . . . or for the not Precise Practice of the Rites . . . [London], 1605. This and the following work are good examples of the violent Puritan reaction to the 1604 canons.

Certaine Demandes with Their Grounds. Drawne out of Holy Writ, and Propounded "in Foro Conscientiae" by Some Religious Gentlemen unto the Reverend Fathers, Richard [Bancroft] *Archbishop of Canterbury . . .* London, 1605.

A. Ar., *The Practise of Princes.* [Amsterdam], 1630. The standards of acceptable kingly rule are set forth.

b. Richard Baxter.

A Christian Directory. Or a Summ of Practical Theologie, and Cases of Conscience. London, 1673. A classic summary of Puritan virtue written by a post-1630 divine.

c. Paul Bayne[s].

Briefe Directions unto a Godly Life . . . London, 1637.
Christian Letters of Mr. Paul Bayne. London, 1628.
A Commentarie upon the First and Second Chapters of Saint Paul to the Colossians . . . together with Divers Places of Scripture Briefly Explained. London, 1634. This and the following commentary comprise Baynes' magnum opus.

An Entire Commentary upon the Whole Epistle of St. Paul to the Ephesians . . . Edinburgh, Nichol, 1866. Indispensable for the early 17th-century Puritan conception of law.

d. William Bradshaw.

Humble Motives for Association to Maintaine Religion Established . . . [London], 1601. Illustrates Puritan support of the established church.

A Myld and Iust Defense of Certeyne Arguments, at the Last Session of Parliament Directed to that Most Honorable High Court, in Behalfe of the Ministers Suspended . . . [London], 1606.

Several Treatises of Worship & Ceremonies. Cambridge, 1660. A collection of Bradshaw's major works. Most important for this study are: *English Puritanisme*, on the essentials of the early 17th-century Puritanism; *Twelve General Arguments, Proving the Ceremonies Unlawful;* and *A Protestation of the King's Supremacy*, on the powers of the governor of the church.

e. William Brewster, ed.

An Abridgement of that Booke which the Ministers of Lincolne Diocese Delivered to His Maiestie. . . . an Apologie for Themselves . . . that Refuse the Subscription and Conformitie. [Leyden], 1617.

f. Richard Byfield.

The Power of the Christ of God . . . London, 1641. This and the following work are mid-century statements that demonstrate, among other things, Presbyterian theocratic aims.

A Short Treatise Describing the True Church of Christ . . . London, 1653.

g. Nathanael Carpenter.

Achitophel. Or, the Picture of a Wicked Politican. [London], 1629.

h. Daniel Featley.

A Parallel. Of New-Old Pelagiarminian Error . . . London, 1626. Both this and the following work are good examples of the Puritan attack on theological Arminianism.

Pelagius Redivius. Or Pelagius Raked Out of the Ashes by Arminius and His Schollers. London, 1626.

i. Thomas Gataker.

An Anniversarie Memoriall of Englands Delivery from the Spanish Invasion . . . London, 1626.

An Answer to Mr. George Walker's Vindication . . . *wherein He Chargeth* . . . *Mr. Gataker with Socinianism* . . . London, 1642. A defense of Calvinist orthodoxy.

The Christian Man's Care. A Sermon on Mathh. 6:33 . . . London, 1637. A moving sermon preached on "Seek ye first the kingdom of God."

David's Instructor . . . London, 1620.

David's Remembrancer. A Meditation on Psalme 13.1 . . . London, 1637. A devotional sermon preached to members of the legal profession at Serjeants Inn.

A Discours Apologetical . . . London, 1654. An attack on an astrologist, emphasizing that God's will is known in the Bible not in the stars.

God's Eye on His Israel . . . London, 1645. A discussion of the rigid moral life required of the elect.

God's Parley with Princes . . . *Two Sermons upon the 3 Last Verses of the 82. Psalme* . . . London, 1620. On the limitations of kingly rule. Both sermons were preached at Serjeants Inn and contain admonitions to judges as well as princes.

Iacobs Thankfulnesse to God . . . London, 1624.

The Ioy of the Iust . . . London, 1623. A description of the Puritan "good life."

Noah. His Obedience the Ground of It . . . *A Meditation on Hebrewes 11.7. Delivered in a Sermon at Lincolnes-Inne.* London, 1637.

Opera Critica. 2 vols. Trajecti ad Rhenum, 1697–98. A collection of Gataker's works in literary criticism. The most important part for this study is Gataker's edition of Marcus Aurelius' *De Rebus Suis, sive de Eis Qae ad Se Pertinere Censebat, Libri XII* (*Meditations* or *Conversations with Himself*). In a commentary on this work Gataker heartily approves the Stoic concept of divine sovereignty.

et al., *A Serious and Faithfull Representation of the Judgements of Ministers of the Gospell* . . . *to the*

Generall and His Councell of Warre. London, 1649. A post-1630 work in which Gataker joined with other Puritans to urge restraint on the New Model Army.

Shadowes without Substance . . . London, 1646. An attack on John Saltmarsh, Puritan liberal and mystic.

A Sparke toward the Kindling of Sorrow for Sion. A Meditation on Amos 6:6 . . . *Preached at Serjeants Inne* . . . London, 1621.

The Spirituall Watch. Or Christs Generall Watch-Word . . . London, 1622. A good example of Puritan eschatology.

True Contentment in the Gaine of Godlines . . . London, 1620.

j. John Goodwin.

The Obstructours of Justice. Or a Defense of the Honourable Sentence Passed upon the Late King, by the High Court of Justice. London, 1649. A famous mid-century "liberal" Puritan defends the execution of the king and incurs the wrath of orthodox Puritans.

k. William Gouge.

The Workes . . . *in Two Volumes. The First, Domesticall Duties. The Second, the Whole Armour of God.* London, 1627. Contains many tracts on Puritan morality. Two on the believer's fight with the devil are especially revealing: *Of Arming a Christian Soldier* and *Of the Meanes to Use Spirituall Armour Aright.*

The Saint's Sacrifice. Or, a Commentary on the CXVI Psalme. . . . London, 1632.

l. Richard Holdsworth.

Praelectiones Theologicae, ed. Richard Pearson. London, 1661. Contains "Oratio . . . in Vesperiis Comitiorum, apud Cantabrigienses . . ." Holdsworth's moving July 1641 commencement address.

A Sermon Preached in St. Maries in Cambridge. Upon . . . the Day of His Majesties Happy Inauguration. Cambridge, 1642.

The Valley of Vision. Or, A Clear Sight of Sundry

Sacred Truths Delivered in Twenty-One Sermons.
London, 1651. The authenticity of all the sermons is
in question.

m. John Preston.

*The Breast-Plate of Faith and Love . . . Expressed in
Good Works . . .* London, 1634. An important
treatise (18 sermons) on the Puritan concept of
works.

The Deformed Forme of a Formall Profession . . .
Edinburgh, 1634. A sermon on godliness.

Foure Godly and Learned Treatises . . . 3d ed. London, 1633. Sermons chiefly on self-denial. Three were
preached at Lincoln's Inn.

*Life Eternall. Or, a Treatise of the Knowledge of the
Divine Essence and Attributes . . .* 3d ed. London,
1633. Thirteen of the 18 sermons were preached on
the "I am that I am" text of Exodus 3:13–15.

The New Covenant. Or the Saints' Portion . . . 4th ed.
London, 1630. Contains Preston's so-called "covenant" theology.

*The Position of John Preston . . . concerning the
Irresistibleness of Converting Grace.* London, 1654.

*Remaines of that Reverend and Learned Divine, John
Preston . . .* 2d ed. London, 1637.

*The Saints Daily Exercise. A Treatise Unfolding the
Whole Dutie of Prayer . . .* 4th ed. London, 1630.

The Saints Qualification . . . London, 1633. Sermons
on Christian "humiliation" and sanctification.

*A Sermon Preached at a Generall Fast before the
Commons-House of Parliament. The Second of Iuly,
1625.* London, 1633.

*Sermons Preached before His Maiestie. And upon Other
Speciall Occasions.* London, 1633.

*Two Godly and Learned Treatises upon Mortification
and Humiliation.* 3d ed. London, 1634.

n. William Prynne.

*Anti-Arminianisme. Or, the Church of Englands Old
Antithesis to New Arminianisme.* 2d ed. London, 1630.
An example of the Puritan attack on Anglican "lib-
eral" theology.

A Brief Survay and Censure of Mr. Cozens His Couzen-ing Devotions . . . London, 1628. A harsh attack on John Cosin and his "popish" writings.

Canterburies Doom. Or the . . . *History of the* . . . *Tryall* . . . *of William Laud* . . . London, 1646.

God, No Impostor, nor Deluder . . . London, 1629. Sharp criticism of free will and universal divine grace. The nine Articles of Lambeth (Nov. 1595) are included in this edition, pp. 35–7.

Healthes: Sicknesse. Or, a Compendious and Brief Discourse; Proving the Drinking, and Pledging of Healthes, to be Sinfull . . . London, 1628.

The Perpetuitie of a Regenerate Mans Estate. London, 1627. Once elected, a saint cannot totally fall from grace.

The Unlovelinesse of Love-Lockes . . . London, 1628.

o. John Rainolds, or Reignolds.

The Iudgement of Doctor Reignolds concerning Episcopacy, whether It Be God's Ordinance . . . London, 1641. An Elizabethan Presbyterian attacks the *ius divinum* claim supposedly put forth by Archbishop Bancroft.

p. John Saltmarsh.

Reasons for Unitie, Peace, and Love. With an Answer . . . *to a Book of Mr. Gataker* . . . London, 1646. A mid-century Puritan mystic defends his conception of universal grace.

q. Thomas Scott, or Scot.

The Workes . . . Utrick (Utrecht), 1624. A complete copy of this unique work exists in the Houghton Library of Harvard University. Nearly all the tracts are important for an understanding of early 17th-century Puritanism. Significant for this study are: *Vox Regis; The High-Waies of God and the King. Wherein All Men Ought to Walke in Holinese Here to Happiness Hereafter;* and *The Proiector. Teaching a Direct, Sure, and Ready Way to Restore the Decayes of the Church and State.*

r. Richard Sibbes, or Sibs.

The Complete Workes . . . , ed. Alexander B. Grosart. 7 vols. Edinburgh, Nichol, 1862–64. The contents are primarily sermons preached by the foremost devotional preacher of the age. Sibbes' long work *The Bruised Reed and Smoking Flax* deserves careful study for the meaning of Puritan piety.

s. Anthony Wotton.

A Dangerous Plot Discovered . . . London, 1626. This and the following work are attacks on Richard Montagu the Anglican bishop.

t. John Yates.

Ibis ad Caesarem. Or a Submissive Appearance before Caesar; in Answer to Mr. Mountagues Appeale, in the Points of Arminianisme and Popery, Maintained by Him . . . London, 1626.

u. Later collections and editions.

William Haller, ed., *Tracts on Liberty in the Puritan Revolution, 1638–1647.* 3 vols. New York, Columbia University Press, 1934. This work relates to the post-1630 period—indispensable for tracing the development of Puritanism in the 17th century.

William Haller and Godfrey Davies, eds., *The Leveller Tracts, 1647–1653.* New York, Columbia University Press, 1944.

Albert Peel and Leland H. Carlson, eds., *The Writings of Robert Harrison and Robert Browne.* London, Allen and Unwin, 1953. Part of a projected collection of Elizabethan nonconformist texts.

Arthur S. P. Woodhouse, *Puritanism and Liberty, Being the Army Debates (1647–9) from the Clarke Manuscripts with Supplementary Documents.* 2d ed. Chicago, University of Chicago Press, 1951. Prefaced by a first-rate introduction.

2. *Anglican.*

a. George Abbot.

An Exposition upon the Prophet Jonah. Contained in

Certaine Sermons . . . London, 1600. Detailed exe-
gesis, very similar to Puritan biblical sermons.
*Cheap-Side Crosse Censured and Condemned by a Letter
Sent from the Vicechancellour and Other Learned
Men . . . of Oxford . . . Concerning the Said
Crosse, in the Yeere 1600* . . . London, 1641. A
Puritan-like denunciation of an image by the future
archbishop of Canterbury.
*A Treatise of the Perpetuall Visibilitie, and Succession
of the True Church in All Ages.* London, 1624.

b. Lancelot Andrewes.
Sermons [etc.], in *Library of Anglo-Catholic Theology.*
Vols. *1–11.* Oxford, Parker, 1841–54.

c. Richard Bancroft.
Dangerous Positions and Proceedings . . . *within This
Iland of Britaine.* London, 1640.
*A Sermon Preached at Paules Crosse the 9. of Februarie
. . . Anno. 1588.* London, 1588. Bancroft declares
the *ius divinum* of episcopacy, or so it appeared to
Puritan interpreters.
A Survey of the Pretended Holy Discipline . . . Lon-
don, 1593.
Tracts Ascribed to Richard Bancroft, ed. Albert Peel.
Cambridge, The University Press, 1953.

d. John Cosin.
The Works . . . in *Library of Anglo-Catholic Theology.* Vols. 34–8. Oxford, Parker, 1843–55. High Anglicanism is prevalent in these works which deal with
doctrine, church history, and ritual. The Puritans
especially attacked *A Collection of Private Devotions
. . . Called the Hours of Prayer*, London, 1627.

e. John Donne.
LXXX Sermons . . . London, 1640.
Fifty Sermons . . . *The Second Volume.* London, 1644.
Paradoxes, Problems, Essayes, Characters . . . *Epi-
grams.* London, 1652.
Poems, &c. . . . *with Elegies on the Author's Death
. . .* London, 1669.
XXVI Sermons . . . *The Third Volume.* London, 1660.

f. Richard Hooker.

The Works of That Learned and Judicious Divine, Mr. Richard Hooker. With an Account of His Life and Death, by Isaac Walton, ed. John Keble. 3 vols. 3d ed. Oxford, The University Press, 1845. Hooker's magnum opus is *Of the Laws of Ecclesiastical Polity.* The eight books of the work (the authenticity of some sections is in question) antedate the period of this study. Nonetheless, Hooker's reasoned arguments from the *Laws* continue to sound throughout the Jacobean age. Some of the books were not published until after the author's death in 1600.

g. William Laud.

The Works . . . , in *Library of Anglo-Catholic Theology.* Vols. *56–64.* Oxford, Parker, 1847–60.

h. Richard Montagu.

Appello Caesarem . . . London, 1625. Montagu appeals to the crown for protection in his propagation of the Arminian doctrine.

A Gagg for the New Gospell? No: A New Gagg for an Old Goose . . . London, 1624. Written against the Roman Catholic Matthew Kellison. The work drew Puritan fire for its supposed defense and definition of Protestantism.

Immediate Addresse unto God Alone . . . London, 1624. First delivered in a sermon before the king.

i. James Ussher.

The Whole Works . . . with a Life of the Author, and an Account of His Writings, by Charles Richard Elrington . . . 17 vols. Dublin, Hodges, 1864. Ussher, archbishop of Armagh and primate of Ireland, was the most Puritan of the Anglican hierarchy in regard to theology, morals, and church polity.

C. LEGAL WORKS.

Francis Bacon, *The Elements of the Common Lawes of England, Branched into a Double Tract. The One Containing a Collection of Some Principall Rules and Maximes . . . the Other the Use of the Common Law . . .* London, 1639.

Edward Coke, *The . . . Institutes of the Laws of England.*
London, 1797. Indispensable for an understanding of the
common law tradition. The work is divided into four Parts.
Pts. 2 and 4 ("Containing the Exposition of Many Ancient,
and Other Statutes . . ." and "Concerning the Jurisdiction of Courts . . .") are crucial for this study.

———, *The Reports of Sir Edward Coke, Knight. In Thirteen Parts* [1572–1616], ed. J. H. Thomas and J. F.
Fraser. 6 vols. London, Butterworth, 1826. The authoritative reports of the period.

John Cowell, *The Institutes of the Lawes of England, Di-
gested into the Method of the Civill or Imperiall Institutions* . . . , trans. W. G. London, 1651. This and the following account of England's laws were written by a civil
law sympathizer of royalist persuasion.

———, *The Interpreter. Or Booke Containing the Significa-
tion of Words. Wherein Is Set Foorth the True Meaning of
All, or the Most Part . . . as Are Mentioned in the Law
Writers, or Statutes . . .* London, 1607.

John Doddridge, *The English Lawyer Describing a Method
for the Managing of the Laws of This Land and Expressing the Best Qualities Requisite in the Student, Practizer,
Judges and Fathers of the Same.* London, 1631. An account by a student of both law and theology.

———, *The Lawyer's Light. Or, a Due Direction for the
Study of the Law; for Methode, Choyce of Bookes Mod-
erne, Selection of Authours of More Antiquitie, Application of Either, Accomodation of Divers Other Usefull
Requisits . . .* London, 1629.

William Dugdale, *Origines Juridiciales. Or, Historical Memorials of the English Laws, Courts of Justice . . . Innes
of Court and Chancery.* 2d ed. London, 1671.

Henry Finch, *A Description of the Common Laws of England, According to the Rules of Art, Compared with the
Prerogatives of the King.* London [1759]. A royalist sympathizer describes the law of the land. The original law
French edition appeared in 1613.

Nicholas Fuller, *The Argument of Nicholas Fuller . . . in
the Case of Tho. Lad, and Rich. Mansell His Clients.
Wherein It Is Plainly Proved, that the Ecclesiasticall Commissioners Have No Power by Their Commission, to Im-*

prison, or to Fine Any of His Majesties Subjects, or to Put Them to the Ex Officio. London, 1641. The tract was first published in 1607.

[Andrew Horn], *The Mirror of Justices,* ed. William J. Whittaker, intro. Frederic W. Maitland. Publications of the Selden Society, London, Quaritch, 1895. The "Mirrour," supposedly written by Horn (d. ca. 1328), was often cited by Coke in the *Institutes,* 2d Pt.

Jenkensius Redivivus. Or, the Works of That Grave, Learned, Truly-Loyal, and Courageous Judge [David] *Jenkins whilst a Prisoner in the Tower . . . by Command of the Rebellious Long-Parliament.* London, 1681. The royalist position on the law made clear.

[James Morice], *A Briefe Treatise of Oathes Exacted by Ordinaries and Ecclesiasticall Judges, to Answere Generallie to All such Articles or Interrogatories, as Pleaseth them to Propound. And of their Forced and Constrained Oathes ex Officio, wherein Is Proved that the Same Are Unlawful.* [Middelburg, 1590.] This attack on the oath ex officio was answered by Richard Cosin who upheld the position of the crown and the high church party.

William Noye, *A Treatise of the Principall Grounds and Maximes of the Lavves of This Kingdome.* London, 1642. A helpful work by the famous reporter of Lincoln's Inn.

John Selden, *Of the Judicature of Parliaments, A Posthumous Treatise. Wherein the Controversies and Precedents Belonging to that Title, Are Methodically Handled.* London, n. d.

————, *An Historical and Political Discourse of the Laws and Government of England, from the First Times to the End of the Reign of Queen Elizabeth . . . ,* ed. Nathaniel Bacon. 5th ed. London, 1760.

————, *Table-Talk. Being the Discourses of John Selden, Esq.; or His Sense of Various Matters of Weight and High Consequence; Relating Especially to Religion and State.* 2d ed. London, 1696.

D. BIOGRAPHIES.

Simeon Ashe, *Gray Hayres Crowned with Grace. A Sermon Preached . . . Aug. 1. 1654. At the Funerall of . . .*

Thomas Gataker . . . together with His . . . Life . . .
London, 1655. The best early 17th-century source on
Gataker.

*The Letters and the Life of Francis Bacon including All His
Occasional Works* . . . , ed. James Spedding. 7 vols. London, Longmans, 1861–74.

Thomas Ball, *The Life of the Renowed Doctor Preston . . .*
Oxford, Parker, 1885 (1st ed. 1628). One Puritan lavishly
praises another.

Richard Baxter, *Reliquiae Baxterianae, or, Mr. Richard
Baxter's Narrative of the Most Memorable Passages of
His Life and Times.* London, 1696. A valuable source for
17-century Puritanism.

Samuel Clarke, *A Collection of the Lives of Ten Eminent Divines.* London, 1662. Clarke includes John Cotton, William Gouge, Thomas Gataker, and James Ussher in his
biographical survey.

———, *The Lives of Sundry Eminent Persons in This Later
Age. In Two Parts. I. Of Divines. II. Of Nobility and
Gentry of Both Sexes . . .* London, 1683.

Simonds D'Ewes, *The Autobiography and Correspondence* . . . , ed. James O. Halliwell. 2 vols. London, Bentley, 1845. An important work by a man who was an ardent
lay Puritan, a common lawyer, and a parliamentarian.
The book gives an excellent picture of the early 1600's.
D'Ewes lived 1602–50.

Thomas Fuller, *The Church History of Britain. From the
Birth of Jesus Christ Until the Year 1648 . . .* , ed. J. S.
Brewer. 6 vols. Oxford, The University Press, 1845.

———, *The History of the Worthies of England*, ed. P.
Austin Nuttall. 3 vols. London, Tegg, 1840. Fuller de-
scribes breezily William Gouge, Richard Sibbes, John
Preston, Edward Coke, Simonds D'Ewes, and William
Prynne, and many others.

E. PARLIAMENTARY RECORDS AND COLLECTIONS.

William Cobbett, ed., *Cobbett's Parliamentary History of
England. From the Norman Conquest, in 1066, to the Year,
1803.* 36 vols. London, Longmans, 1806–20. An inaccurate
selection from and summary of earlier sources. Vol. *1*
covers 1066–1625, and *2* 1625–42.

Thomas Crew, ed., *The Proceedings and Debates of the House of Commons in the Sessions of Parliament, Begun the Twentieth of January, 1628, and Ended by the Dissolution the Tenth of March Following* . . . London, 1707. A generally reliable edition of parliamentary records.

Thomas Fuller, ed., *The Soveraign's Prerogative and the Subject's Priviledge.* London, 1658. Various material from the two sessions of Charles' important third Parliament, 1628–29. Parliament did not meet again until 1640.

Journals of the House of Commons. [London], 1803. This "official" record of proceedings is fragmentary and inaccurate. Vol. *1* covers 1547–1628, and *2* the period just before the outbreak of hostilities.

Journals of the House of Lords. n.p., n.d. Fragmentary like the above. Vol. *3* covers 1620–28.

Wallace Notestein, Frances H. Relf, Hartley Simpson, eds., *Commons Debates, 1621.* 7 vols. New Haven, Yale University Press, 1935. A classic edition of parliamentary records. All sources for this crucial Parliament are covered.

Wallace Notestein and Frances H. Relf, eds., *Commons Debates for 1629, Critically Edited, and an Introduction Dealing with Parliamentary Sources for the Early Stuarts.* Minneapolis, University of Minnesota, 1921. Indispensable.

The Parliamentary or Constitutional History of England. From the Earliest Times to the Restoration of King Charles II. 24 vols. 2d ed. London, 1762–63. A clumsy collection of sources. Vols. *5–8* cover 1603–40; the last volume contains an index.

David Harris Willson, ed. and intro., *The Parliamentary Diary of Robert Bowyer, 1606–1607.* Minneapolis, University of Minnesota Press, 1931.

F. OTHER POLITICAL, LEGAL, AND ECCLESIASTICAL DOCUMENTS.

The Bible. That Is, the Holy Scriptures Conteined in the Old and New Testament. Translated according to the Ebrew and Greeke . . . with Most Profitable Annotations upon All Hard Places and Other Things of Great Importance. London, Barker, 1608. One of the many English translations of the Genevan Bible which was the household Bible of Puritanism in the late 16th and early 17th centuries.

Edward Cardwell, ed., *A History of Conferences and Other Proceedings Connected with the Revision of the Book of Common Prayer. From the Year 1558 to the Year 1690* . . . 3d ed. Oxford, The University Press, 1849. A dependable collection and commentary.

———, ed., *Synodalia. A Collection of Articles of Religion, Canons, and Proceedings of Convocations in the Province of Canterbury, from the Year 1547 to the Year 1717.* 2 vols. Oxford, The University Press, 1842. Invaluable for ecclesiastical research.

The Charge of the Commons of England, against Charls Stuart, King of England, of High Treason, and other High Crimes, Exhibited to the High Court of Justice. London, 1648. The charge read to Charles by Solicitor General John Cook displays the political radicalism of the mid-century.

William Cobbett [or Thomas B. Howell], ed., *A Complete Collection of State Trials . . . from the Earliest Period to the Year 1783* . . . 21 vols. London, Longmans, 1816–26. A necessary reference work, although inaccurate in many entries as later scholarship has shown. Vols. *2* and *3* apply to this study.

The Convocation Book of MDCVI. Commonly Called Bishop Overall's Convocation Book . . . Oxford, Parker, 1844. A helpful collection of the 1606 proceedings in convocation.

Charles H. Firth, ed. and intro., *Stuart Tracts, 1603–1693.* Westminster, Constable, 1903. Highly selective.

Charles W. Foster, ed. and intro., *The State of the Church in the Reigns of Elizabeth and James I as Illustrated by Documents Relating to the Diocese of Lincoln.* [Lincoln], Lincoln Record Society, 1926.

Samuel R. Gardiner, ed., *The Constitutional Documents of the Puritan Revolution 1625–1660* . . . 3d ed. Oxford, Clarendon Press, 1906. An indispensable one-volume work.

———, ed., *Documents Relating to the Proceedings against William Prynne, in 1634 and 1637* . . . [Westminster], Camden Society, 1877.

Charles H. McIlwain, ed. and intro., *The Political Works of*

James I. Reprinted from the Edition of 1616. Cambridge, Harvard University Press, 1918. A first-rate collection and introductory essay.

A Perfect Narrative of the whole Proceedings of the High Court of Iustice in the Tryal of the King in Westminster Hall . . . with the Several Speeches of the King, Lord President, and Solicitor General. London, 1649.

George W. Prothero, ed., *Select Statutes and Other Constitutional Documents Illustrative of the Reigns of Elizabeth and James I . . .* Oxford, Clarendon Press, 1894. A useful one-volume collection.

John Rushworth, ed., *Historical Collections. Of Private Passages of State, Weighty Matters in Law, Remarkable Proceedings in . . . Parliaments . . .* 7 vols. 4 pts. London, 1659–1701. Materials not readily found elsewhere are located easily in this generally dependable collection.

Joseph R. Tanner, *Constitutional Documents of the Reign of James I, A. D. 1603–1625. With an Historical Commentary.* Cambridge, The University Press, 1930. Both editing and commentary in this and the following work are excellent.

————, *Tudor Constitutional Documents, A. D. 1485–1603. With an Historical Commentary.* 2d ed. Cambridge, The University Press, 1930.

III. LATER STUDIES.

A. UNPUBLISHED PH.D. DISSERTATIONS.

Waldo Beach, "The Meaning and Authority of Conscience in Protestant Thought of Seventeenth-Century England." Yale, 1944.

Mark H. Curtis, "Oxford and Cambridge in Transition. An Essay on Changing Relationships between the English Universities and English Society, 1558–1642." Yale, 1953. A significant re-evaluation of the universities, with special attention to undergraduate education.

Charles S. McCoy, "The Covenant Theology of Johannes Cocceius." Yale, 1956.

Archibald S. Foord, "The Development of the Parliamentary Opposition. Chapters in the History of 'His Majesty's

Loyal Opposition.' " Yale, 1942. An excellent study of the
opposition in the unreformed Parliaments, 1714–1830.

William W. McKee, "The Idea of Covenant in Early English
Puritanism, 1580–1643." Yale, 1948. Helpful biographies
and classifications of English and some American Puritans.

Lowell H. Zuck, "Anabaptist Revolution through the Covenant in Sixteenth-Century Continental Protestantism."
Yale, 1954.

B. ENGLISH HISTORICAL STUDIES (SOCIAL, POLITICAL,
ECCLESIASTICAL).

George B. Adams, *The Origin of the English Constitution.*
New Haven, Yale University Press, 1912.

John W. Allen, *English Political Thought, 1603–1660.* 2
vols. London, Methuen, 1938.

John B. Black, *The Reign of Elizabeth, 1558–1603.* Oxford,
Clarendon Press, 1936.

Stanley B. Chrimes, *English Constitutional History.* London, Oxford University Press, 1947.

————, *English Constitutional Ideas in the Fifteenth Century.* Cambridge, The University Press, 1936.

Godfrey Davies, *The Early Stuarts, 1603–1660.* Oxford,
Clarendon Press, 1937.

Albert V. Dicey, *Introduction to the Study of the Law of the
Constitution,* ed. and intro. E. C. S. Wade. 9th ed. London,
Macmillan, 1950. A classic work by the Vinerian Profes-
sor of English Law at Oxford, first published in 1885.

Samuel R. Gardiner, *The First Two Stuarts and the Puritan
Revolution,* 1603–1660. 8th ed. New York, Scribners,
1888.

————, *History of England from the Accession of James I
to the Outbreak of the Civil War, 1603–1642.* 10 vols.
London, Longmans, 1883–84. The standard history of the
period. Later historians have picked only a few quarrels
with Gardiner. Vol. *10* is a complete index.

George P. Gooch, *Political Thought in England. From Bacon
to Halifax.* New York, Holt, 1914.

John W. Gough, *Fundamental Law in English Constitutional
History.* Oxford, Clarendon Press, 1955. A helpful survey
carried up to the 18th century.

———, "Fundamental Law in the Seventeenth Century," *Political Studies*, *1*, No. 2 (June 1953).

———, *John Locke's Political Philosophy, Eight Studies*. Oxford, Clarendon Press, 1950.

W. H. Greenleaf, "James I and the Divine Right of Kings," *Political Studies*, *5*, No. 1 (Feb. 1957). A new discussion of the philosophical foundations in James' theory of divine right.

William H. Hutton, *The English Church from the Accession of Charles I to the Death of Anne (1625–1714)*. London, Macmillan, 1903.

Rufus M. Jones, *Mysticism and Democracy in the English Commonwealth*. Cambridge, Harvard University Press, 1932.

Wilbur K. Jordan, *The Development of Religious Toleration in England from the Accession of James I to the Convention of the Long Parliament (1603–1640)*. London, Allen and Unwin, 1936.

Russell Kirk, "Burke and the Philosophy of Prescription," *Journal of the History of Ideas*, *14*, No. 3 (June 1953).

Marshall M. Knappen, *Constitutional and Legal History of England*. New York, Harcourt, Brace, 1942.

Herbert J. McLachlan, *Socinianism in Seventeenth-Century England*. London, Oxford University Press, 1951.

Hugh N. MacLean, "Fulke Greville: Kingship and Sovereignty," *Huntington Library Quarterly*, *16*, No. 3 (May 1953).

Frederic W. Maitland, *The Constitutional History of England*. Cambridge, The University Press, 1908.

Richard H. Malden, *The English Church and Nation*. London, S.P.C.K., 1952.

David Mathew, *The Jacobean Age*. London, Longmans, 1938.

William F. Mitchell, *English Pulpit Oratory from Andrewes to Tillotson. A Study of Its Literary Aspects*. London, S.P.C.K., 1932.

Christopher Morris, *Political Thought in England. Tyndale to Hooker*. New York, Oxford University Press, 1953.

George L. Mosse, "Change and Continuity in the Tudor Constitution," *Speculum*, *22*, No. 1 (Jan. 1947).

———, "The Influence of Jean Bodin's *Republique* on English Political Thought," *Medievalia et Humanistica, 5* (July 1948).

————, *The Struggle for Sovereignty in England. From the Reign of Queen Elizabeth to the Petition of Right.* East Lansing, Mich., Michigan State College Press, 1950.

Wallace Notestein, *The English People on the Eve of Colonization, 1603–1630.* New York, Harper, 1954. A brilliant social history.

Wallace Notestein and Roland G. Usher, "The Stuart Period. Unsolved Problems," *Annual Report of the American Historical Association for the Year 1916,* Vol. *1.*

Walther Rothschild, *Der Gedanke der geschriebenen Verfassung in der englischen Revolution.* Tubingen, Mohr, 1903.

Alfred L. Rowse, *The England of Elizabeth. The Structure of Society.* New York, Macmillan, 1951.

————, *The Expansion of Elizabethan England.* New York, St. Martin's Press, 1955. An interesting account written from an anti-Puritan point of view.

Ernest G. Rupp, *Studies in the Making of the English Protestant Tradition, Mainly in the Reign of Henry VIII.* Cambridge, The University Press, 1947.

Max A. Shepard, "The Political and Constitutional Theory of Sir John Fortescue," *Essays in History and Political Theory. In Honor of Charles Howard McIlwain.* Cambridge, Harvard University Press, 1936.

Walter M. Simon, "John Locke: Philosophy and Political Theory," *American Political Science Review, 45,* No. 2 (June 1951).

Lacey B. Smith, *Tudor Prelates and Politics, 1536–1558.* Princeton, Princeton University Press, 1953.

William Stubbs, *The Constitutional History of England, in Its Origin and Development.* 3 vols. 5th ed. Oxford, Clarendon Press, 1891–96.

Joseph R. Tanner, *English Constitutional Conflicts of the Seventeenth Century, 1603–1689. Cambridge,* The University Press, 1928.

George M. Trevelyan, *England under the Stuarts.* 17th ed. New York, Putnam, 1938.

————, *Illustrated English Social History.* 4 vols. London, Longmans, 1949–52.

Roland G. Usher, *The Reconstruction of the English Church.* 2 vols. New York, Appleton, 1910.

———, *The Rise and Fall of the High Commission.* Oxford, Clarendon Press, 1913.

Cicely V. Wedgwood, *The King's Peace, 1637–1641.* London, Collins, 1955.

Bertie Wilkinson, *Constitutional History of England, 1216–1399.* 3 vols. London, Longmans, 1948.

David H. Willson, *King James VI and I.* New York, Holt, 1956.

Arthur S. P. Woodhouse, "Religion and Some Foundations of English Democracy," *Philosophical Review, 61,* No. 4 (Oct. 1952).

Francis D. Wormuth, *The Royal Prerogative, 1603–1649. A Study in English Political and Constitutional Ideas.* Ithaca, N.Y., Cornell University Press, 1939.

Louis B. Wright, *Middle-Class Structure in Elizabethan England.* Chapel Hill, N.C., The University of North Carolina Press, 1935.

Perez Zagorin, *A History of Political Thought in the English Revolution.* London, Routledge, 1954.

C. STUDIES OF CALVINISM AND PURITANISM.

Roland H. Bainton, "Congregationalism: From the Just War to the Crusade in the Puritan Revolution," *Andover Newton Theological School Bulletin, 35,* No. 3 (April 1943).

Jerald C. Brauer, "Puritan Mysticism and the Development of Liberalism," *Church History, 19,* No. 3 (Sept. 1950).

———, Reflections on the Nature of English Puritanism," *Church History, 23,* No. 2 (June 1954).

Champlin Burrage, *The Church Covenant Idea. Its Origin and Its Development.* Philadelphia, American Baptist Publication Society, 1904.

———, *The Early English Dissenters in the Light of Recent Research (1550–1641).* 2 vols. Cambridge, The University Press 1912.

Isabel M. Calder, ed. and intro., *Activities of the Puritan Faction of the Church of England 1625–33.* London, S.P.C.K., 1957. The basic documents relating to the lawsuit between the crown and certain Puritans, lawyers, and merchants who were attempting to control the "lay impropriations" of the established church.

Douglas Campbell, *The Puritan in Holland, England, and America*. 2 vols. 4th ed. New York, Harper, 1893.

Henry W. Clark, *History of English Nonconformity from Wiclif to the Close of the Nineteenth Century*. 2 vols. London, Chapman, 1911–13.

Winnifred Cockshott, *The Pilgrim Fathers. Their Church and Colony*. London, Methuen, 1909.

Charles D. Cremeans, *The Reception of Calvinistic Thought in England*. Urbana, Ill., University of Illinois Press, 1949.

Godfrey Davies, "Arminian versus Puritan in England, ca. 1620–1640," *Huntington Library Bulletin*, No. 5 (April 1934).

———, "English Political Sermons, 1603–1640," *Huntington Library Quarterly*, *3*, No. 1 (Oct. 1939).

Horton Davies, *The Worship of the English Puritans*, Westminster, Deere, 1948.

Henry M. Dexter, *The England and Holland of the Pilgrims*. Boston, Houghton Mifflin, 1905.

Everett H. Emerson, "Calvin and Covenant Theology," *Church History*, *25*, No. 2 (June 1956).

Collected Papers of Herbert D. Foster. Historical and Biographical Studies. [New York], priv. print., 1929. Five of the seven papers deal with Calvinism.

Joseph Frank, *The Levellers. A History of the Writings of Three Seventeenth-Century Social Democrats: John Lilburne, Richard Overton, William Walwyn*. Cambridge, Harvard University Press, 1955.

Allen French, *Charles I and the Puritan Upheaval. A Study of the Causes of the Great Migration*. London, Allen and Unwin, 1955.

Mary I. Fry and Godfrey Davies, "William Prynne in the Huntington Library," *Huntington Library Quarterly*, *20*, No. 1 (Nov. 1956).

Charles H. George, "A Social Interpretation of English Puritanism," *Journal of Modern History*, *25*, No. 4 (Dec. 1953).

William Haller, *Liberty and Reformation in the Puritan Revolution.* New York, Columbia University Press, 1955.
———, *The Rise of Puritanism . . . 1570–1643.* New York, Columbia University Press, 1938.
A. Edward Harvey, *Martin Bucer in England. Inaugural-Dissertation zur Erlangung der Doktorwürde der hohen philosophischen Fakultät der Universität Marburg.* Marburg, Bauer, 1906.
Jack H. Hexter, "The Problem of the Presbyterian Independents," *American Historical Review, 44,* No. 1 (Oct. 1938).
Constantin Hopf, *Martin Bucer and the English Reformation.* Oxford, Blackwell, 1946.
George L. Kittredge, "A Note on Dr. William Ames," *Publications of the Colonial Society of Massachusetts, 13* (1910–11).
Marshall M. Knappen, *Tudor Puritanism. A Chapter in the History of Idealism.* Chicago, University of Chicago Press, 1939.
Perry Miller, *Orthodoxy in Massachusetts, 1630–1650. A Genetic Study.* Cambridge, Harvard University Press, 1933. The first half of this work deals with 16th- and 17th-century England and is indispensable.
Irvonwy Morgan, *The Nonconformity of Richard Baxter.* London, Epworth, 1946.
Samuel E. Morison, *The Puritan Pronoas. Studies in the Intellectual Life of New England in the Seventeenth Century.* New York, New York University Press, 1936.
George L. Mosse, "The Assimilation of Machiavelli in English Thought: The Casuistry of William Perkins and William Ames," *Huntington Library Quarterly, 17,* No. 4 (Aug. 1954).
———, *The Holy Pretence. A Study in Christianity and Reason of State from William Perkins to John Winthrop.* Oxford, Blackwell, 1957.
———, "The Importance of Jacques Saurin in the History of Casuistry and the Enlightenment," *Church History, 25,* No. 3 (Sept. 1956).
———, "Puritan Political Thought and the 'Cases of Conscience,' " *Church History, 23,* No. 2 (June 1954).

————, "Puritanism and Reason of State in Old and New England," *William and Mary Quarterly*, 3d series, *9*, No. 1 (Jan. 1952).

Daniel Neal, *The History of the Puritans, or Protestant Nonconformists. From the Reformation in 1517 to the Revolution in 1688*, ed. John O. Choules. 2 vols. New York, Harper, 1844.

H. Richard Niebuhr, "The Idea of Covenant and American Democracy," *Church History, 23*, No. 2 (June 1954).

Wilhelm Pauck, *Des Reich Gottes auf Erden: Utopie und Wirklichkeit. Eine Untersuchung zu Butzers "De Regno Christi" und zur englischen Staatskirche des 16. Jahrhunderts*. Berlin, de Greuyter, 1928.

Andrew F. Scott Pearson, *Church & State. Political Aspects of Sixteenth-Century Puritanism*. Cambridge, The University Press, 1928.

————, *Thomas Cartwright and Elizabethan Puritanism, 1535–1603*. Cambridge, The University Press, 1925.

Theodore C. Pease, *The Leveller Movement*. Washington, D.C., American Historical Association, 1916.

D. B. Robertson, *The Religious Foundations of Leveller Democracy*. New York, King's Crown Press, 1951.

Wilhelm Schenk, *The Concern for Social Justice in the Puritan Revolution*. London, Longmans, 1948.

Richard Schlatter, "The Higher Learning in Puritan England," *Historical Magazine of the Protestant Episcopal Church, 23*, No. 2 (June 1954).

Alan Simpson, "Saints in Arms: English Puritanism as Political Utopianism," *Church History, 23*, No. 2 (June 1954).

————, *Puritanism in Old and New England*. Chicago, University of Chicago Press, 1955.

Chard P. Smith, *Yankees and God*. New York, Hermitage, 1954.

Bard Thompson, "Bucer Study since 1918," *Church History, 25*, No. 1 (March 1956).

Leonard J. Trinterud, "The Origins of Puritanism," *Church History, 20*, No. 1 (March 1951).

Roland G. Usher, *The Presbyterian Movement in the Reign of Queen Elizabeth as Illustrated by the Minute Book of the Dedham Classis, 1582–1589.* London, Royal Historical Society, 1905.

Robert Vaughan, *English Nonconformity.* London, Jackson, 1862.

Williston Walker, *The Creeds and Platforms of Congregationalism.* New York, Scribner, 1893.

Sheldon S. Wolin, "Calvin and the Reformation: The Political Education of Protestantism," *American Political Science Review,* *51,* No. 2 (June 1957).

Louis B. Wright, "Propaganda against James I's 'Appeasement' of Spain," *Huntington Library Quarterly,* *6,* No. 2 (Feb. 1943).

D. WORKS ON THE COMMON LAW AND THE INNS OF COURT.

William P. Baildon, ed., *The Records of the Honorable Society of Lincoln's Inn. The Black Books.* 4 vols. London, Lincoln's Inn, 1897–1902.

William V. Ball, *Lincoln's Inn. Its History and Traditions.* London, Stevens, 1947.

William Blackstone, *Commentaries on the Laws of England. In Four Books.* 4 vols. 11th ed. London, 1791.

Francis Cowper, *A Prospect of Gray's Inn.* London, Stevens, 1951.

Reginald J. Fletcher, ed., *The Pension Book of Gray's Inn. (Records of the Honourable Society),* *1569–1800.* 2 vols. London, Stevens, 1901–10.

William P. Goard, *The Law of the Lord. Or the Common Law.* London, Covenant, 1928.

G. D. G. Hall, "Bate's Case and 'Lane's Reports': The Authenticity of a Seventeenth-Century Legal Text," *Bulletin of the John Rylands Library Manchester,* *35,* No. 2 (March 1953).

———, "Impositions and the Courts, 1554–1606," *Law Quarterly Review,* *69,* No. 274 (April 1953).

William Herbert, *Antiquities of the Inns of Court and Chancery . . . with a Concise History of the English Law.* London, Vernor, 1804.

William S. Holdsworth, *A History of English Law.* 13 vols.

London, Methuen, 1903–52. The later volumes of this classic work were completed after Holdsworth's death in 1944. Edward Patton has compiled a valuable one-volume index for the whole study.

Charles H. Hopwood and Charles T. Martin, eds., *Middle Temple Records, 1501–1703.* 4 vols. London, Butterworth, 1904–05.

Gerald B. Hurst, *Lincoln's Inn Essays.* London, Constable, 1949.

———, *A Short History of Lincoln's Inn.* London, Constable, 1946.

Frederick A. Inderwick, ed., *A Calendar of the Inner Temple Records, 1505–1714.* 3 vols. London, Sotheran, 1896–1901.

Frederic W. Maitland, *English Law and the Renaissance.* Cambridge, The University Press, 1901.

———, "Wyclif on English and Common Law," *Law Quarterly Review, 12,* No. 45 (Jan. 1896).

Mary Hume Maguire, "Attack of the Common Lawyers on the Oath *ex officio* as Administered in the Ecclesiastical Courts in England," in *Essays in History and Political Thought. In Honor of Charles Howard McIlwain,* Cambridge, Harvard University Press, 1936.

Arthur von Mehren, "The Judicial Conception of Legislation in Tudor England," in Paul L. Sayre, ed., *Interpretations of Modern Legislative Philosophies. In Honor of Roscoe Pound.* New York, Oxford University Press, 1947.

Charles F. Mullett, "Coke and the American Revolution," *Economica, 12,* No. 38 (Nov. 1932).

William B. Odgers, et al., *Six Lectures on the Inns of Court and of Chancery.* London, Macmillan, 1912.

———, "A Sketch of the History of the Four Inns of Court," in Paul Vinogradoff, ed., *Essays in Legal History.* London, Oxford University Press, 1913.

Robert R. Pearce, *A History of the Inns of Court and Chancery* . . . London, Bentley, 1848.

Theodore F. T. Plucknett, *A Concise History of the Common Law.* 5th ed. Boston, Little, Brown, 1956.

———, "Ellesmere on Statutes," *Law Quarterly Review, 60,* No. 239 (July 1944).

——, *Legislation of Edward I.* Oxford, Clarendon Press, 1949.

——, *Statutes and Their Interpretation in the First Half of the Fourteenth Century.* Cambridge, The University Press, 1922.

Frederick Pollock, *The Origins of the Inns of Court. An Address Given to Canadian Guests at Lincoln's Inn.* Oxford, The University Press, 1931.

——, "The Transformation of Equity," in Paul Vinogradoff, ed., *Essays in Legal History.* London, Oxford University Press, 1913.

Herbert Pope, "The Fundamental Law and the Power of the Courts," *Harvard Law Review, 27*, No. 1 (Nov. 1913).

Roscoe Pound, "Common Law and Legislation," *Harvard Law Review, 21*, No. 6 (April 1908).

Charles H. Randall, Jr., "Sir Edward Coke and the Privilege against Self-Incrimination," *South Carolina Law Quarterly, 8*, No. 4 (summer 1956).

M. Sarfatti, "Roman Law and Common Law. Forerunners of a General Unification of Law," *International and Comparative Law Quarterly, 3*, Pt. 1 (Jan. 1954).

Faith Thompson, *Magna Carta. Its Role in the Making of the English Constitution, 1300–1629.* Minneapolis, University of Minnesota Press, 1948.

Samuel E. Thorne, "The Constitution and the Courts. A Reëxamination of the Famous Case of Dr. Bonham," in Conyers Read, ed., *The Constitution Reconsidered.* New York, Columbia University Press, 1938. Also found under title, "Dr. Bonham's Case," *Law Quarterly Review, 54*, No. 216 (Oct. 1938).

——, "Courts of Record and Sir Edward Coke," *University of Toronto Law Journal, 2*, No. 1 (1937).

——, ed. and intro., *A Discourse upon the Exposicion & Understandinge of Statutes. With Sir Thomas Egerton's Additions.* San Marino, Calif., Huntington Library, 1942.

——, ed. and intro., *Readings and Moots at the Inns of Court in the Fifteenth Century.* Publications of the Selden Society, London, Quaritch, 1954, Vol. *1* contains an excellent 68-page introduction followed by readings, appendices, and tables of statutes and cases. Vol. 2 will deal in a more general way with medieval legal education.

————, "St. Germain's 'Doctor and Student,'" *The Library*, 4th series, *10*, No. 4 (March 1930).

————, "Tudor Social Transformation and Legal Change," *New York University Law Review*, *26*, No. 1 (Jan. 1951).

Paul Vinogradoff, "Reason and Conscience in Sixteenth-Century Jurisprudence," *Law Quarterly Review*, *24*, No. 96 (Oct. 1908).

Harvey Wheeler, "Calvin's Case (1608) and the McIlwain-Schuyler Debate," *American Historical Review*, *61*, No. 3 (April 1956).

Percy H. Winfield, *The Chief Sources of English Legal History*. Cambridge, Harvard University Press, 1925.

E. BIOGRAPHIES.

D. M. Barratt, "The Library of John Selden and Its Later History," *Bodleian Library Record*, *3*, Nos. 31–3, (March–Dec. 1951).

Catherine D. Bowen, *The Lion and the Throne. The Life and Times of Sir Edward Coke (1552–1634)*. Boston, Little, Brown, 1957. An engaging and dependable study of the great jurist.

John C. Campbell, *The Lives of the Chief Justices of England*. 4 vols. New York, Cockcroft, 1873. Begins with the Conquest and terminates in the early 19th century.

————, *The Lives of the Lord Chancellors and Keepers of the Great Seal of England. From the Earliest Times till the Reign of Queen Victoria*. 8 vols. London, Murray, 1847–69.

Charles H. and Thompson Cooper, *Athenae Cantabrigienses*. 3 vols. Cambridge, Bell, 1858–1913. A survey of the lives of important Cambridge men from 1500 to 1611.

William S. Holdsworth, "The Influence of Coke on the Development of English Law," in Paul Vinogradoff, ed., *Essays in Legal History*, London, Oxford University Press, 1913.

Charles W. James, *Chief Justice Coke, His Family & Descendants at Holkham*. London, Country Life, 1929.

Cuthbert W. Johnson, *The Life of Sir Edward Coke, Lord*

Chief Justice of England in the Reign of James I with Memoirs of His Contemporaries. 2 vols. London, Colburn, 1837.

Ethyn W. Kirby, *William Prynne, a Study in Puritanism.* Cambridge, Harvard University Press, 1931.

Marshall M. Knappen, ed. and intro., *Two Elizabethan Puritan Diaries. By Richard Rogers and Samuel Ward.* Chicago, American Society of Church History, 1933.

Arthur R. Ladell, *Richard Baxter, Puritan and Mystic.* London, S.P.C.K., 1925.

Walter H. Lyon and Herman Block, *Edward Coke, Oracle of the Law.* Boston, Houghton Mifflin, 1929.

James Spedding, *An Account of the Life and Times of Francis Bacon. Extracted from the Edition of His Occasional Writings.* 2 vols. Boston, Houghton Mifflin, 1878.

Leslie Stephen and Sidney Lee, eds., *Dictionary of National Biography.* 63 vols. with errata and supplements. New York, Macmillan, 1885——.

H. R. Trevor-Roper, *Archbishop Laud, 1573–1645.* London, Macmillan, 1940.

John Tulloch, *English Puritanism and Its Leaders: Cromwell, Milton, Baxter, Bunyon.* Edinburgh, Blackwood, 1861.

Williston Walker, *Ten New England Leaders.* New York, Silver, 1901.

Anthony à Wood, *Athenae Oxonienses. An Exact History of All the Writers and Bishops Who Have Had Their Education in the University of Oxford,* ed. Philip Bliss. 5 vols. in 4, new ed. London, Rivington, 1813–20.

Humphrey W. Woolrych, *Lives of Eminent Serjeants-at-Law of the English Bar.* 2 vols. London, Allen, 1869.

Louis B. Wright, "William Perkins: Elizabethan Apostle of 'Practical Divinity,' " *Huntington Library Quarterly, 3,* No. 2 (Jan. 1940).

F. STUDIES OF PARLIAMENT.

E. R. Adair, "The Petition of Right," *History, 5,* No. 18 (July 1920).

Carleton K. Allen, *Law in the Making.* 5th ed. Oxford, Clarendon Press, 1952.

Douglas Brunton and D. H. Pennington, *Members of the Long Parliament*. Cambridge, Harvard University Press, 1954.

Strathearn Gordon, *Our Parliament*. New York, Hansard Society, 1945.

Harold Hulme, "The Winning of Freedom of Speech by the House of Commons," *American Historical Review, 61*, No. 4 (July 1956).

Margaret A. Judson, "Henry Parker and the Theory of Parliamentary Sovereignty," in *Essays in History and Political Theory. In Honor of Charles Howard McIlwain*. Cambridge, Harvard University Press, 1936.

George W. Keeton, *The Passing of Parliament*. London, Benn, 1952.

Edward T. Lampson, "Some New Light on the Growth of Parliamentary Sovereignty: *Wimbish versus Taillebois*," *American Political Science Review, 35*, No. 5 (Oct. 1941).

R. A. MacKay, "Coke—Parliamentary Sovereignty or the Supremacy of the Law?" *Michigan Law Review, 22*, No. 3 (Jan. 1924).

Geoffrey Marshall, "What Is Parliament? The Changing Concept of Parliamentary Sovereignty," *Political Studies, 2*, No. 3 (Oct. 1954).

Charles H. McIlwain, *The High Court of Parliament and Its Supremacy. An Historical Essay on the Boundaries between Legislation and Adjudication in England*. New Haven, Yale University Press, 1910. An excellent study whose influence still is felt.

John E. Neale, *Elizabeth I and Her Parliaments, 1559–1581*. London, Cape, 1953.

———, *The Elizabethan House of Commons*. London, Cape, 1949.

———, "Parliament and the Articles of Religion, 1571," *English Historical Review, 67*, No. 265 (Oct. 1952).

Wallace Notestein, *The Winning of the Initiative by the House of Commons*. London, Oxford University Study, 1924. A first-rate essay.

"Parliamentary Opposition. Art. I—Hansard's Parliamentary Debates," *Edinburgh Review Or . . . Critical Journal, 101*, No. 205 (Jan. 1855).

Albert F. Pollard, *The Evolution of Parliament*. 2d ed. New York, Longmans, 1926.

Frances H. Relf, *The Petition of Right*. Minneapolis [University of Minnesota Press], 1917.

Faith Thompson, *A Short History of Parliament, 1295–1642*. Minneapolis, University of Minnesota Press, 1953.

Roland G. Usher, *The Institutional History of the House of Commons, 1547–1641*. N.p., 1924.

David H. Willson, *The Privy Councillors in the House of Commons, 1604–1629*. Minneapolis, University of Minnesota Press, 1940.

G. WORKS ON THE UNIVERSITIES, LEARNING, AND LITERATURE.

Douglas Bush, *English Literature in the Earlier Seventeenth Century, 1600–1660*. Oxford, Clarendon Press, 1945.

Charles C. Butterworth, *The English Primers, 1529–1545*. Philadelphia, University of Pennsylvania Press, 1953.

The Poems of Richard Corbet, ed. Octavius Gilchrist. 4th ed. London, Longmans, 1807.

George E. Corrie, *Brief Historical Notices of the Interference of the Crown with the Affairs of the English Universities*. Cambridge, The University Press, 1839.

Memorials of the Life of George Elwes Corrie . . . Drawn Principally from His Diary and Correspondence, ed. M. Holroyd. Cambridge, The University Press, 1890.

George Dyer, *History of the University and Colleges of Cambridge. Including Notices Relating to the Founders and Eminent Men*. 2 vols. London, Longmans, 1814.

——, *The Privileges of the University of Cambridge. Together with Additional Observations on Its History, Antiquities, Literature, and Biography*. 2 vols. London, Longmans, 1824.

Strickland Gibson, ed. and intro., *The Great Charter of Charles I to the University of Oxford. (3 March 1636)* Oxford, The University Press [1932]. Opinion by William S. Holdsworth.

John Griffiths, ed., *Enactments in Parliament Specially Concerning the Universities of Oxford and Cambridge*. Oxford, Clarendon Press, 1869.

Hiram Haydn, *The Counter-Renaissance*. New York, Scribner, 1950.

John H. Marsden, ed., *College Life in the Time of James the First, as Illustrated by an Unpublished Diary of Sir Symonds D'Ewes*. London, Parker, 1851.

James B. Mullinger, *Cambridge Characteristics in the Seventeenth Century. Or, the Studies of the University and Their Influence on the Character and Writings of the Most Distinguished Graduates during That Period*. London, Macmillan, 1867.

———, *A History of the University of Cambridge*. London, Longmans, 1888.

———, *St. John's College*. London, Robinson, 1901.

———, *The University of Cambridge. From the Earliest Times . . . to the Decline of the Platonist Movement*. 3 vols. Cambridge, The University Press, 1873–1911. A necessary starting point for an understanding of the development of Cambridge University.

John Nichols, *The Progresses, Processions, and Magnificent Festivities of King James the First*. 3 vols. in 4. London, Nichols, 1828. Contains many references to the universities.

Millicent Barton Rex, *University Representation* [in the House of Commons] *in England, 1604–1690*. New York, Barnes, 1954. Other volumes are planned which will bring this excellent account down to the abandonment of university representation in 1948.

Evelyn S. Shuckburgh, *Emmanuel College*. London, Robinson, 1904.

Joe W. Ashley Smith, *The Birth of Modern Education. The Contribution of the Dissenting Academies, 1660–1800*. London, Independent Press, 1954.

Theodore Spencer, *Shakespeare and the Nature of Man*. New York, Macmillan, 1949.

Eustace M. W. Tillyard, *The Elizabethan World Picture*. London, Chatto, 1943.

Helen C. White, *English Devotional Literature* [prose], *1600–1640*. Madison, Wis., University of Wisconsin Press, 1931.

———, et al., eds., *Seventeenth-Century Verse and Prose*. New York, Macmillan, 1951–52.

———, *Social Criticism in* [English] *Popular Religious*

Literature of the Sixteenth Century. New York, Macmillan, 1944.

————, *The Tudor Books of Private Devotion.* Madison, Wis., University of Wisconsin Press, 1951.

James F. Willard, *The Royal Authority and the Early English Universities.* Philadelphia [University of Pennsylvania], 1902.

Basil Willey, *The Seventeenth-Century Background. The Thought of the Age in Relation to Religion and Poetry.* New York, Doubleday, 1953 (1st ed. 1934).

George H. Williams, et al., *The Harvard Divinity School. Its Place in Harvard University and in American Culture.* Boston, Beacon Press, 1954.

H. STUDIES OF CHRISTIAN THOUGHT AND THE ROLE OF THE CHURCH IN SOCIETY.

James T. Addison, "Early Anglican Thought, 1559–1667," *Historical Magazine of the Protestant Episcopal Church,* *22,* No. 3 (Sept. 1953).

Ernest Barker, *Church, State and Study. Essays.* London, Methuen, 1930.

George K. Clark, *The English Inheritance. An Historical Essay.* London, S.C.M. Press, 1950.

Ebenezer T. Davies, *The Political Ideas of Richard Hooker.* London, S.P.C.K., 1946.

John N. Figgis, *Churches in the Modern State.* London, Longmans, 1913.

Frank S. B. Gavin, *Seven Centuries of the Problem of Church and State.* Princeton, Princeton University Press, 1938.

Yung chi Ho, *The Origin of Parliamentary Sovereignty or 'Mixed' Monarchy, Being a Study of the Political Implications of Calvinism and Bodinism.* Shanghai, The Commercial Press, 1935.

Frederick D. Maurice, *Social Morality. Twenty-One Lectures.* London, Macmillan, 1869.

James H. Nichols, *Democracy and the Churches.* Philadelphia, Westminster Press, 1951.

Helmut Richard Niebuhr, *Christ and Culture.* New York, Harper, 1951.

————, *The Kingdom of God in America,* Chicago, Willett, 1937.

Samuel E. Stumpf, "Christian Theology and Juristic Thought," *Journal of Religion, 30*, No. 1 (Jan. 1950).

———, *Democracy and the Christian Faith.* Nashville, Tenn., Vanderbilt University Press, 1950.

———, *A Democratic Manifesto. The impact of Dynamic Christianity upon Public Life and Government.* Nashville, Tenn., Vanderbilt University Press, 1954.

Paul Tillich, *The Protestant Era,* concluding essay and trans. James L. Adams. Chicago, University of Chicago Press, 1948.

Ernst Troeltsch, *Protestantism and Progress. A Historical Study of the Relation of Protestantism to the Modern World,* trans. W. Montgomery. New York, Putnam, 1912.

———, *The Social Teaching of the Christian Churches,* trans. Olive Wyon. 2 vols. New York, Macmillan, 1931.

John Tulloch, *Rational Theology and Christian Philosophy in England in the Seventeenth Century.* 2 vols. Edinburgh, Blackwood, 1872.

Louis B. Wright, *Religion and Empire. The Alliance between Piety and Commerce in English Expansion, 1558–1625.* Chapel Hill, N.C., University of North Carolina Press, 1943.

I. WORKS ON LAW, SOVEREIGNTY, AND JURISPRUDENCE.

James L. Adams, "The Law of Nature in Greco-Roman Thought," *Journal of Religion, 25,* No. 2 (April 1945).

———, "The Law of Nature: Some General Considerations," *Journal of Religion, 25,* No. 2 (April 1945).

John Austin, *Lectures on Jurisprudence. Or the Philosophy of Positive Law,* ed. and rev. Robert Campbell. 2 vols. 5th ed. London, Murray, 1885.

Roland H. Bainton, "The Appeal to Reason and the American Constitution," in Conyers Read, ed., *The Constitution Reconsidered.* New York, Columbia University Press, 1938.

William A. Banner, "National Law and Social Order," in John Wild, ed., *The Return to Reason. Essays in Realistic Philosophy.* Chicago, Regnery, 1953.

Stanley I. Benn, "The Uses of 'Sovereignty,'" *Political Studies, 3,* No. 2 (June 1955).

Jean J. Burlamaqui, *The Principles of National and Politic Law*, trans. Thomas Nugent. 5th ed. Cambridge, The University Press, 1807.

Huntington Cairns, *Law and the Social Sciences*. New York, Harcourt, Brace, 1935.

————, *Legal Philosophy from Plato to Hegel*. Baltimore, Johns Hopkins Press, 1949.

Hsü-Ching Chen, *Recent Theories of Sovereignty*. Canton, China, 1929.

Francis W. Coker, *Organismic Theories of the State. Nineteenth-Century Interpretations of the State as Organism or as Person*. New York, Longmans, 1910.

Edward S. Corwin, "The 'Higher Law' Background of American Constitutional Law," *Harvard Law Review*, *42*, Nos. 2 and 3 (Dec. 1928 and Jan. 1929).

John Dickinson, "A Working Theory of Sovereignty," *Political Science Quarterly*, *42*, No. 4 (Dec. 1927).

Reginald A. Eastwood and George W. Keeton, *The Austinian Theories of Law and Sovereignty*. London, Methuen, 1929.

Otto F. von Gierke, *Das deutsche Genossenschaft*. 4 vols. Berlin, Weidmann, 1868–1913.

————, *Die Genossenschaftstheorie und die deutsche Rechtsprechung*. Berlin, Weidmannsche Buchhandlung, 1887.

————, *Natural Law and the Theory of Society, 1500–1800*, trans. and intro. Ernest Barker. 2 vols. Cambridge, The University Press, 1934. Contains an essay by Ernst Troeltsch, "The Ideas of Natural Law and Humanity in World Politics," trans. Ernest Barker.

John C. Gray, *The Nature and Sources of the Law*. 2d ed. New York, Macmillan, 1921.

Charles G. Haines, *The Revival of Natural Law Concepts. A Study of the Establishment and of the Interpretation of Limits on Legislatures with Special Reference to the Development of Certain Phases of American Constitutional Law*. Cambridge, Harvard University Press, 1930.

William S. Holdsworth, *Some Lessons from Our Legal History*. New York, Macmillan, 1928.

Hans Kelsen, *General Theory of Law and State*, trans. Anders Wedberg. Cambridge, Harvard University Press, 1945.

Paul H. Kocher, "Francis Bacon on the Science of Jurisprudence," *Journal of the History of Ideas*, *18*, No. 1 (Jan. 1957).

Harold J. Laski, *Authority in the Modern State*. New Haven, Yale University Press, 1919.

———, *The Foundations of Sovereignty and Other Essays*. New York, Harcourt, Brace, 1921.

———, *The State in Theory and Practice*. New York, Viking, 1935.

———, *Studies in Law and Politics*. New Haven, Yale University Press, 1932.

———, *Studies in the Problem of Sovereignty*. New Haven, Yale University Press, 1917.

Earl Latham, "The Group Basis of Politics. Notes for a Theory," *American Political Science Review*, *46*, No. 2 (June 1952).

John D. Lewis, *The Genossenschaft-Theory of Otto von Gierke*. Madison, Wis., University of Wisconsin Press, 1935.

William S. Livingston, "A Note on the Nature of Federalism," *Political Science Quarterly*, *67*, No. 1 (March 1952).

Charles H. McIlwain, "A Fragment on Sovereignty," *Political Science Quarterly*, *48*, No. 1 (March 1933).

———, "Sovereignty Again," *Economica*, *6*, No. 18 (Nov. 1926).

John T. McNeill, "Natural Law in the Teaching of the Reformers," *Journal of Religion*, *26*, No. 3 (July 1946).

Charles E. Merriam, Jr., *History of the Theory of Sovereignty since Rousseau*. New York, Columbia University Press, 1900.

Sobei Mogi, *Otto von Gierke, His Political Teaching and Jurisprudence*. London, King, 1932.

Baron de Montesquieu, *The Spirit of the Laws*, trans. Thomas Nugent, rev. J. V. Prichard, intro. O. W. Holmes. 2 vols. New York, Appleton, 1900.

John A. Mourant, *The Physiocratic Conception of Natural Law*. Chicago, University of Chicago, 1943.

John C. Murray, "The Problem of Pluralism in America," *Thought*, *29*, No. 113 (summer 1954).

Natural Law Forum, *1*, No. 1 (July 1956), *2*, No. 1 (1957).

Alessandro Passerin d'Entrèves, *Natural Law. An Intro-

duction to Legal Philosophy. London, Hutchinson's University Library, 1951.

Edwin W. Patterson, "Historical and Evolutionary Theories of Law," *Columbia Law Review, 51*, No. 6 (June 1951).

Roscoe Pound, *The Spirit of the Common Law*. Francestown, N. H., Marshall Jones, 1921.

George H. Sabine, "Pluralism: A Point of View," *American Political Science Review, 17*, No. 1 (Feb. 1923).

Max A. Shepard, "Sovereignty at the Crossroads: A Study of Bodin," *Political Science Quarterly, 45*, No. 4 (Dec. 1930).

Leo Strauss, *Natural Right and History*. Chicago, University of Chicago Press, 1953.

Paul Vinogradoff, "Aims and Methods of Jurisprudence," *Columbia Law Review, 24*, No. 1 (Jan. 1924).

————, *Common-Sense in Law*. New York, Holt, 1914.

————, *Custom and Right*. Oslo, Aschehoug, 1925.

————, *Outlines of Historical Jurisprudence*. London, Oxford University Press, 1920–22.

H. W. R. Wade, "The Basis of Legal Sovereignty," *Cambridge Law Journal*, Nov. 1955.

Paul W. Ward, *Sovereignty, a Study of a Contemporary Political Notion*. London, Routledge, 1928.

John D. Wild, *Plato's Modern Enemies and the Theory of Natural Law*. Chicago, University of Chicago Press, 1953.

Westel W. Willoughby, *The Fundamental Concepts of Public Law*. New York, Macmillan, 1924.

Benjamin F. Wright, *American Interpretations of Natural Law. A Study in the History of Political Thought*. Cambridge, Harvard University Press, 1931.

J. MISCELLANY.

John W. Allen, *A History of Political Thought in the Sixteenth Century*, 3d ed. London, Methuen, 1951.

The Works of Francis Bacon, Lord Chancellor of England. With a Life of the Author by Basil Montagu. 3 vols. New York, Worthington, 1884.

The Works of the Right Honorable Edmund Burke. Rev. ed. Boston, Little, Brown, 1865–67.

William F. Church, *Constitutional Thought in Sixteenth-*

Century France. Cambridge, Harvard University Press, 1941.

William A. Dunning, *A History of Political Theories from Luther to Montesquieu.* New York, Macmillan, 1905.

John N. Figgis, *The Divine Right of Kings.* 2d ed. Cambridge, The University Press, 1914.

———, *Studies of Political Thought from Gerson to Grotius, 1414–1625.* 2d ed. Cambridge, The University Press, 1916.

Otto F. von Gierke, *Political Theories of the Middle Age,* trans. and intro. Frederic W. Maitland. Cambridge, The University Press, 1900.

John W. Gough, *The Social Contract. A Critical Study of Its Development.* Oxford, Clarendon Press, 1936.

John H. Hallowell, *Main Currents in Modern Political Thought.* New York, Holt, 1950.

———, *The Moral Foundation of Democracy.* Chicago, University of Chicago Press, 1954.

Wilfrid Harrison, "Texts in Political Theory," *Political Studies, 3,* No. 1 (Feb. 1955).

Georg Jellinek, *Allgemeine Staatslehre.* Berlin, Häring, 1900.

Arthur D. Lindsay, *The Essentials of Democracy.* London, Oxford University Press, 1929.

———, *The Modern Democratic State.* 1st American ed. New York, Oxford University Press, 1947.

Leslie Lipson, "The Two-Party System in British Politics," *American Political Science Review, 47,* No. 2 (June 1953).

The Collected Papers of Frederic William Maitland, ed. H. A. L. Fisher. 2 vols. Cambridge, The University Press, 1911.

Charles H. McIlwain, *Constitutionalism. Ancient and Modern.* Rev. ed. Ithaca, N.Y., Cornell University Press, 1947.

———, *Constitutionalism & the Changing World.* Cambridge, The University Press, 1939.

———, *The Growth of Political Thought in the West. From the Greeks to the End of the Middle Ages.* New York, Macmillan, 1932.

George H. Sabine, *A History of Political Theory.* Rev. ed. New York, Holt, 1950.

Francis D. Wormuth, *The Origins of Modern Constitution-alism.* New York, Harper, 1949.

Iohannis Wyclif, *Tractatus de Officio Regis,* ed. Alfred W. Pollard and Charles Sayle. London, Wyclif Society, 1887.

INDEX

Abbot, Arch. George, 68, 70; sympathetic to Puritan theology, 20; supports crown, 67

Absolute, the: nature of, Puritans and lawyers on, 125 and n. *See also* Authority

Absolutism: in Hobbes, 129; Whigs employ, 161–2. *See also* Divine right of kings

Allegiance, 140–1. *See also* Authority

Allen, J. W., 45, 60 n., 156 n. 19

America, 5, 10, 22; Puritan exodus to, 3; Independents leave for, 14; Ames important for, 14 n.; fundamental law in, 45

Ames, William: general importance of, but not specifically here, 14 and n.; translates Bradshaw, *English Puritanisme,* 24 n.; covenant leader, 31; uses natural law, 131

Ancien régime, 149

Andrewes, Launcelot, 21 n. 18

Anglicans, 87; similar to Puritans, 13, 16–18; partly espouse Calvinism, 20; differ from Puritans, 20–5; give in to crown, universities, 39; support crown, finances and church, 67; not interested in preaching, 75; theology of, supported by crown, 78–81

Anglo-Saxon, 117

Anne, Queen, 167

Ante-nati, the, 115. *See also Post-nati,* case of the

Antinomian, 24. *See also* Arminians

Antiquarians, 41

Antoninus, Marcus Aurelius: Gataker attracted to, 27, 27 n. 32

Apology and Satisfaction (1604), 153

Aquinas. *See* Thomas Aquinas

Arians, 21. *See also* Arminians

Arminians, 14 n.; Anglicans so called, inadequacy of term, 21, 40; Puritans are when preaching, 22 n. 19; receive crown's favor, 73, 78–81; on authority, 80–2; cited in Parliament, 82. *See also* Church of England; Cosin; High church party; Montagu

Army, New Model, 147

Articles of Religion, 1628 edition of, 68 and n. 13, 78 and n.

Articuli Cleri, 90 and n., 91–3

Ashby vs. White, case of, 161 n.

Attainder, bill of, 153

Aurelius. *See* Antoninus, Marcus Aurelius

Austin, John: sovereignty theory of, 162, 166–7; contribution of, 163; monism of 172, 175 and n. 5

Authority, 107; of crown's new church law, 71–2; in doctrine, 80–1; divine, crown usurps, 85; final, 114–19; final, Puritans and lawyers differ on, 125 and n.; of old laws today, 164–5; "loyal opposition" on, 167–70, 168 n.; how justified, 174; Puritans and lawyers on, 179–80; distributive, 137, 141–8, 150–5, 160–71, 162–3. *See also* Bible; Church, the; Courts; Law, common; Crown; Parliament

Authors, anonymous, 12, 69, 73. "Lawes of England, The," 121–2, 122 n.

Axioms, 137, 139

Bacon, Francis, 2, 42; harangues judges, 59–60, 89; consults with judges, 96–7, 99; arguments in Bate's Case, 105 n.; impeached, 151

Bancroft, Arch. Richard: opposes Presbyterians, 13; reformer, 18; deprivations during administration, 70; role in prohibitions issue, 89–94; supports divine right of kings, 91